An ADHD Primer

Second Edition

An ADHD Primer

Second Edition

Lisa L. Weyandt
The University of Rhode Island

LEA LAWRENCE ERLBAUM ASSOCIATES, PUBLISHERS
2007 Mahwah, New Jersey   London

Lawrence Erlbaum Associates, Inc., Publishers
10 Industrial Avenue
Mahwah, New Jersey 07430
www.erlbaum.com

Cover design by Tomai Maridou

Library of Congress Cataloging-in-Publication Data

Weyandt, Lisa L.
    An ADHD primer / Lisa L. Weyandt. — 2nd ed
        p.   cm.
    Includes bibliographical references and indexes.
    ISBN 0-8058-4969-6 (cloth : alk. paper)
    ISBN 0-8058-4970-X (pbk : alk. paper)
    1. Attention-deficit hyperactivity disorder—Popular works.   I. Title.

RJ506.H9W49   2006
618.92′8589—dc22   2006040991
                                                                CIP

Books published by Lawrence Erlbaum Associates are printed on acid-free paper, and their bindings are chosen for strength and durability.

Printed in the United States of America
10 9 8 7 6 5 4 3 2 1

To my son, Sebastian,
an extraordinary boy.

CONTENTS

FOREWORD

Thousands of scientific papers exist on attention deficit hyperactivity disorder (ADHD) making it among the most well-studied psychological disorders of children. Research on adults with ADHD is also rapidly increasing giving us a clearer picture of the adult stage of the disorder that is both consistent with what has been found in children with ADHD while differing from it in some important ways. As a consequence of this growing literature, numerous books have appeared on ADHD which raises an obvious question, "why write another one?" The answer is that either these books are exceptionally large handbooks or compendiums of this vast literature that are arduous and time consuming to plow through if one wishes to understand this literature. Or they are relatively brief and in many cases superficial renderings in trade book format for the lay-reader that give but a cursory sense of what our science has to say about the disorder. For the intelligent reader who hungers for more than a mere anecdote-filled trade book based chiefly on clinical or lay observations but has not the time to wrestle with the Sumo-sized handbooks on the disorder that contain more scientifically based information, there are few if any "executive summaries" in book form like the one you hold in your hand at this moment. Lucky for you and fortunate for us all, Dr. Weyandt has wisely addressed this need with her exceptionally well-written, pithy, efficient, and economical book aimed at this largely neglected market for the time-harried, educated public.

Here you will find, in short order, the facts of the matter with regard to the nature, diagnosis, associated risks, causes, assessment, and treatment of the disorder, expertly conveyed yet down-right stingy with your time—our field at an educated glance, as it were. Here is what you need to know about this disorder just when you needed to know it. It is shorn of time-wasting, lengthy clinical cases and anecdotes. It is also free of obscurantist clinical opinions loosely anchored, if at all, to the science of the matter and conveyed with such condescension or circumlocution as to long for some version of a "time out" for clinician-writers who cannot possibly get to their point. Not here. Dr. Weyandt is just the professional to convey what we know about ADHD with great clarity and respect for your time and intelligence. As I discerned over the years I have known her, she is a clinical scientist with an incisive intellect who can get to the meat of matters in a heart beat, conveying the essence of a complex literature with great ease and simplicity while still respecting the controversies and limitations that abound in the clinical science on ADHD. As one who is known to be a stickler for time management, I admire this among the many qualities I most appreciate about her work. If you like your bourbon or scotch straight and unadulterated, your red wines seductively bold, deeply complex, and lasting in a finish that commands yet another sip, and your conversations respectfully direct, challenging, well-crafted, and eye-openingly educational, then you are going to love this tidy little book.

As Dr. Weyandt notes here, ADHD is more than just a problem with attention, impulsive control, or activity levels. Those with the disorder have considerable problems with greater variation in their performance of various tasks, with holding information in mind that is needed to remember goals and guide behavior toward them, with manipulating such information, with organizing their actions and various sub-routines in their pursuit of their goals, with managing their emotions or motivations as well as others, and with planning for the future or problem-solving along the way when confronted with unexpected obstacles to their goals. And their ability to organize their behavior relative to time's passage, deadlines, appointments with others, and numerous other instances of temporal responsibilities are consistently inadequate. All of this suggests a broader cognitive impairment associated with the disorder than the term *attention deficits* and a broader behavioral difficulty than the term *hyperactivity* seem to convey.

Modern theorists and researchers working in the field of ADHD have taken considerable notice of these facts and have identified working memory, the larger domain of executive functioning (of which working memory is a component), and self-regulation (which the executive functions appear to provide to humans) as areas of deficiencies in the disorder. They are constructs that also better explain the myriad symptoms and impairments associated with its life course. Contrary to the public's opinion that this is just some disorder-de-jour comprised mostly of inattentiveness, the real science being done in this field shows ADHD to be as serious and complex in its own way as are disorders like autism, bipolar disorder, or schizophrenia. For among our many psychological abilities that distinguish humans from primates or other mammals is our unique gift for self-regulation—ADHD is its nemesis. As a developmental disorder of self-regulation and its hand-maiden, executive functioning, ADHD is complex and adversely affects a wide swath of major life activities, increasingly so from childhood to adulthood. This complexity and seriousness are nicely captured here and are followed up with numerous recommendations for how best to manage the disorder, all scientifically based.

If you would know something well, teach it to others. My congratulations to Dr. Weyandt for obeying E. Tryon's admonition while producing this book with skill and effort. And my thanks to her for providing us a timely and tightly written statement of what we know about ADHD and what we can do about it. Thank you, Lisa.

—*Russell A. Barkley, Ph.D.*
Research Professor of Psychiatry
SUNY Upstate Medical University (Syracuse, NY)
and
Clinical Professor of Psychiatry
Medical University of South Carolina (Charleston, SC)

PREFACE

Attention-Deficit/Hyperactivity Disorder is one of the most well-known and controversial disorders of childhood. ADHD is characterized by developmentally inappropriate level of inattention, hyperactivity, and impulsivity, and affects approximately 3% to 7% of the school-age population and 2% to 4% of the adult population. Outspoken critics claim that the disorder is fraudulent, while the scientific evidence clearly supports the validity of the disorder, as do professional groups such as the American Academy of Pediatrics, American Psychological Association, American Medical Association, National Association of School Psychologists, and the U.S. Surgeon General. Research across genetic, behavioral, neuroanatomical, neuropsychological, and neuroimaging disciplines support the existence of ADHD. Long-term studies have found that children, adolescents, and adults with ADHD are at significantly greater risk for academic, behavioral, occupational, and psychological problems compared to those without the disorder. Numerous types of treatments are available for ADHD, with some more supported by research than others. Identification and diagnosis of ADHD is not simple and requires a thorough assessment process. Misconceptions and questions abound in the media as well as in the scientific community concerning the etiology, diagnosis and treatment of ADHD. An ADHD Primer addresses each of these areas from a scientific perspective.

An ADHD Primer is intended for students enrolled in teacher certification programs, graduate students enrolled in research and applied training programs, and educators, counselors, psychologists, physicians, parents, and individuals with ADHD. This revised text summarizes the literature concerning ADHD across the lifespan with regard to assessment, diagnosis, etiology, and treatment. It is packed with current, practical, and useful information that will help professionals as well as individuals with the disorder better understand and respond to ADHD. One of the greatest strengths of *An ADHD Primer* is that it contains tables and appendixes many that can be photocopied, as well as numerous up-to-date references and resources for the reader who desires more information about ADHD. Although many books have been written about ADHD, most of the texts have been written from a clinical perspective or for a select audience (i.e., parents, teachers, clinicians, researchers, or individuals with ADHD). Many of the available texts are either non-research based or are heavily researched based and time-consuming to digest. As a university professor with both clinical and research experience, I am frequently called upon to share the 'facts' about ADHD in children, adolescents, college students, and adults. *An ADHD Primer* is intended to capture what is known about ADHD from a scientific perspective and to convey this knowledge in a concise, straightforward, and user-friendly manner.

Acknowledgments

I wish to acknowledge and thank the many authors, researchers, and publishers who gave permission for their work to be included in this book. I would also like to express my appreciation of CWU undergraduate student Sarah Dunkin, and CWU graduate students Michelle Lillard and Teresa Vance, for their research skills and organizational assistance. Michelle Lillard's assistance with the permissions process and development of the index was invaluable. Special thanks are owed to the children, adolescents, college students, and adults with ADHD, as well as their families, who inspired me to write this primer. I would like to extend my gratitude to Dr. Russell Barkley for writing the foreword for *An ADHD Primer*, and for his unwavering dedication to the scientific study of ADHD, Lastly, I would like to thank my editor Steve Rutter at LEA, for his support and encouragement throughout the publication process.

1

Attention-Deficit/ Hyperactivity Disorder— What Is It?

He never sits still; he is constantly in motion.
She never pays attention, and she talks incessantly.
He cannot hold down a job.
She is not doing well in school. The teachers say she is lazy.
He does not follow through on anything, and he loses everything.
He is so disorganized!
She has been this way as long as I can remember.

Description

Although these statements can be true of most children, adolescents, and adults at some point in their lives, they are typical concerns expressed by parents, teachers, spouses, and siblings about individuals with *attention-deficit/hyperactivity disorder* (*ADHD*). ADHD, as it is currently defined by the American Psychiatric Association (2000), is characterized by persistent and developmentally inappropriate problems with attention, impulsivity, and hyperactivity that cause impairment in one's life. The presence, absence, or combination of these three symptoms reflects the severity and subtype of ADHD. Research findings indicate that ADHD is a lifelong condition that impacts an individual's educational, social, and occupational life.

Does ADHD Exist?

In the year 2000, the National Institutes of Health (NIH) released a consensus statement concerning the diagnosis and treatment of ADHD (National Institutes of Health, 2000) and indicated that "despite the progress in assessment, diagnosis and treatment of children and adults with ADHD, the disorder has remained controversial. . . . The controversy raises questions concerning the literal existence of the disorder" (p. 182). This concern mirrors the views expressed by others such as Armstrong (1995), who has questioned the authenticity of ADHD, and Baughman (2004), a neurologist, who is the author of a video entitled "ADHD—Total 100% Fraud." Although the concern may be well intended, research across behavioral, genetic, neuropsychological, and neurophysiological disciplines supports the existence of ADHD; and a diagnosis of ADHD can be made reliably using various assessment methods discussed in later chapters. In fact, the NIH consensus statement after thorough review of the scientific evidence concludes that ADHD is a valid disorder and this perspective is endorsed by the American Academy of Pediatrics, the American Medical Association, the American Psychiatric Association, the American Psychological Association, the National Association of School Psychologists, the U.S. Surgeon General, and others. In 2002, a consortium of international scientists addressed the assertion that ADHD is a fraud by reviewing the scientific evidence to the contrary and issued the International Consensus Statement on ADHD (2002).

Admittedly, there is not an objective, conclusive "test" for the disorder, but nor is there an objective test for the common cold or many clinical conditions such as autistic disorder, depression, Tourette's disorder, and obsessive compulsive disorder. Like the common cold, depression, and other disorders, a diagnosis of ADHD is based on the presence and severity of symptoms. In the case of ADHD, the symptoms have an early onset; are chronic, pervasive, and developmentally inappropriate; and cause significant impairment in an individual's life.

ADHD is the most frequently studied disorder of childhood, and volumes of scientific evidence attest to the existence of the disorder (e.g., Asherson, 2004; Brown et al., 2005; Wolraich et al., 2005). To deny the existence of ADHD can do far more harm than good. Long-term studies, for example, have found that children, adolescents, and adults with ADHD—compared to those without the disorder—are at significantly greater risk for academic, behavioral, and social problems (see Developmental Information later in this chapter). Early identification and intervention are essential to improving the outcome of individuals with the disorder, and educators often play a key part in both of these tasks. As Satterfield, Satterfield, and Cantwell (1981) noted, and more recently Foy and Earls (2005), the classroom teacher is a major determining factor in whether a student is correctly diagnosed with ADHD and whether they succeed or fail in the classroom.

Background Information

According to Dr. Roscoe Dykman (2005) the symptoms now associated with ADHD have been recognized in children since the 1800s and, in fact, appeared in a nursery rhyme written by Heinrich Hoffman in 1863. George Still (1902), a physician who presented a series of papers to the Royal College of Physicians, is typically credited for formally identifying ADHD symptoms in children, although others have also been recognized as pioneers in the field (see Dykman, 2005, for a review of the historical information). Following Still's work, clinicians and researchers asserted that these symptoms were likely due to brain damage, and, despite lack of physiological evidence for this claim, the term *minimal brain dysfunction* (*MBD*) emerged during the late 1940s and the 1950s (e.g., Brown et al., 1962; Clements & Peters, 1962; Strauss & Lehtinen, 1947). During the 1960s, the research focus shifted to the overt, hyperactivity symptoms. In 1968, the second edition of the *Diagnostic and Statistical Manual* (*DSM-II*) was published (American Psychiatric Association, 1968) and for the first time included the diagnostic category *hyperkinetic reaction disorder of childhood*. Ac-

TABLE 1.1   Historical Information

1902	Symptoms Described by Dr. George Still
1950	Minimal Brain Dysfunction (MBD) Focus on Hyperactivity Symptoms
1968	*DSM-II;* Hyperkinetic Reaction Disorder of Childhood Focus Remained on Hyperactivity Symptoms
1980	*DSM-III;* Attention-Deficit Disorder (ADD) ADD With Hyperactivity ADD Without Hyperactivity
1987	*DSM-III-R;* Attention-Deficit Hyperactivity Disorder ADHD With Levels of Severity Noted Mild, Moderate, and Severe Undifferentiated ADD
1994	*DSM-IV;* Attention-Deficit/Hyperactivity Disorder ADHD: Combined Type ADHD: Predominately Inattentive Type ADHD: Predominately Hyperactive-Impulsive Type

Note: From Weyandt (2001).

cording to the *DSM-II*, the central hallmarks of the disorder were hyperactivity, distractibility, and attention problems. It was believed at this time that children would outgrow the disorder by adolescence.

During the 1970s, the research emphasis shifted from hyperactivity to attention problems. This focus was reflected in the new diagnostic label, *attention deficit disorder (ADD)*, published in the third edition of the *DSM* (American Psychiatric Association, 1980). According to *DSM-III*, two subtypes of ADD existed—*ADD with or without hyperactivity*. In 1987, the *DSM-III* was revised (*DSM-III–R*), and, although the label remained the same (i.e., *ADD*), the emphasis was now on the presence and pervasiveness of three core symptoms—inattention, impulsivity, and hyperactivity (American Psychiatric Association, 1987). *ADD without hyperactivity* was no longer recognized as a specific subtype of ADD and was instead categorized as *undifferentiated ADD*. In 1994, the fourth edition of the *DSM* was released, and the diagnostic category *ADD* was changed to *ADHD (attention-deficit/hyperactivity disorder)*. Three new subtypes were delineated—*ADHD, predominately inattentive type; ADHD, predominately hyperactive-impulsive type;* and *ADHD, combined type* (see Table 1.1 for a summary of this information).

Differences in Subtypes

Research indicates that the three ADHD subtypes can be reliably diagnosed (see Table 1.2) and may have clinically meaningful differences. For example, a study by Morgan, Hynd, Riccio, and Hall (1996) found that children with ADHD, combined type, have more behavioral and acting out problems, while

TABLE 1.2   Diagnostic Criteria for Attention-Deficit/Hyperactivity Disorder

A. Either (1) or (2):

 (1) six (or more) of the following symptoms of inattention have persisted for at least 6 months to a degree that is maladaptive and inconsistent with the developmental level:

 Inattention
 (a) Often fails to give close attention to details or makes careless mistaken in school work, work, or other activities
 (b) often has difficulty sustaining attention in tasks or play activities
 (c) often does not seem to listen when spoken to directly
 (d) often does not follow through on instructions and fails to finish school work, chores, or duties in the workplace (not due to oppositional behavior or failure to understand instructions)
 (e) often has difficulty organizing tasks and activities
 (f) often avoids, dislikes, or is reluctant to engage in tasks that require sustained mental effort (such as school work or homework)
 (g) often loses things necessary for tasks or activities (e.g., toys, school assignments, pencils, books, or tools)
 (h) is often easily distracted by extraneous stimuli
 (i) is often forgetful in daily activities

 (2) six (or more) of the following symptoms of hyperactivity-impulsivity have persisted for at least 6 months to a degree that is maladaptive and inconsistent with developmental level:

 Hyperactivity
 (a) often fidgets with hands or feet or squirms in seat
 (b) often leaves seat in classroom or in other situations in which remaining seated is expected
 (c) often runs about or climbs excessively in situation in which it is inappropriate (in adolescents or adults, may be limited to subjective feelings of restlessness)
 (d) often has difficulty playing or engaging in leisure activities quietly
 (e) is often "on the go" or often acts as if "driven by a motor"
 (f) often talks excessively

 Impulsivity
 (g) often blurts out answers before questions have been completed
 (h) often has difficulty awaiting turn
 (i) often interrupts or intrudes on others (e.g., butts into conversations or games)

B. Some hyperactive-impulsive or inattentive symptoms that caused impairment were present before age 7 years.

C. Some impairment from the symptoms is present in two or more settings (e.g., at school [or work] and at home).

D. There must be clear evidence of clinically significant impairment in social, academic, or occupational functioning.

E. The symptoms do not occur exclusively during the course of a Pervasive Developmental Disorder, Schizophrenia, or other Psychotic Disorder and are not better accounted for by another mental disorder (e.g., Mood Disorder, Anxiety Disorder, Dissociative Disorder, or a personality Disorder).

Code based on type:

314.01 Attention-Deficit/Hyperactivity Disorder, Combined Type: if both Criteria A1 and A2 are met for the past 6 months

314.00 Attention-Deficit/Hyperactivity Disorder, Predominately Inattentive Type: if Criterion A1 is met but Criterion A2 is not met for the past 6 months

314.01 Attention-Deficit/Hyperactivity Disorder, Predominately Hyperactive-Impulsive Type: if Criterion A2 is met but Criterion A1 is not met for the past 6 months

Coding note: For individuals (especially adolescents and adults) who currently have symptoms that no longer meet full criteria. "In Partial Remission" should be specified.

Source: Reprinted with permission from the *Diagnostic and Statistical Manual of Mental Disorders Text Revision*, Fourth Edition. Copyright 2000 American Psychiatric Association.

children with ADHD, predominately inattentive type, have fewer behavioral but more learning problems. More recently, Carlson and Mann (2002) reported that children with ADHD inattentive subtype were rated by teachers as having fewer behavioral problems but higher levels of anxiety, depression, unhappiness, and withdrawn behavior. Bauermeister, Matos, and Reina (1999) found the family is impacted differently depending on the ADHD subtype a child or adolescent might have. Specifically, Bauermeister and colleagues found that mothers of children with ADHD, combined type, reported (a) more negative feelings such as frustration, and less positive feelings toward their children; and (b) a greater negative impact on family social life and relationship with teachers, compared to mothers of children with ADHD, predominately inattentive type. With regard to age and subtype, studies suggest that the predominately hyperactive-impulsive subtype is most often associated with younger children and the predominately inattentive type is associated with older children in the United States as well as in other countries (McBurnett et al., 1999; Nolan, Gadow, & Sprafkin, 2001; Pineda et al., 1999). On behavioral tasks, several studies have found performance differences among children with different subtypes of ADHD. For example, Collings (2003) reported that children with ADHD combined type committed a greater percentage of omission errors on a continuous performance task, and their performance deteriorated more quickly, relative to children with ADHD inattentive type (and children without ADHD). Todd et al. (2002) studied achievement and cognitive performance of a sample of child and adolescent twins with ADHD and found that those with the combined subtype and inattentive subtype made significantly worse grades and achievement testing scores, and had an increased use of special education services compared to those twins with hyperactive/impulsive subtype of ADHD. Clark and colleagues (Clark, Barry, McCarthy, & Selikowitz, 2001) compared EEG recordings of children with ADHD combined type versus inattentive type and reported that those with combined type had an increase in fast-wave activity in the frontal regions of the brain. Although these findings are inconclusive, they do suggest that distinct physiological differences may exist between different subtypes of ADHD. Murphy, Barkley, and Bush (2002) conducted one of the few studies to compare subtype differences among young adults with ADHD (ages 17–27) and found that those with ADHD combined type were more likely than those with inattentive subtype to have been arrested, attempted suicide, to have oppositional defiant disorder, and hostility problems. These authors as well as others have suggested that the greater impulsivity associated with the combined subtype may increase the likelihood that young adults with ADHD will engage in antisocial behavior. It is important to note, however, that Murphy, Barkley, and Bush found that young adults with ADHD combined and inattentive subtypes did not differ on a number of dimensions such as co-existing psychiatric conditions, psychological distress, use of mental health services, and use of illegal drugs. In addition, a number of studies have failed to find cognitive or behavioral differences between individuals with subtypes of ADHD (e.g., Corkum & Siegel, 1993; Milich, Balentine, & Lynam, 2002) and the majority of studies have been conducted with children. Furthermore, some studies have reported subtype differences on a few but not all neuropsychological tasks (Schmitz et al., 2002). Additional research is needed to determine whether distinct behavioral, cognitive, academic, and neurophysiological differences exist among children, adolescents, and adults with different subtypes of ADHD.

Current Criteria

The *DSM-IV* was published in 1994 and the *DSM-IV* Text Revision was released in 2000. The diagnostic criteria for ADHD did not change from the fourth edition to the Text Revision of the *DSM* and the current diagnostic criteria appear in Table 1.2. The diagnostic criteria for ADHD require that an individual display significant *and* developmentally inappropriate levels of inattention, hyperactivity, and impulsivity. These symptoms must be present early in life; exist in two or more settings; and cause social, educational, or occupational impairment. It is important to recognize that nearly everyone is inattentive, hyperactive, or impulsive in some situations and that the mere presence of ADHD symptoms does not equal a "disorder." Furthermore, symptoms associated with ADHD, particularly inattention, can also be characteristic of many other disorders such as learning disabilities, sleep disorders, substance use, and emotional problems, to name a few. As Gordon and Barkley (1999) aptly stated, "inattention as a symptom resembles fever or chest pains in that its presence alone does little to narrow the field of diagnostic possibilities" (p. 2). To arrive at a valid ADHD diagnosis, a thorough evaluation is required.

DSM-IV Limitations

The current diagnostic criteria are an improvement over *DSM-III–R* (1987) criteria as they are based on research studies and they include a requirement of impairment in social, academic, or occupational functioning. Problems remain, however, as some experts in the field argue that ADHD, predominately inattentive type should be a separate, distinct, and independent disorder from ADHD (Barkley, 1998, p. 65). Indeed, results from several studies suggest that, statistically, *DSM* criteria tend to fall into two, rather than three, categories. For example, Beiser, Dion, and Gotowiec (2000) examined parent and teacher ratings of 1,555 Native and 489 non-Native children from the United States and Canada and found a two-factor solution; attention versus hyperactive-impulsive symptoms. Similar findings have been reported with Icelandic children (Magnusson, Smari, Gretarsdottir, & Prandardottir, 1999), Brazilian children (Rohde et al., 2001), and others (e.g., DuPaul, McGoey, Eckert, & Van Brackle, 2001; Wolraich, Lambert, Baumgaertel, et al., 2003). The usefulness and stability of the ADHD, predominately hyperactive-impulsive, subtype has also been questioned. For example, Lahey, Pelham, Loney, Lee, and Willcutt (2005) conducted an 8-year longitudinal study of 4- to 6-year olds who met *DSM-IV* criteria for ADHD and found that most children, over time, continued to meet diagnostic criteria for the disorder. Of the three subtypes, however, children with the hyperactive-impulsive subtype rarely met the criteria for this subtype over time. An additional problem with the current diagnostic criteria concerns the questionable developmental appropriateness of the items for children, adolescents, and adults. For example, earlier research by Hart, Lahey, Loeber, Applegate, and Frick (1995) indicated that the symptoms of ADHD changed during childhood and adolescence and specifically that problems with attention remain relatively persistent while hyperactivity and impulsivity symptoms appear to decline with age. More recently, Biederman, Mick, and Faraone (2000) followed 128 boys with ADHD for a period of 4 years and also found that ADHD symptoms tended to decline with age, and the most significant decline in symptoms was with hyperactive, impulsive symptoms. Similar age-related changes have been reported by others (e.g., Drechsler, Brandeis, Foldenyi, Imhof, & Steinhausen, 2005; Kato, Nichols, Kerivan, & Huffman, 2001). These findings, however, are likely due in part to the diagnostic criteria which are not age-referenced and are limited in number with regard to hyperactivity and impulsivity relative to inattention (i.e., nine for inattention, six for hyperactivity, and three for impulsivity). Indeed, Spencer, Biederman, Wilens, and Faraone (2002) suggested that the current criteria for ADHD may minimize, or underestimate, the actual rate of persistence of ADHD into adulthood. Given the concerns expressed in the literature and the ongoing research in this area, it is likely that the diagnostic criteria for ADHD will be revised in future editions of the *DSM* and reflect more age-appropriate items. It is also likely that the subtypes will be revised and may reflect statistical studies that support two primary dimensions (attention, impulsivity/hyperactivity) rather than three.

Prevalence of ADHD and ADHD Symptoms

According to the American Psychiatric Association (2000), ADHD is estimated to affect 3% to 7% of the U.S. school-age population and affects all ethnic and socioeconomic groups. This percentage varies, however, depending on (a) the diagnostic criteria and methods used by clinicians and researchers to define and assess ADHD, and (b) whether researchers actually assess the prevalence of *the disorder* or merely the presence of ADHD symptoms. Studies differ also with respect to the age and gender of the individuals examined, geographic location, criteria used to define ADHD (e.g., *DSM* versions), raters (e.g., teachers, parents, pediatricians), settings (e.g., home, school, clinics), assessment tools, cut-off scores indicative of ADHD, as well as other aspects. As Rowland, Lesesne, and Abramowitz (2002) aptly stated, "basic epidemiologic information about the distribution of ADHD across the population by age, sex, race, and socio-economic status remains inadequately described" (p. 162). With regard to age, for example, the American Psychiatric Association (2000) estimates 3% to 7% of school-age children have ADHD while estimates of ADHD in adults is substantially lower (i.e., 1% to 2%) (Biederman, 2004; Kooij et al., 2005).

The CDC (2005) recently reported that 4.4 million children ages 4 to 17 were reported to have a diagnosis of ADHD in 2003, and of these 2.5 million (56%) were treated with medication. Similar numbers of males and females were prescribed medication (56.8% and 55.0%). Prevalence rates varied by state with the lowest prevalence of ADHD in Colorado (5%) and the highest in Alabama (11%). With regard to ethnicity, ADHD appears in all ethnic groups but as Stevens, Harman, and Kelleher (2004) found, ethnic and regional differences exist in primary care visits for children with ADHD. Specifically, the researchers found that an ADHD diagnosis and a stimulant prescription were less likely to be made with Hispanic American children than White American children. Interestingly, their results also revealed that stimulants were prescribed more frequently for children with ADHD in the south and west than in the northeast. A later study using data from 1997 to 2000 produced similar findings and revealed that African American children with ADHD were less likely to take stimulant medication compared to White-American children (Stevens, Harman, & Kelleher, 2005). Bussing and colleagues (Bussing, Gary, Mills, & Garvan, 2003) reported that African-American parents expressed fewer worries about ADHD-related school problems and were more unsure about the causes and treatments for ADHD compared to Caucasian parents. As Samuel et al. (1999) noted, very little is known about ADHD in African-American children and the same can be said about Hispanic-American and other minority groups with ADHD.

When studies examine the prevalence of ADHD *symptoms*, the percentages vary and in some cases tend to be higher or lower than the estimates provided by the American Psychiatric Association (Katusic et al., 2005). For example, in 1996 Lavigne and colleagues found that 2% of preschool children in a primary care sample met the *DSM-IV* (1994) criteria for ADHD. In a recent review of the literature, however, Conner (2002) reported that the prevalence of ADHD symptoms in preschoolers in the United States varies from 2% to 59% depending on whether community or clinic-referred children are studied. Pineda et al. (1999) found a higher rate of ADHD symptoms among 6- to 11-year-old children than 12- to 17-year-old adolescents, and Nolan, Gadow, and Sprafkin (2001) found very few adolescents reported significant problems with hyperactivity and impulsivity (only 0.8%). With regard to the prevalence of ADHD symptoms in young adults Weyandt, Rice, and Linterman (1995) found a substantial percentage of college students reported significant levels of ADHD symptoms (i.e., 7%). This percentage dropped, however, when both childhood symptoms and current symptoms were considered (2.5%). More recently, DuPaul, Schaughency, Weyandt, Tripp, et al. (2001) examined the prevalence of ADHD symptoms in college students from three countries (Italy, New Zealand, and the United States) and found the prevalence rates varied from 0% (Italian females) to 8.1% (New Zealand males).

As mentioned previously, a variety of factors contribute to the discrepant findings among studies including the methods used to identify ADHD symptoms. This is a crucial factor to consider as relying on a single method can result in overidentification and misleading information. For example, using teacher ratings as the only source of information, Werry and Quay (1971) found 30% of the boys and 12% of the girls in their study were rated as overactive, while 43% of the boys and 25% of the girls were rated as having attention span problems! Wolraich, Hannah, Pinnock, Baumgaertel, and Brown (1996), using teacher ratings based on *DSM-IV* criteria, found a prevalence rate of 11.4% for children in kindergarten through Grade 5. The most common subtype found in their study was ADHD, predominately inattentive type (5.4%), followed by the combined type (3.6%) and hyperactive-impulsive type (2.4%). In 2001, Nolan et al. asked teachers to complete a *DSM-IV* symptom inventory for 3,006 school children between the ages of 3 and 18 and found an overall prevalence rate of 15.8%. The highest prevalence rate was for the inattentive subtype (9.9%) followed by the hyperactive-impulsive and combined subtypes of ADHD (9.9% and 3.9% respectively). Prevalence rates were higher for African-American students (39.5%) compared to White students (14.2%). Reid and colleagues (2001) also found that African-American boys and girls were two to three times more likely to be rated by teachers as having significantly greater attention and impulsivity problems than European Americans and suggested that African-American children are at greater risk for being inaccurately identified as having ADHD. It is important to note that these studies only assessed the presence of ADHD symptoms and did not conduct clinical evaluations for the disorder. In fact, when additional information *is* gathered, such as degree of impairment, pervasiveness, onset, and ratings from multiple informants (e.g., teacher and parent), these figures drop substantially to about 1% to 4% (Barkley, 1998), which is more consistent with the 3% to 7% suggested by the American Psychiatric Association. This issue of identification and assessment of ADHD will be thoroughly addressed in chapter 3.

Prevalence of ADHD Symptoms in Other Countries

The prevalence of ADHD in other countries has also been investigated, and, as in the United States, statistics vary depending on factors such as age of the individuals investigated, gender, raters (e.g., parents, teachers) and diagnostic criteria employed. In some countries the prevalence rates are substantially higher than those reported in the United States, while other studies report similar prevalence rates. In Germany, for example, Baumgaertel, Wolraich, and Dietrich (1995) reported a prevalence of 10.9% using teacher ratings and *DSM-III–R* (1987) criteria. Similar findings were reported in a Canadian study, with an ADHD prevalence rate of 9% in boys and 3.3% in girls (Szatmari, 1992). In Japan, Kanbayashi, Nakata, Fujii, Kita, and Wada (1994) reported a prevalence rate of 7.7% of children ages 4 to 12, using parent ratings and *DSM-III–R* criteria, and similar findings were reported by teacher ratings of children age 6 to 12 living in Hong Kong (Luk, Leung, & Lee, 1988). The prevalence of ADHD in Bangkok, Thailand among a sample of 353 students was recently reported to be 6.5% (Benjasuwantep, Ruangdaraganon, & Visudhiphan, 2002). Studies conducted in New Zealand have yielded mixed results, with ADHD prevalence rates ranging from 2% to 6% in school-age children, and 4% to 6% in adolescents (Schaughency, McGee, Raja, Feehan, & Silva, 1994). Studies in Australia have reported a 7.5% prevalence rate for ADHD among children ages 6 to 17, based on parent ratings (Graetz et al., 2001). In India, Bhatia, Nigam, Bohra, and Malik (1991) reported that 29.2% of adolescents ages 11 and 12 displayed significant ADHD symptoms. The prevalence rate of ADHD in Norway is similar to U.S. statistics, with ADHD occurring in approximately 3% to 4% of school-age children (Kløve, 1989). Rohde and colleagues from Brazil (1999) reported that approximately 5.8% of students ages 12 to 14 have ADHD, with a slightly higher percentage of males than females having the disorder. Pineda and colleagues (1999) reported that of a sample of 540 children living in Manizales, Colombia, 19.8% of boys and 12.3% of girls ages 6 to 11 met *DSM-IV* (1994) criteria based on parental ratings alone. Disruptive behavior disorders, most commonly ADHD, have been reported to affect 11.1% of a sample of children in Valencia, Spain (Andrés, Catala, & Gómez-Beneyto, 1999). Recently, a study of 600 Ukrainian children reported an overall prevalence rate of 19.8% for ADHD with the highest subtype ratings for ADHD hyperactive-impulsive type (8.5%) followed by the inattentive type (7.2%), and combined type (4.2%) based on parent and teacher ratings (Gadow et al., 2000). The prevalence of ADHD symptoms in Italian children has been investigated as well, and Mugnaini et al. (2005) recently reported an overall prevalence rate of 7.1% in first graders based on teacher reports. The most common subtype of ADHD was the inattentive type (3.5%) followed by the hyperactive-impulsive and combined subtypes (2.3% and 1.3%). In this study, males were more likely to meet *DSM-IV* criteria for ADHD than females (10.4% vs. 3.8%). Kadesjö, Kadesjö, Hägglöf, and Gillberg (2001) from Sweden also reported gender differences with respect to ADHD symptoms in children ages 3 to 7, and noted that only 6% of the children who met the criteria for ADHD "appeared normal" with regard to attention and activity level at clinical examination (p. 1027). A study conducted in Ethiopia found that living in an urban area was significantly associated with ADHD, and that children between the ages of 10 and 14 were three times more likely to have ADHD compared to younger children (Ashenafi, Kebede, Desta, & Alem, 2000). Perhaps one of the lowest rates of ADHD was reported by Brownell and Yogendran (2001), who investigated physicians' diagnosis rates for ADHD in the province of Manitoba and found an overall rate of 1.52%.

In summary, ADHD symptoms appear in children, adolescents, and adults from various countries throughout the world. A variety of factors contribute to the inconsistent rates among studies. An important distinction is whether prevalence rates reflect the prevalence of ADHD symptoms or actual diagnosed cases of ADHD. Although estimates vary, the generally accepted rate is 3% to 7% for children in the United States as reported by the American Psychiatric Association (2000). Some have questioned whether ADHD is "on the rise" in the United States and elsewhere in the world.

Increased Incidence of ADHD?

The question of whether the incidence of ADHD is on the rise is difficult to assess for several reasons. First, the diagnostic criteria have changed considerably over the years, making comparison studies extremely problematic. Second, it is difficult to determine whether physicians and clinicians are more knowledgeable and better trained at recognizing and diagnosing the disorder, or whether they are making faulty diagnoses as claimed by some (e.g., Breggin, 1998a). Third, given the media attention and proliferation of material on the subject available to parents, teachers, and the general public, more referrals for ADHD assessment are likely to occur and, consequently, individuals with ADHD may be identified who otherwise would have remained undiagnosed. However, research comparing the frequency of ADHD diagnoses using *DSM-III–R* (1987) and *DSM-IV* (2000) criteria does suggest that more children are *diagnosed* with ADHD relative to a decade ago (e.g., Wolraich et al., 1996; Wolraich, Hannah, Baumgaertel, & Feurer, 1998). For example, in a study comparing the classification rates of *DSM-III–R* and *DSM-IV* among preschoolers, Byrne, Bawden, Beattie, and DeWolfe (2000) found that 16% of the preschoolers identified as having ADHD would not have been classified as having ADHD using *DSM-III–R* criteria. Barbaresi et al. (2004) reported a 7.5% cumulative incidence of ADHD in 19-year-olds living in Rochester, Minnesota. Although it is uncertain whether the incidence of ADHD is increasing or whether it is more accurately being diagnosed, recent findings suggest that teachers are likely to identify children as having ADHD when they do not have the disorder. Specifically, Havey, Olson, McCormick, and Cates (2005) found that nearly 24% of students were identified by teachers as meeting *DSM-IV* criteria for ADHD, compared to the expected rate of 3% to 7% (APA, 2000). Similar findings were reported by Glass and Wegar (2000) who found teachers overidentified ADHD in students. Glass and Wegar also found that medication was the preferred form of treatment by teachers for students with ADHD.

Studies conducted in clinic settings also support that more children are diagnosed with ADHD compared to a decade or more ago. For example, Robinson, Sclar, Skaer, and Galin (1999; Robinson, Skaer, Sclar, & Galin, 2002) reported that the number of office visits documenting a diagnosis of ADHD increased from nearly 950,000 in 1990 to more than 2 million in 1995, and to more than 3 million by 1998. This study also reported a 2.3-fold increase in office-based visits documenting ADHD, with a 3.9-fold increase in the number of girls diagnosed with ADHD and a 2.2-fold increase in the number of boys diagnosed with ADHD. Critics have used this information to fuel the argument that ADHD does not exist and is simply a way of justifying the control of children with drugs (Breggin, 1998b, 2001). In response to these claims, as well as due to public concern, the American Medical Association's Council of Scientific Affairs evaluated the diagnosis and treatment of ADHD. The council concluded that ADHD is *not* overdiagnosed and the actual number of children treated for ADHD falls at the lower end of the prevalence range (Couzin, 2004; Goldman, Genel, Bezman, & Slanetz, 1998). (See chapter 4 for additional information on this topic.)

Developmental Information

Prenatal, Infancy, and Toddlerhood

Leslie, age four, is described by his parents as a "handful and has been that way since day one." As an infant, Leslie was a difficult baby; he cried frequently, slept irregularly, and was generally a "fussy baby." During toddlerhood, Leslie had numerous "accidents" and was much more active than other two-year-olds. He began attending preschool at four years of age, and his teachers frequently complained that he was unruly and "very mischievous." After attending preschool for one month, Leslie's preschool teachers indicated that he was too disruptive and did not appear "ready" for preschool.

As indicated by Leslie's case, children with ADHD typically exhibit ADHD symptoms early in life and sometimes can be identified as early as preschool. Although *DSM-IV-TR* (1994) criteria require that the onset of ADHD symptoms occur before age seven, most children are identified during the school-age years (i.e., elementary school). Work by Barkley, Fischer, Edelbrock, and Smallish (1990), however, suggests that the average age of onset of symptoms is three to four years of age. Several studies have attempted to identify infancy variables that might be predictive of the development of ADHD in childhood. Although no "infancy profile" exists, several factors have been associated with the development of ADHD, including maternal smoking and alcohol use during pregnancy, premature delivery, low birth weight, delayed motor development, and strong intensity of response during infancy (e.g., Barkley, DuPaul, & McMurray, 1990; Breslau et al., 1996; Hartsough & Lambert, 1985). Recently, McGrath et al. (2005) conducted a longitudinal study of low birth weight infants to determine factors that might be predictive of ADHD at a later age (age four). Results indicated that birth weight, gestational age, and medical and neurological status were all associated with attention problems and hyperactivity at age four. Bhutta and colleagues (2002) conducted a meta-analysis of preterm infants and cognitive and behavioral outcomes and found that 81% of preterm infants had increased risk of cognitive and behavior problems, and more than twice the risk for ADHD. Other studies have found that infant regulatory problems at the age of 3 months are predictive of hyperactive symptoms in childhood (e.g., Becker, Holtman, Laucht, & Schmidt, 2004), and severe sleep problems during infancy are highly predictive (1 in 4) of ADHD by age five (Crabtree, Ivanenko, & Gozal, 2003; Thunstrom, 2002). It is crucial to note that these findings are only correlational and do not have a direct relationship with ADHD. In other words, some children with ADHD do not have a history of regulatory problems during infancy, were not of low birth weight, etc., and by the same token, many children with these problems during infancy do not develop ADHD. What can be concluded is that certain characteristics during infancy increase the risk of a child developing ADHD later in life.

During the preschool years, children with ADHD are typically excessively active, impulsive, accident prone, demanding, and frequently do not adapt well to environmental changes (Fraser, 2002). Byrne and colleagues (2003) reported that the most common type of ADHD in preschool children is the hyperactive-impulsive subtype. In addition, Wilens, Biederman, Brown, et al. (2002) reported that the most common type of psychopathology in preschoolers is ADHD and that most preschoolers with ADHD have at least one or more additional disorders (e.g., conduct, oppositional, mood, anxiety disorders). Preschool children with ADHD have also been found to be more aggressive, noncompliant, and defiant and are often described as having a negative temperament (e.g., Campbell & Ewing, 1990). Research also indicates that preschool age children with ADHD are more likely to have problems with oppositional behavior than children without ADHD and to engage in behaviors that places them at greater risk for physical injury (Byrne, Bawden, Beattie, & DeWolfe, 2003; Gadow, Sprafkin, & Nolan, 2001). These behaviors are obviously problematic in a preschool setting, and children with ADHD are at greater risk for expulsion from preschool settings, which increases the likelihood that these children will develop social and academic problems. Indeed, DuPaul, McGoey, Eckert, and Van Brakle (2001) found that preschool children with ADHD scored significantly lower on a test of preacademic skills than children without the disorder. DuPaul and colleagues also found that children with ADHD were less socially skilled, exhibited more problem behaviors, and were more noncompliant during school tasks. Kathleen Fraser (2002) recently reviewed public-school administrative records and conducted interviews with educators who worked with preschoolers diagnosed with ADHD and found that certain factors were associated with a better school adjustment for these children (e.g., structure, gentle and consistent adult assistance, acceptance, gross motor activities) while other factors were associated with less favorable outcomes (e.g., multiple caregivers, unreasonable expectations, unavailable and uninvolved parents). Barkley, Shelton, Crosswait, et al. (2002) conducted a 3-year follow-up study of preschool children with ADHD and found that those children with aggressive and oppositional defiant behavior in addition to their ADHD symptoms were at substantially greater risk for academic, social, and behavior problems. In summary, the literature indicates that ADHD symptoms are often present during the preschool years and that children with the disorder are more likely to have social, behavior, and academic difficulties. Preschool children with ADHD and aggressive, defiant behaviors, appear to be at the greatest risk for maladjustment in preschool and later years.

Childhood

More information is available about ADHD in childhood than any other developmental period. Given that most classrooms contain at least 20 children, it has been estimated that one to two children with ADHD will be found in a typical classroom (DuPaul & Stoner, 1994, 2003). Based on long-term studies, it is clear that ADHD symptoms generally persist during the elementary school years, with additional problems emerging such as poor social skills, problems with peer relationships, and in more severe cases, conduct problems, and aggressive behavior. Hoza and colleagues (2005) recently found that peers of children with ADHD rated those with the disorder as less well liked, more often rejected, and as having fewer friends than comparison children without the disorder. Research has also found that girls with ADHD tend to have fewer friends and greater difficulty maintaining friendships compared to girls without the disorder (Blachman & Hinshaw, 2002). Stroes, Alberts, and van der Meere (2003) found that boys with ADHD demonstrated poor social attention (e.g., less eye contact, talking while adult was talking) during conversation with a nonfamiliar adult compared to boys without ADHD. Lawrence and colleagues (2002) reported that boys with ADHD exhibited more self-talk while playing video games compared to boys without the disorder. Wolraich, Lambert, Baumgaertel, et al. (2003) recently studied teacher ratings of approximately 21,000 children in three countries (United States, Spain, Germany) and found that children with the most inattention problems also had significant academic

problems while those with behavior problems tended to have significant problems across all three core symptoms of ADHD (inattention, impulsivity, hyperactivity). Research has also found that teachers tend to rate boys as having more
ADHD symptoms than girls (Hartung et al., 2002; Havey, Olson, McCormick, &
Cates, 2005). Hinshaw (2002) studied preadolescent girls with ADHD and
found they were more likely to have been retained at least one grade level, had
lower academic achievement, and more acting out behaviors than non-ADHD
girls. Hinshaw also reported that those with the inattentive subtype of ADHD
were more socially isolated than girls without ADHD and those with the combined type were the most socially rejected by their peers. Other studies have
reported similar findings with boys with ADHD, and most have also found co-
existing problems during the elementary school years such as learning disabilities (e.g., Seidman, Biederman, Monuteaux, Doyle, & Faraone, 2001). Reading
disability is the most common type of learning problem with these children,
and their mathematical achievement tends to be lower that that of their peers
(Riccio, Hynd, Cohen, Hall, & Molt, 1994; Zentall & Smith, 1993; Palacios &
Semrud-Clikeman, 2005). Pastor and Reuben (2002) studied national prevalence rates of ADHD in the United States and found 3% of children in the study
were diagnosed with ADHD, while 4% were diagnosed with ADHD and learning disability. Due to their academic underachievement and/or learning disabilities, it is not uncommon for children with ADHD to require a tutor or begin
receiving special education during elementary school.

In addition to learning difficulties, research has found that children with
ADHD tend to have problems organizing and expressing their thoughts in a
fluent manner (Barkley, Cunningham, & Karlsson, 1983; Hinshaw, 2002; Purvis
& Tannock, 1997). These expressive language problems appear to be related to
cognitive processes such as poor planning and organizational skills (i.e., executive functions) rather than to an underlying speech and language disorder (although children with ADHD can have co-existing language impairments).
Many studies have found executive function deficits in preschool age children,
elementary age children, adolescents, and more recently young adults with
ADHD (e.g., Fischer, Barkley, Smallish, & Fletcher, 2005; Mahone et al., 2005;
Seidman, Biederman, et al., 2005; Willcutt, Brodsky, et al., 2005). Preliminary
studies also suggest that executive function deficits may emerge early in life
and persist over time, however, it is important to note that executive function
deficits are not unique to ADHD and are characteristic of other disorders such
as traumatic brain injury, autistic disorder, and Tourette's disorder to name a
few (Fischer et al., 2005; Levin & Hanten, 2005; Weyandt, 2005a).

With respect to language, research suggests that children with ADHD may
have delays in internalized speech (i.e., "self-talk" or self-directed speech), and
some argue that internalized speech is essential for children to control and gov-
ern their own behavior (Barkley, 1998; Berk & Potts, 1991). In the classroom,
teachers often describe children with ADHD as disorganized, distractible,
spacey, and restless. Research supports that children with ADHD tend to make
more noises and inaudible speech sounds than children without the disorder
(Berk & Potts, 1991). They are often criticized for not following through on assignments and being inconsistent and careless in their schoolwork. These problems have led some to question whether children with ADHD have lower intelligence and/or memory deficits. Research concerning intelligence and ADHD

has found mixed results, with some studies finding that children with ADHD fall below average, while other studies have found their performance to be average or above average on standardized IQ tests. As with non-ADHD children, intelligence is likely to vary greatly among individuals, and group findings can be misleading (Faraone, Biederman, Lehman, Keenen, et al., 1993; Faraone, Biederman, Lehman, Spencer, et al., 1993; Faraone, Biederman, & Monuteaux, 2002; Shaw & Brown, 1990; Webb & Latimer, 1993).

With regard to memory, studies generally have not found short-term and long-term memory deficits with children with ADHD; however, several studies have reported that these children have problems with *working memory* (i.e., being able to retain information in memory while working on a problem) (e.g., Bauermeister et al., 2005; Martinussen, Hayden, Hogg-Johnson, & Tannock, 2005). In addition, the more complex the tasks and the greater the demands for organizing and remembering information, the more difficulty these children appear to have (Amin, Douglas, Mendelson, & Dufresne, 1993). Jonsdottir, Bouma, Sergeant, and Scherder (2005) recently questioned whether working memory deficits were characteristic of children with ADHD or whether working memory deficits are actually associated with underlying language impairments. Martinussen et al. (2005), however, recently reviewed 26 studies published between 1997 and 2003 (i.e., meta-analysis) and concluded that working memory impairments are characteristic of ADHD and are independent of language problems and intelligence level. In 2000, Lorch et al. compared the comprehension of televised stories in boys with and without ADHD and found that groups showed similar levels of cued recall when queried about the story. However, when recall tasks required more detailed knowledge (e.g., relations among events), children with ADHD performed more poorly.

Although there has been speculation that individuals with ADHD may be more creative than children without ADHD, very few empirical studies have addressed this issue. In 1993, Funk, Chessare, Weaver, and Exley studied the performance of boys with and without ADHD (ages 8 to 11) on a creative thinking task and found no significant difference between the groups. These researchers also found that methylphenidate (Ritalin) did not improve creative thinking performance in boys with ADHD. Recently, Professors Dione Healey and Julia Rucklidge from the University of Canterbury studied 33 children with ADHD compared to those without the disorder on several creativity tests (Healey & Rucklidge, 2005). Results were similar to Funk and colleagues with no measurable difference between the groups on the creativity tasks. Thus, these findings, as with intelligence, suggest that although some individuals with ADHD may be highly creative, as a group, research does not support the idea that individuals with ADHD are more creative than the general public.

In addition to being at greater risk for learning disabilities, children with ADHD often have co-existing psychiatric disorders such as conduct disorder, oppositional defiant disorder, major depression, anxiety disorders, and less frequently, bipolar disorder, obsessive compulsive disorder, and Tourette's disorder (e.g., Faraone, Biederman, & Monuteaux, 2002; Geller et al., 2003; Kadesjö, Hägglöf, Kadesjö, & Gillberg, 2003; Mannuzza, Klein, Abikoff, & Moulton, 2004; Sukhodolsky et al., 2003). Of these disorders, conduct disorder appears to be most common in children with ADHD, which places them at even greater risk for antisocial behavior, peer rejection, and academic failure. Overall, the research clearly indicates that children with ADHD who have co-existing internalizing (e.g., anxiety) and externalizing (e.g., conduct disorder) disorders are at significantly greater risk for social, academic, and behavior problems. In addition, Klassen, Miller, and Fine (2004) recently reported that the problems children with ADHD have significantly impact the overall quality of life of the child with the disorder and also the family. Specifically, Klassen and colleagues found that parents of children with ADHD, especially those with comorbid conduct disorder, had compromised emotional health and the family had poorer cohesion. In other words, in families of children with ADHD, the quality of life of the child, parents, and family as a unit is often compromised compared to families without children with ADHD.

ADHD is the most frequently studied disorder of childhood, and research has examined the performance of children with ADHD on a plethora of measures and a review of these studies is beyond the scope of this book. The studies have ranged, however, from motor skills to reading comprehension of students with ADHD. For example, studies have found that boys with ADHD compared to those without ADHD, demonstrate poorer performance on tasks that assess fine motor skills (Pitcher, Piek, & Hay, 2003). Children with ADHD also tend to overestimate their performance on tasks such as the ability to solve mazes (Ohan & Johnston, 2002). Hoza and colleagues (2002) also found that boys with ADHD tended to overestimate their scholastic competence, social acceptance, and behavioral performance, and they did so in the domains in which they were most impaired. Hoza et al. suggested that these inflated self-perceptions of boys with ADHD may serve a protective role given the likelihood of failure in terms of academic, social, and behavioral functioning. The common theme among studies with children with ADHD is that they are at greater risk for academic, behavioral, and social problems compared to their same-age peers without ADHD. Guevara and colleagues (2003) recently reported that children with behavior disorders, such as ADHD, incurred health services expenditures similar to children with physical conditions, and had greater expenditures for office-based visits and prescription medications.

Adolescence

> Tanya, age 14, is in the seventh grade. She was retained in first grade because her teachers thought that she was not achieving to expectations and was "extremely immature." Tanya continued to have attention problems in second grade and primarily earned letter grades of C. Her second grade teacher described Tanya as "a dreamer" and "very disorganized." Tanya was diagnosed as having ADD in third grade and began receiving special educational services at that time. Tanya took medication for several years but stopped taking it during the end of the sixth grade because she was concerned that her friends were making fun of her. At the beginning of seventh grade, Tanya was doing well academically and behaviorally, but, after the first quarter, her grades began to slip and she was frequently assigned to detention for inappropriate behavior in the classroom.

Although it was previously believed that children with ADHD would outgrow their symptoms with the onset of puberty, studies suggest that the majority continue to display these symptoms throughout adolescence (Barkley,

Anastopoulos, Guevremont, & Fletcher, 1991; Barkley, Fischer, Edelbrock, & Smallish, 1990; Biederman, Faraone, Milberger, Curtis, et al., 1996). As indicated in Tanya's case, adolescents with ADHD typically have a history of academic and social problems, and females more often than males are likely to suffer from ADHD, predominately inattentive type. Faraone, Biederman, and Monuteaux (2002) recently compared ADHD symptoms in children and adolescents and concluded "the presentation of a clinically referred ADHD syndrome does not vary dramatically between children and adolescents" (p. 10). However, the manner in which ADHD symptoms are expressed during adolescence compared to childhood appears to change. For example, according to *DSM-IV-TR* (2000) criteria as well as research studies, hyperactivity symptoms tend to decrease in adolescence; however, feelings of internal restlessness may increase (American Psychiatric Association, 2000; Hart, Lahey, Loeber, Applegate, & Frick, 1995; Iwaszuk et al., 1997; Weyandt et al., 2003). In most cases, attention and impulsivity problems persist throughout adolescence, and adolescents with ADHD are at greater risk for social, behavioral, and academic problems. For example, research by Biederman, Faraone, Milberger, Guite, et al. (1996) and others has found that nearly 45% of adolescents with ADHD also have conduct disorder and/or oppositional defiant disorder and engage in deviant behaviors such as stealing and fire setting. In addition, Faraone, Biederman, and Monuteaux (2002) reported that 59% of a sample of adolescents with ADHD had coexisting anxiety disorders, 30% major depression, and 21% suffered from bipolar disorder.

In 1993, Barkley, Guevremont, Anastopolous, DuPaul, and Shelton found that adolescents with ADHD were significantly more likely to be involved in automobile accidents and receive more speeding ticket violations than adolescents without ADHD. In 2002, Barkley, Murphy, DuPaul, and Bush took a more in-depth look at driving knowledge, performance, and accidents in a group of adolescents and young adults with ADHD compared to a group of control subjects from the community. Results indicated that the ADHD group reported more traffic citations for speeding, crashes, and license suspensions. The ADHD group also achieved lower scores on a test of driving decision making and rules compared to the community control group.

With regard to substance use, a number of studies have reported adolescents with ADHD are at greater risk for substance use and abuse including cigarettes, alcohol, and drugs such as marijuana (Barkley, Fischer, Edelbrock, & Smallish, 1990; Chilcoat & Breslau, 1999; Loney, Kramer, & Milich, 1981; Tercyak, Lerman, & Audrain, 2002). In substance abuse treatment settings, it has been estimated that 30% to 50% of adolescents have ADHD (Gordon, Tulak, & Troncale, 2004). Research indicates that severity of ADHD symptoms and presence of conduct and antisocial behavior increases the likelihood that adolescents with ADHD will use and abuse substances (Molina & Pelham, 2003).

Because of this increased risk of substance use *and* the use of stimulants in the treatment of ADHD, many have questioned whether the use of stimulants in childhood increases the risk of drug use in adolescence (i.e., gateway drug). In this regard studies have produced interesting findings. For example, Barkley, Fischer, Smallish, and Fletcher (2003) studied 147 children with ADHD for 13 years and asked about their use of various drugs during adolescence and young adulthood. Results revealed that children treated with stimulants during childhood had no greater risk of trying drugs by adolescence and no greater frequency of drug use during adulthood than those not treated with stimulants. Biederman, Wilins, Mick, et al. (1999) reported an 85% reduction risk for Substance Abuse Disorder in adolescents with ADHD who had been treated with stimulants compared to those who had not been treated. Recently, Wilens, Faraone, Biederman, and Gunawardene (2003) conducted a meta-analysis of studies that investigated the relationship between use of stimulants to treat ADHD in childhood and later substance abuse. Results revealed a 1.9-fold *reduced* risk of Substance Abuse Disorder in youths who were treated with stimulants earlier in life compared to those with ADHD who did not receive such treatment.

Academically, adolescents with ADHD are more likely to be underachievers, retained in one or more grades, or suspended or expelled from school and are at greater risk for dropping out of school. Adolescents with ADHD who are not aggressive or defiant and come from families where there is stability, greater marital satisfaction, and good parenting skills, tend to have fewer social, academic, and behavior problems in adolescence (Fischer, Barkley, Fletcher, & Smallish, 1993). Research clearly indicates that adolescents with ADHD who also have conduct disorder are at significantly greater risk for maladjustment and antisocial behavior as well as poor academic performance (Jensen et al., 2001; Wilson & Marcotte, 1996). (See Arthur Robin's 1998 book *ADHD in Adolescents: Diagnosis and Treatment* for more information about teenagers with ADHD.)

Adulthood

Information concerning the prevalence of ADHD in the adult population is limited relative to what is known about the prevalence of ADHD in children. As mentioned previously, it was commonly believed that children with ADHD would outgrow the symptoms by adolescence. Based on well-designed follow-up studies, it is now clear that the majority (70% to 85%) of children with ADHD are likely to continue to display ADHD symptoms throughout adolescence (e.g., Barkley, Fischer, Edelbrock, & Smallish, 1990; Biederman, Faraone, Milberger, Guite, et al., 1996). Fewer follow-up studies have been conducted with adults, and of those that have been conducted, findings have been variable with some studies reporting only 6% of cases persist into adulthood, while other studies have reported that the majority of cases persist into adulthood (e.g., Barkley, Fischer, Smallish, & Fletcher, 2002; Wilens, Biederman, & Spencer, 2002). Factors that appear to predict whether ADHD persists into adulthood include severity of ADHD in childhood and treatment and interventions during childhood, as well as family history of ADHD, co-existing psychiatric problems, and psychosocial adversity (Biederman, 2005; Kessler et al., 2005). If ADHD is a biologically based disorder, it is unclear why ADHD does not persist into adulthood in all cases. There are several plausible explanations for these findings including (a) the diagnosis was invalid, (b) a lack of age appropriate diagnostic criteria, (c) the symptoms remit over time, (d) assessment and diagnostic criteria differ among studies, and (e) early interventions help to ameliorate the condition by enhancing coping skills and/or altering physiologic pathways that contributed to the expression of the initial symptoms.

In contrast to follow-up studies, studies that assess the prevalence of ADHD symptoms in adults consistently find that a 2% to 4% prevalence rate for all subtypes of ADHD in the adult population (e.g., Heiligenstein, Conyers, Berns, & Smith, 1998; Murphy & Barkley, 1996; Weyandt, Rice, & Linterman, 1995). This percentage is more consistent with *DSM-IV-TR* (2000) estimates and supports findings from follow-up studies that indicate that the majority of children with ADHD continue to display significant symptoms throughout elementary school and into adolescence (e.g., Lahey, Pelham, Loney, Lee, & Willcutt, 2005; Wilens, Biederman, & Spencer, 2002). Relative to what is known about the cognitive, social, and behavioral functioning of children and adolescents with ADHD, less empirical information is available about the disorder in adults. Adults with ADHD typically report problems with attention, impulsivity, and internal feelings of restlessness (Weiss & Hechtman, 1993). As Mick, Faraone, and Biederman (2004) noted, most adults continue to have substantial ADHD symptoms and high levels of dysfunction across social, behavioral, and occupational areas. Several studies suggest that inattention problems are more persistent in adulthood than impulsivity and hyperactivity, although, as discussed previously in this chapter, this finding may be due in part to a lack of age appropriate diagnostic criteria for adults.

McGough, Smalley, et al. (2005) and Mannuzza, Klein, Bessler, Malloy, and Hynes (1997) found that adults with ADHD completed fewer years of education and had lower ranking occupational positions than adults without ADHD. The most common occupation of the adults with ADHD was skilled labor followed by physical labor. Similar outcome findings have been reported by other studies (e.g., Hechtman, Weiss, Perlman, & Amsel, 1984). In addition to lower educational and occupational status, Howell, Huessy, and Hassuk (1985) found that adults with ADHD had poorer social adjustment and antisocial behavior, as was reported by Mannuzza, Gittelman-Klein, Bessler, Malloy, and LaPadula (1993). More recently, Murphy, Barkley, and Bush (2002) found that adults with ADHD were less likely to have graduated from college, achieved fewer years of formal education, were more likely to have received special education services in high school, reported greater levels of psychological distress, and had a higher rate of drug dependence than young adults without the disorder. A number of studies have reported that ADHD is common among the male prison population, and compared to inmates without the disorder, those with ADHD report more emotional and psychiatric problems (e.g., Eyestone & Howell, 1994; Rasmussen, Almvik, & Levander, 2001; Retz et al., 2004; Rosler et al., 2004).

In terms of substance use and abuse, research indicates that adults with ADHD are at greater risk for substance use and abuse and chemical dependency (Shekim, Asarnow, Hess, Zaucha, & Wheeler, 1990; Wilson & Levin, 2001). Pomerleau and colleagues (2003) reported that cigarette smokers are overrepresented among adults with ADHD, and Coger, Moe, and Serafetinides (1996) suggested that adults with ADHD are more likely to use and become addicted to nicotine as a form of self-medication (i.e., trying to treat their own symptoms of ADHD). According to Carroll and Rounsaville (1993), up to 35% of patients seeking treatment for cocaine dependence have a history of ADHD. Schubiner (2005) recently reported that 20% to 40% of adults with ADHD have a history of Substance Abuse Disorder and 20% to 30% of adults seeking treatment for Substance Abuse Disorder have co-existing ADHD. Wilens (2004) noted that adults with ADHD transition more rapidly to dependence than adults without ADHD, and treatment of substance abuse in adults with ADHD is often more difficult and lasts longer.

Similar to adolescence, comorbidity problems such as low self-esteem, major depression, anxiety disorders, and bipolar disorders have also been found in adults with ADHD (Biederman, Faraone, Milberger, Guite, Mick, et al., 1996; Kennemer & Goldstein, 2005; Nierenberg et al., 2005). McGough, Smalley, et al. (2005) recently found that 87% of adults with ADHD had at least one co-existing disorder and 56% had two or more co-exiting disorders (e.g., depression, anxiety, substance use). Other studies have reported that adults with ADHD are more likely to be fired from jobs, have greater difficulty getting along with co-workers, and are more likely to experience relationship and intimacy problems than adults without ADHD (Barkley, 2002). Lomas and Gartside (1997) studied ADHD among homeless veterans and found that an alarming 62% of their sample met clinical criteria for ADHD. Collectively these studies indicate that ADHD can be a life-long condition and adults with ADHD are at risk for occupational, social, and interpersonal problems.

Positive Outcomes.   It is important to note that the outcome is not so bleak for all individuals with ADHD. With early identification and treatment, it is possible for individuals with the disorder to lead productive and successful lives. For example, studies suggest that children with ADHD who are medicated during childhood and adolescence are less likely to use substances and engage in deviant behavior than those who are not medicated (Barkley, Fischer, Smallish, & Fletcher, 2003; NIH, 2000). Perwien and colleagues (2004) recently found that children with ADHD treated with medication showed enhanced quality of life based on their ratings on the Child Health Questionnaire, compared to children who received a placebo. Also those with a later onset of symptoms and less severity of symptoms are likely to fair better in adolescence and adulthood (Connor et al., 2003). It is also important to point out that substance use and antisocial behavior are associated with academic and social problems in all students, not just those with ADHD. However, medication and additional interventions such as behavior management, social skills training, and parent training can improve the social and academic difficulties that are characteristic of children and adolescents with ADHD (e.g., Hinshaw et al., 2000). As Spencer (2004) recently noted, ADHD can be effectively treated across the life cycle, and medication can be just as effective with adults with ADHD as it is with children. Hesslinger et al. (2002) found too that a structured skill training program designed specifically for adults with ADHD, resulted in positive outcomes in adults who participated in the program. Also, despite the findings that suggest adults with ADHD are more likely to have employment difficulties, Mannuzza, Gittelman-Klein, Bessler, et al. (1993, 1997) found that most adults with ADHD *were* employed and were working in manual labor positions such as carpenters, electricians, plumbers, painters, or mechanics. A small percentage had earned a college degree and held professional positions. With regard to job performance, preliminary studies suggest that adults with ADHD are often rated similarly in work adequacy (e.g., Weiss & Hechtman, 1993) although more studies are needed in this area.

Hartmann (1993) and others have even asserted that ADHD symptoms may be *advantageous* in certain situations (e.g., high-intensity jobs, brainstorming) and were especially useful in the distant past for activities such as hunting and gathering. For example, a recent article by Cohen and Bailer appearing in *Fire Chief* magazine (1999) suggests that a higher-than-expected percentage of firefighters may have ADHD, yet perform well on the job. Hartmann (1993) claims that adults with ADHD are highly creative, are intrinsically motivated, are insightful, and have a high tolerance for ambiguity. He also argues that the symptoms of individuals with ADHD tend to fit poorly with current cultural and employment expectations such as conformity, passivity, and desk-jobs. Research studies consistently indicate, however, that individuals with ADHD tend to be highly impulsive, be poor planners and problem solvers, and have difficulty sustaining their attention over time. It is difficult to imagine how these qualities would enhance one's hunting or gathering abilities. Linterman and Weyandt (2001) found that adults with ADHD were *not* superior to adults without ADHD on a computer task designed to measure divided attention skills as Hartmann (1993) may predict. Clearly, scientific studies are needed to determine whether individuals with ADHD are truly drawn to and excel at certain types of jobs as has been touted in the media. Although the idea that some types of employment may be better suited to individuals with ADHD makes intuitive sense, research is needed to properly address this issue.

College Students With ADHD.   As mentioned previously, high school students with ADHD are at greater risk for dropping out, although some do pursue a college education. For example, Mannuzza et al. (1997) found in their study that 12% of the adults with ADHD had received a bachelor's degree. Although the precise number of college students with ADHD is unknown, it is estimated that ADHD *symptoms* affect 2% to 4% of the college student population (DuPaul, Schaughency, Weyandt, Tripp, Kiesner, Ota, & Stanish, 2001; Heiligenstein, Conyers, Berns, & Smith, 1998; Weyandt, 1995; Weyandt, Rice, & Linterman, 1995). What is unknown at this time is what percentage of college students actually have ADHD. It has been reported that the number of college students requesting accommodations for ADHD under the Americans with Disabilities Act (ADA) has increased substantially (Wolf, 2001). The actual percentage of college students receiving disability support services for ADHD varies across universities and is likely influenced by factors such as the size of the university and the types of services provided. In general, approximately 25% of students receiving disability support services receive services for ADHD and this percentage has increased substantially since 1975 (Wolf, 2001). To help address this issue, Gordon, Barkley, and Murphy (1997) have prepared documentation guidelines for an ADHD-based accommodations request (see Table 1.3).

Accommodations for College Students With ADHD.   Accommodations for college students vary across universities but typically include adjustments such as a distraction-free room, increased time for taking exams, altered exam format, note-taking services, recording devices, adaptive technology, and books on tape (Javorsky & Gussin, 1994; Ranseen, 1998; Weyandt & DuPaul, in press). The usefulness of these methods is questionable given that they are mainly based on common sense and not scientific studies. If fact, few scientific studies

TABLE 1.3   Suggestions for Preparing Documentation Supporting an ADHD-Based Request for Accommodations Under the Americans With Disabilities Act

1. **Establish evidence that ADHD-type symptoms arose in childhood.**
   a. Indicate you employed *DSM-IV* criteria retrospectively.
   b. Report approximate age of onset. (Although appearance of symptoms after age 7 is acceptable, there must be some evidence of impariment at least by middle school or early high school. Except in highly unusual circumstances, claims of adult onset are generally unacceptable.)
   c. Provide compelling information beyond the client's self-report that ADHD symptoms significantly interfered with the individual's academic *and* social functioning. If someone experienced serious impairment, there will be a long paper trail of prior referrals, comments on multiple report cards, and past attempts at intervention. In addition to information from parents, you should also attempt to provide corroborating evidence from individuals outside of the family.
   d. Document all prior accommodations and treatments. If there were none, explain why not.

2. **Establish evidence that symptoms currently meet *DSM-IV* criteria in their nature and severity.**
   a. Indicate that you employed *DSM-IV* criteria and report the number of symptoms endorsed for current functioning.
   b. Offer hard evidence (supervisor's reports, performance reviews, test histories, academic record, statements by disinterested parties, etc.) that the individual suffers significant impairment in comparison to the general population across current educational or occupational settings. Your write-up should be specific about the nature and extent of poor adjustment. Also, keep in mind that problems taking certain kinds of educational tests, like multiple choice formats, are not in themselves sufficient evidence of pervasive impairment.
   c. Remember that the diagnosis of Adult ADHD hinges far more on evidence of childhood history and current impairment than on any particular profile of psychological test scores. While testing may be useful in ruling out alternate explanations for underperformance (particularly insufficient cognitive abilities), it cannot alone justify an ADHD diagnosis. Requests for accommodations based primarily on testing will likely be denied.

3. **Establish evidence that current remediation does not lead to sufficient improvement in function.**
   a. Provide a history of past treatments and their outcome.
   b. Indicate in which important ways these treatments have not produced relief from symptoms. If current treatments are successful, why are accommodations necessary?

4. **Provide a rationale for the kinds of accommodations requested.**
   a. Indicate on what basis the accommodations you recommend are sensible. For example, if you suggest additional testing time, explain the scientific basis for this accommodation. You can also provide evidence from your client's history that certain accommodations have proved successful.

5. **If you are not a physician or do not hold a terminal degree in clinical psychology, indicate why you are qualified to render this diagnosis. (Specifically, what training qualifies you to conduct a differential diagnosis of mental illness.)**

Source: Reprinted with permission from ADHD on trial, *The ADHD Report*, 4, 1–4.

have been conducted with college students with ADHD, and there is a need for basic research in this area. Questions remain, for example, as to what percentage of college students with ADHD seek accommodations, whether they experience academic, social, or behavioral difficulties; choose certain areas of study more than others; complete a college degree or drop out; develop effective coping strategies; rely on support services; or seek counseling services and so on.

Studies With College Students With ADHD.   Compared to other populations with ADHD, a dearth of information exists regarding ADHD in college students. Weyandt and DuPaul (in press) recently reviewed the academic, psychological, and neuropsychological findings with college students with ADHD and concluded, in general, college students with ADHD are at greater risk for academic and psychological difficulties. With regard to neuropsychological functioning, however, college students with ADHD tend to perform similar to their non-ADHD peers on neuropsychological tasks including intelligence tests (e.g., Weyandt, Mitzlaff, & Thomas, 2002; Weyandt, Rice, Linterman, Mitzlaff, & Emert, 1998). Cognitively, studies suggest that these students with ADHD have more intrusive thoughts than college students without ADHD (Shaw & Giambra, 1993), and are internally restless compared to college students without the disorder (Weyandt et al., 2003). Researchers have speculated that college students with ADHD may be physiologically underaroused, have poor inhibitory control, are easily bored and, as a result, they are more susceptible to external as well as internal distractions such as task-unrelated thoughts (Shaw & Giambra, 1993). Hines and Shaw (1993) reported that college students with ADHD are at greater risk for using drugs to escape uncomfortable thoughts.

With regard to emotional expression, Ramirez et al. (1997) found that college students who self-reported ADHD symptoms had higher levels of anger and inappropriate ways of expressing anger compared to college students without significant ADHD symptoms. Weyandt, Rice, Linterman, Mitzlaff, and Emert (1998) found that college students with ADHD reported more adjustment problems than college students without ADHD but did not differ significantly from college students without ADHD on a number of tasks thought to measure attention and impulsivity. Healy (2000) found that college students with ADHD took fewer credits, had lower GPAs, and reported more difficulty paying attention in lecture than college students without the disorder. Healy also found that 88% of the students with ADHD reported significant problems with psychological distress, and these students reported using alcohol significantly more often than students without ADHD. Other studies have also reported that college students with ADHD or ADHD symptomology are more likely to report greater psychological distress compared to students without the disorder (e.g., Heiligenstein & Keeling, 1995; Richards, Deffenbaucher, & Rosen, 2002). Clearly, more research is needed to better understand ADHD in this subpopulation of adults with ADHD. (Table 1.4 summarizes common characteristics of individuals with ADHD.)

Gender Information

According to the American Psychiatric Association (2000) boys are more likely to be diagnosed with ADHD than girls, with ratios ranging from 2:1 to 9:1 depending on the subtype of ADHD. Other studies have provided male–female

TABLE 1.4   Common Characteristics of Individuals With ADHD

Early Childhood
Excessive activity level
Talking incessantly
Difficulty paying attention
Difficulty playing quietly
Impulsive and easily distracted
Academic underachievement
Poor social skills

Middle Childhood
Excessive fidgeting
Difficulty remaining seated
Messy and careless work
Failure to follow instructions
Failure to follow through on tasks
Academic underachievement
Poor peer relationships

Adolescence
Feelings of restlessness
Difficulty engaging in quiet sedentary activities
Forgetful and inattentive
Impatience
Engaging in potentially dangerous activities
Academic underachievement
Poor peer relationships

Adulthood
Feelings of restlessness
Difficulty engaging in quiet sedentary activities
Frequent shifts from one uncompleted activity to another
Frequent interrupting or intruding on others
Avoidance of tasks that allow for little spontaneous movement
Relationship difficulties
Anger management difficulties
Frequent changes in employment

Note: From Weyandt (2001).

ratios of 3:1 in the general population, and 6:1 in children referred to clinics (Gaub & Carlson, 1997). Historically, research has supported that girls with ADHD tend to be less hyperactive, have fewer acting out problems, are less likely to have a learning disability, and are more likely than boys to have ADHD predominately inattentive type (Biederman, Mick, Faraone, Bratton, Doyle, et al., 2002). Boys tend to be more hyperactive, have more acting out and aggression problems, and fewer attention and anxiety problems than girls with ADHD (Levy, Hay, Bennett, & McStephen, 2005; Newcorn et al., 2001). These findings have led some to question whether girls with ADHD represent a "silent minority" that is underidentified and underserved compared to boys with ADHD (Berry, Shaywitz, & Shaywitz, 1985). Recently, however, research by Joseph Biederman and colleagues at Massachusetts General Hospital, Boston, found that ADHD combined type was predominant in both boys and girls, and girls had the same relative risk for adverse outcomes as boys with ADHD (e.g., Biederman, Kwon, Aleardi, et al., 2005; Biederman & Faraone, 2004). These results also have been substantiated in Taiwanese children with ADHD (Yang, Jong, Chung, & Chen, 2004). Work by Carlson, Tamm, and Gaub (1997) found it was not uncommon for girls with ADHD to also have coexisting disruptive behavior problems. Seidman and colleagues (2005) noted that boys and girls with ADHD demonstrate more neuropsychological deficits than children without the disorder, however, boys and girls with ADHD perform similar to each other on these neuropsychological tasks. Graetz, Sawyer, and Baghurst (2005) studied more than 2,000 children age 6 to 13 who met *DSM-IV-TR* criteria for ADHD in Australia and found that boys and girls did not differ on core symptoms, comorbidity, or impairment. Girls, however, did report more somatic complaints than boys. Some support that during adolescence and adulthood, females may be more prone to depression and anxiety disorders, while males may have more difficulty with behavior problems and antisocial behaviors, however this finding is not unique to ADHD but is true of males and females in the general population (Biederman et al., 1993; Gershon, 2002; Rucklidge & Tannock, 2001). In addition, Biederman et al. (2004) recently studied 219 adults with ADHD and concluded that higher rates of depression, anxiety, substance use disorders, and antisocial personality disorders were associated with ADHD in *both* genders. Learning disabilities (e.g., reading, math) appear to be equally prevalent in males and females with ADHD, although they are more common among males than females in the general population. Recent research has found different patterns of cortical activity in adolescent males and females based on EEG recordings (Hermens, Kohn, Clarke, Gordon, & Williams, 2005) although the clinical relevance of these findings is unclear. What is clear is that ADHD affects both males and females, and children, adolescents, and adults with the disorder are at greater risk for academic, behavior, and interpersonal problems. For more information concerning gender and ADHD, see Gaub and Carlson (1997), Rucklidge and Kaplan (1997), and Gershon (2002).

Legal Issues

Three federal laws pertain to the legal rights of individuals with ADHD: (a) the Individuals with Disabilities Education Act (IDEA, 1990, 1997 amendments, 2004); (b) Section 504 of the Rehabilitation Act (1973); and (c) the Americans with Disabilities Act (ADA, 1990). A summary of the implications of these laws follows; however, for more detailed information concerning these laws and entitlements, see Latham and Latham (1992, 1999), Clay (1998), or www.ed.gov.

IDEA

In 1991, the U.S. government (Department of Education) issued an important document outlining the conditions under which individuals with ADHD are eligible for special services under IDEA and Section 504 (Davila, Williams, & MacDonald, 1991). In summary, the document specifies that public schools are required to provide a free and appropriate education for all children with disabilities (IDEA). Children with ADHD may be eligible for special services under IDEA based on three categories: (a) specific learning disability, (b) serious emotional disturbance, and (c) other health impaired. To qualify for one of these categories, school systems are required to follow federal evaluation guidelines, describe the disability, explain how the disability adversely affects educational performance, develop an individualized educational plan (IEP), and explain how the goals and objectives of the IEP will be achieved and measured. More specifically, to qualify for special services under "specific learning disability" or "serious emotional disturbance," students with ADHD must meet the federal and state criteria for these handicapping conditions (i.e., they must have a co-existing learning disability or emotional impairment). To qualify for special services under "other health impaired," IDEA requires that children suffer from chronic or acute impairments that result in limited alertness, which adversely affects educational performance. Given that ADHD is considered a chronic disorder, many individuals could be considered eligible for special services under "other health impaired," provided that the disorder causes impairment in the child's educational performance. School systems that follow federal guidelines for evaluation and classification of disabilities *receive federal funds* to support the special education programs that service these students. According to attorneys Latham and Latham (1999), the number of children who request services under IDEA has grown dramatically. The authors also report that the specific learning disabilities category is the largest category serviced under IDEA; however, the "other health impaired" category is the fastest growing category. On December 3, 2004 President Bush signed into law new IDEA reforms, under the Individuals with Disabilities Improvement Act, now known as Public Law Number 108-446 (IDEA, 2004). Under the new IDEA ADHD is not listed as a separate disability however students will continue to qualify for special educational services under other disabilities as long as the need for services is warranted and impairment is documented according to federal and state guidelines.

Section 504

Unlike IDEA, which outlines disability categories, Section 504 of the Rehabilitation Act defines a disability as a "physical or mental impairment" that limits one or more major life activities (i.e., academic performance) and *is not accompanied by federal funding*. Section 504 clearly indicates that students with ADHD qualify for a free and appropriate education, which may or may not require special educational services, provided that the disorder interferes significantly with the student's learning. According to this law, schools are required to conduct a multidisciplinary evaluation of students with a suspected disability, including ADHD, and to create a plan and accommodations to address the student's needs. As much as possible, schools are encouraged to provide accommodations in regular education classrooms.

According to research by Reid, Maag, Vasa, and Wright (1994) from the University of Nebraska–Lincoln, approximately 50% of students with ADHD receive special education services, and most do not receive services under health impaired (i.e., behavior disordered, learning disabled). The most common type of special education placement for these students is the general education classroom plus resource support. An IDEA/504 flowchart is depicted in Figure 1.1.

IDEA/504 Flow Chart

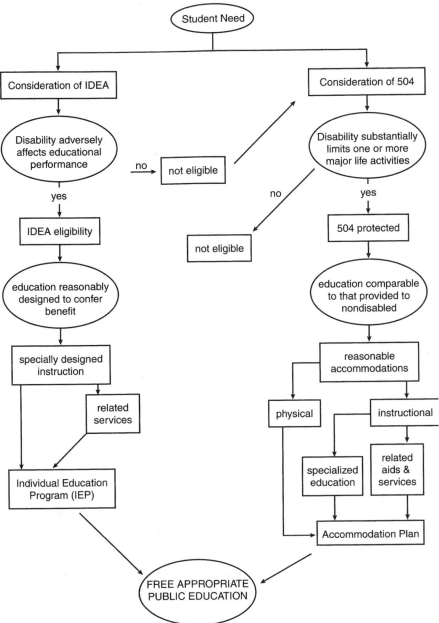

FIGURE 1.1.   IDEA/504 Flow Chart.

Source: From *Student Access: A Resource Guide for Educators: Section 504 of the Rehabilitation Act of 1973* (p. 3a), by Council of Administrators of Special Education, 1992, Reston, VA: Author. Copyright 1992 by Council of Administrators of Special Education. Reprinted with permission.

ADA

It is important to note that the protections of 504 extend to private schools, but religious schools are exempt from the requirements. At the postsecondary level and in the workplace, individuals with ADHD are protected from discrimination and are entitled to educational or occupational accommodations under the Americans with Disabilities Act (ADA). The ADA (1990) was designed to prevent discrimination against individuals with mental, physical, or learning disabilities. To be eligible for coverage under ADA, individuals with ADHD must inform the proper authority of his or her disability. (For a review of the issues relating to accommodation requests by adults with ADHD, see Gordon, Barkley, & Murphy, 1997; Latham & Latham, 2002; and Dr. John Ranseen's 1998 article, "Lawyers with ADHD: The special test accommodation controversy.")

Summary

ADHD is a lifelong disorder characterized by problems with attention, impulsivity, and hyperactivity. It is estimated to affect 3% to 7% of the childhood population, and similar percentages are found in other countries. ADHD can be a debilitating disorder that impacts an individual's academic, social, and occupational life. It is diagnosed more frequently in males than females, and both sexes are at increased risk for interpersonal and psychiatric problems such as depression, anxiety, and substance use disorders. Relative to what is known about ADHD in children, less information is available concerning ADHD in adolescents and adults. Many students with ADHD require special educational services, and early identification and intervention help these individuals attain a more positive outcome. Despite decades of research, critics continue to question the validity of the disorder. Recent advances in technology are helping researchers to better understand the physiological underpinnings of the disorder, which may ultimately help to identify the cause(s) of ADHD. Chapter 2 discusses theories and research concerning the etiology of ADHD.

TEST YOUR KNOWLEDGE ABOUT ADHD

To help assess your knowledge about ADHD, answer True (T) or False (F) to each of the following questions. It may be useful for you to answer the questions before reading this book and again when you have completed the book. You may also wish to photocopy the quiz and encourage colleagues, family members, students, or individuals with ADHD to take the quiz to help them learn more about ADHD.

1. T or F Females are diagnosed with ADHD more frequently than males.
2. T or F Stimulants have been found to improve ADHD symptoms in children, adolescents, and adults.
3. T or F ADHD is present in other cultures.
4. T or F ADHD is synonymous with learning disability.

5. T or F ADHD is caused by diets rich in food additives and sugar.

6. T or F Most individuals with ADHD are of gifted intelligence.

7. T or F Children with ADHD usually outgrow the disorder by adolescence or early adulthood.

8. T or F According to *DSM-IV-TR* criteria, all individuals with ADHD have problems with attention, impulsivity, and hyperactivity.

9. T or F Individuals with ADHD often have coexisting learning disabilities.

10. T or F Individuals with ADHD are at greater risk for dropping out of school and typically complete fewer years of education than their non-ADHD peers.

11. T or F ADHD is caused by poor parenting.

12. T or F Children with ADHD perform best on assignments that are highly detailed and complex.

13. T or F Peer tutoring can improve academic productivity and decrease off-task behavior of children with ADHD.

14. T or F Stimulants have the opposite effect on individuals with ADHD compared to their effect on people without ADHD.

15. T or F ADHD is caused by an imbalance of neurotransmitters in the brain.

16. T or F Most individuals with ADHD are highly creative.

17. T or F Children with ADHD are automatically eligible for special educational services.

18. T or F Ritalin is overprescribed by physicians on a nationwide level.

19. T or F Increasing numbers of college students are requesting special services based on an ADHD diagnosis.

20. T or F Individuals with ADHD can lead successful and productive lives.

Answers: 1(F), 2(T), 3(T), 4(F), 5(F), 6(F), 7(F), 8(F), 9(T), 10(T), 11(F), 12(F), 13(T), 14(F), 15(F), 16(F), 17(F), 18(F), 19(T), 20(T)

Note: From Weyandt (2001).

CHAPTER

2

ADHD—What Causes It?

As technology advances, so does our understanding of the biological under-pinnings of ADHD. The purpose of this chapter is to dispel myths associated with the cause of ADHD and to review factors implicated in the etiology of ADHD.

Myths

Diet

A widely accepted myth is that a poor diet *causes* ADHD. Substances that have been targeted include preservatives, food colorings, aspartame, and additional food additives. In addition to additives, some authors such as Taylor (1990) have suggested that nutritious foods such as peaches and berries should be avoided, as well as tomatoes, cucumbers, and peppers. The theory behind these recommendations is that substances in food, whether natural or additive, are causing ADHD and by removing specific items from the diet ADHD symptoms will be alleviated. This practice stems from a popular diet that was proposed by Dr. Benjamin Feingold during the 1970s. Feingold (1975) claimed that food ad-ditives and preservatives were largely responsible for the development of hy-peractivity in children and recommended that a special diet be followed to treat the disorder. Although a few studies have reported improvement in ADHD symptoms followed dietary restrictions (e.g., Boris & Mandel, 1994; Carter et al., 1993; Schmidt et al., 1997; Schnoll, Burshteyn, & Cea-Aravena, 2003) most well-designed scientific studies have not supported these claims. This is not to say that diet does not affect behavior as proper nutrition clearly influences chil-dren's physical and cognitive development. In addition, some children have genuine food allergies but when treated properly, the allergy symptoms abate. With respect to ADHD, specifically, however, most research indicates that di-etary restrictions, such as those proposed in the Feingold diet, do not substan-tially improve the symptoms of inattention, hyperactivity, and impulsivity. Kavale and Forness (1983) reviewed more than 20 studies that investigated the Feingold diet and concluded that the Feingold diet was an ineffective treatment method. Keith Conners (1980) came to the same conclusion in his book, *Food Ad-ditives and Hyperactive Children*. Despite the fact that scientific studies indicate that diet does not cause ADHD and that restricted diets usually do not improve ADHD symptoms, many families with ADHD children do incorporate the use of alternative treatments including modified diets. Sinha and Efron (2005) for

example, found that 67.6% of families surveyed reported the use of complementary and alternative medicines with their children with ADHD. The most
commonly used approach was modified diet followed by vitamin and/or mineral therapy and dietary supplements.

Sugar and Additional Myths

Sugar has also been identified as an ADHD culprit (Block, 2001), and, again, scientific studies have failed to support this claim. In 1994, Mark Wolraich from
Vanderbilt University and his colleagues published a study in the *New England
Journal of Medicine* and concluded that even when sugar intake exceeds typical
daily levels it does *not* affect children's behavior or cognitive function (Wolraich, Wilson, & White, 1995). Other studies have supported Dr. Wolraich's
findings (e.g., Kanarek, 1994) and Shaywitz et al. (1994) found that aspartame at
greater than 10 times the usual consumption had no significant effect of the cognitive and behavioral functioning of children with ADHD.

   Additional myths have been perpetuated about ADHD, especially on the
Internet, including the idea that fluorescent lighting, tar and pitch, soaps and
detergents, disinfectants, yeast, and insect repellents can induce or worsen
ADHD symptoms. Poor teaching and parenting styles have also been targeted
as the cause of ADHD symptoms. Although it is important to recognize that environmental factors such as teaching and parenting styles can exacerbate or
lessen ADHD symptoms, they do not *cause* the disorder. (Additional information concerning teaching and parenting issues is included in chapter 4.) The
idea that environmental pollutants and substances included in or missing from
one's diet is responsible for ADHD has led to a variety of unusual interventions
such as sensory integration training, mineral and megavitamin supplements,
caffeine, osteopathic therapy, yoga, massage, homeopathy, and use of green,
outdoor spaces (Rojas & Chan, 2005). Most of these interventions are not supported by scientific research but remain popular due to parental good intentions, anecdotal reports, and media attention. Research findings concerning
these interventions are discussed in chapter 5. As mentioned previously, it is
important to note that some individuals do have food allergies or chemical sen-
sitivities and they may be inaccurately diagnosed as having ADHD. Proper
identification and diagnosis of symptoms is crucial so that appropriate treatment can be implemented with individuals with ADHD.

Genetic and Hereditary Factors

Genetic and Chromosomal Factors

In 1993, newspaper headlines read, "Genetic defect found to cause hyperactivity," which was based on an article that appeared in the *New England Journal of
Medicine* (Hauser et al., 1993). In the article, the researchers reported that the
majority of individuals with a rare thyroid disorder (generalized resistance to
thyroid hormone, GRTH) also had ADHD. According to the authors, their intention was not to claim a genetic basis for ADHD but rather to describe an as-

sociation between the two disorders (Hauser et al., 1994). Unfortunately, the findings were misinterpreted, which led to inaccurate news headlines that the genetic basis for ADHD had been established. Although individuals with the thyroid condition may manifest ADHD symptoms, GRTH is not believed to cause ADHD. (For more information on thyroid disease and ADHD, see Bhatara, Kumer, McMillin, & Bandettini, 1994.) Other authors have suggested a link between ADHD and the chromosomal defect, fragile X syndrome. Well-controlled experiments, however, have failed to support this claim (Einfeld, Hall, & Levy, 1991). Although individuals with documented chromosomal abnormalities such as Down's syndrome or fragile X syndrome may display attention and hyperactivity problems, such chromosomal abnormalities are rare in children with ADHD.

To date, no specific gene or combination of genes has been identified as *causing* ADHD. However, collaborative efforts by genetic scientists such as that led by the International ADHD Genetics Consortium have been underway to search for and identify specific genes related to ADHD (Kent, 2004) and as Stevenson, Asherson, Hay, et al. (2005) noted, the genetic study of ADHD has made considerable progress. In general, a large number of studies have found a link between genes involved in the production, regulation, and functioning of the brain chemical (neurotransmitter) *dopamine*, and the behavioral expression of ADHD (Asherson, Kuntsi, & Taylor, 2005; Faraone et al., 2005). For example, earlier molecular genetic research by Lahoste et al. (1996), Sonuhara et al. (1997), and Swanson et al. (1998) suggested that some children with ADHD may have an overrepresentation of a particular dopamine gene (although these results have not been found in all children with ADHD). Other studies have suggested that certain dopamine-related genes may be altered in individuals with ADHD causing dysfunction of the dopamine system and consequently resulting in widespread effects on cellular networks in the brain (e.g., Kirley et al., 2002; Swanson et al., 2000). Since the year 2000, the rate of ADHD genetic studies has been prodigious, and studies have continued to implicate genes that regulate the dopamine system (e.g., Bobb, Castellanos, Addington, & Rapoport, 2005; see Weyandt, 2006, *The Physiological Bases of Cognitive and Behavioral Disorders*, for a review of these genetic studies). In addition to dopamine genes, studies have explored the role of genes that regulate other neurotransmitters such as serotonin and norepinephrine, as well as the role of chemicals that help to break down these neurotransmitters (e.g., MAO, COMT). The findings from these studies have been mixed with some studies reporting an association between alterations of specific genes or related chemicals while other studies report no association (e.g., Mill et al., 2005; Xu et al., 2005; Zhao et al., 2005). Overall, these studies suggest that it is likely that ADHD is caused by a complex combination of genetic factors that interact with environmental factors, and the physiological underpinnings to ADHD are likely to be equally complex (Nigg, Willcutt, Doyle, & Sonuga-Barke, 2005; Willcutt, 2005).

Hereditary Factors

In addition to studies that link genetic alterations to ADHD, familial and twin studies support a hereditary basis for the disorder. For example, numerous studies have examined the rate of ADHD among identical twins, fraternal twins, siblings, relatives, and nonrelated individuals. Studies consistently indicate that ADHD occurs significantly more often in identical relative to fraternal twins (e.g., Gjone, Stevenson, & Sundet, 1996; Goodman & Stevenson, 1989; Sherman, Iacono, & McGue, 1997; Todd et al., 2002). Based on these and other studies, the heritability estimate has been reported to range from .60 to .90 for ADHD, although some studies have reported smaller or larger estimates (Levy et al., 1997; Smalley, 1997; Willcutt, Pennington, & DeFries, 2000). Recently, Larsson, Larsson, and Lichtenstein (2004) conducted a long-term twin study in Sweden and found that ADHD symptoms were highly heritable and remained relatively stable over time. Similar heredity findings were reported by Kuntsi and colleagues (2005) who studied more than 4,000 twin pairs in the United Kingdom.

Familial factors associated with ADHD have also been studied. For example, investigations have looked at siblings of individuals with ADHD, and have found that individuals with ADHD are more likely to have brothers or sisters with the disorder compared to families with no history of ADHD (Biederman et al., 1995). Others have found that ADHD occurs more frequently among siblings with the same parents than in half-brothers and half-sisters (Safer, 1973). Siblings of children with ADHD have also been found to have greater problems with attentional control and controlling impulses during tasks compared to those without a sibling with ADHD (Slaats-Willemse, Swaab-Barneveld, De Sonneville, & Buitelaar, 2005). Doyle, Biederman, Seidman, et al. (2005) recently reported that relatives of girls with ADHD performed more poorly on a battery of neuropsychological tasks than relatives of girls without ADHD. Further evidence that ADHD may be inherited comes from research with biological and nonbiological parents. Biederman et al. (1995) reported that if one biological parent has ADHD, then the likelihood that the child will have ADHD is 57% (similar findings were reported by Frick, Lahey, Christ, Loeber, & Green, 1991). McGough, Smalley, et al. (2005) recently reported that 47% of adults with ADHD had one parent with ADHD while 10% had two affected parents with ADHD. Nigg and Hinshaw (1998) found that boys with ADHD were more likely to have fathers with the disorder and mothers with depression or anxiety problems. Second-degree relatives of a child with ADHD (such as grandparents, aunts, and uncles) have also been found to have ADHD more frequently than relatives of individuals without the disorder (Faraone, Biederman, & Milberger, 1995). Several studies have found that ADHD is more common in biological parents of children with the disorder than in adoptive parents who have children with ADHD (e.g., Alberts-Corush, Firestone, & Goodman, 1986). Sprich and colleagues (2000) at Massachusetts General Hospital in Boston, reported in homes with children with ADHD, 18% of biological parents compared to 6% of adoptive parents.

Numerous studies have found that families with ADHD children have a higher incidence of psychological and psychiatric problems such as depression, anxiety, substance abuse, antisocial disorders, and ADHD. In a review of the literature concerning families of children with ADHD, Lily Hechtman (1996), concluded that ADHD has "strong genetic underpinnings" and that it is critical to diagnose and treat family members as well as the individual with ADHD (p. 350). Because of the type of and number of coexisting problems typically found in families of individuals with ADHD, researchers have suggested that some families may be biologically vulnerable and consequently at greater risk for developing disorders such as ADHD. A predisposition for ADHD, in combination with prenatal exposure to alcohol and nicotine, for example, may increase the likelihood that a child will develop the disorder (Milberger, Biederman, Faraone, Chen, & Jones, 1996). In a recent review of the literature, Doyle, Willcutt, Seidman, Biederman, et al. (2005) from Harvard Medical School, Boston, concluded that ADHD is a "highly heritable disorder with a multifactorial pattern of inheritance" (p. 1324). In other words, research clearly indicates that ADHD runs in families but the manner in which the disorder is genetically transmitter remains elusive.

Neurochemical Factors

Numerous magazine and newspaper articles have reported that ADHD is due to "a chemical imbalance in the brain." Although this explanation is a gross simplification of what is known about brain chemistry and function, these articles are usually referring to chemicals known as *neurotransmitters*. Hundreds of neurotransmitters have been identified and are used by brain cells (neurons) to communicate with each other (see Figure 2.1). Billions of neurons and supporting cells exist in the brain, each with a multitude of connections to other neurons. Communication among these neurons is necessary for thought and behavior to occur, and researchers have attempted to assess the role of various neurotransmitter systems in ADHD. Given the complexity of the brain's neural networks, no single neurotransmitter is likely to account for the variety of symptoms associated with ADHD. Three neurotransmitters that have received the most attention by the scientific community include *serotonin, dopamine*, and *norepinephrine* (e.g., Barr et al., 2002; Liu & Reichelt, 2001; Oades et al., 2005).

Halperin et al. (1997), for example, focused on the neurotransmitter serotonin and found that aggressive boys with ADHD had lower serotonin function than boys without ADHD. More recently, Oades (2000) found increased levels of serotonin (metabolites) in children with ADHD and this was associated with poor performance on an attention task. Other studies, however, investigating serotonin levels in children, adolescents, and adults with ADHD have not substantiated this finding. In addition, lower amounts of serotonin are not unique to ADHD and have been associated with other disorders such as impulsive personality disorders, violent behavior, and depression (see Weyandt, 2006, *The Physiological Bases of Cognitive and Behavioral Disorders* for a review of these serotonin studies).

Compared to serotonin studies, more studies support that *dysregulation* (i.e., faulty functioning) of a class of neurotransmitters known as *catecholamines*, which include norepinephrine, epinephrine, and dopamine are implicated in ADHD (e.g., Pliszka, 2005; Pliszka, McCracken, & Mass, 1996). These neurotransmitters are known to play a critical role in arousal and attention in humans and other animals. Research with individuals who have sustained damage to brain regions that involve these chemical systems has found that these individuals display symptoms analogous to ADHD. In other words, they become impulsive and have problems with organization, attention, and hyperactivity. This idea has been supported by studies that have found lower levels of catecholamine by-products in the urine of children with ADHD compared to

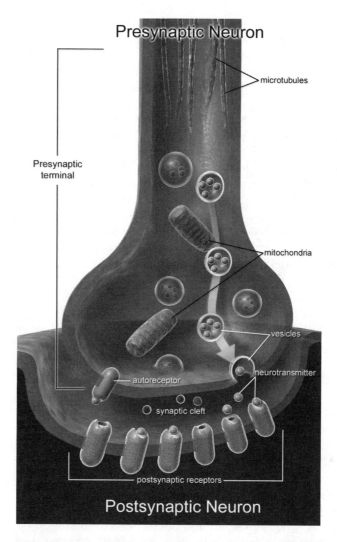

FIGURE 2.1.   Image with neurotransmitters being released at synapse. Copyright Blausen Medical Communications. Reproduced by permission.

children without the disorder (Anderson et al., 2000; Hanna, Ornitz, & Hariharan, 1996; Shekim et al., 1979). In addition, increased levels of these by-products have been found in the urine of individuals with ADHD after they have taken stimulant medication (Lijffijt et al., in press; Mikkelsen, Lake, Brown, Ziegler, & Ebert, 1981). Stimulant medication, which is commonly used to treat ADHD, has been shown to affect the catecholamine systems in the brain. Specifically, brain imaging studies suggest stimulants increase catecholamine levels, particularly dopamine and norepinephrine in both children and adults with ADHD (e.g., Lou, Henriksen, & Bruhn, 1984; Lou et al., 1989; Pliszka, 2005; Schweitzer et al., 2003; Volkow et al., 2001). It is important to point out that abnormal levels of catecholamines have been found in children with other disorders (e.g., Autistic Disorder) and are therefore not necessarily specific to ADHD (e.g., Barthelemy et al., 1988).

Current neurotransmitters theories of ADHD, compared to earlier theories, focus on the interactive effects of neurotransmitters rather than the effects of a single neurotransmitter. For example, Oades (2002; Oades et al., 2005) suggested that serotonin, dopamine, and norepinephrine all contribute to ADHD and it may be that serotonin systems are underactive in children with ADHD while dopamine and norepinephrine levels are overactive. Pliszka (2005) has also theorized that complex interactions between neurotransmitter, genetic, and environmental factors contribute to the etiology of ADHD. Additional chemicals such as cortisol have been investigated, and, in Japan, Kaneko, Hoshino, Hashimoto, Okano, and Kumashiro (1993) found that children with ADHD had significantly lower amounts of this brain substance relative to children without the disorder. These authors suggested that this finding may help to explain the hyperactivity and restlessness associated with ADHD, although studies are needed to substantiate and better understand this finding. It is important to note that not all research studies examining urine or brain activity in individuals with ADHD have reported significant findings, and thus the neurochemical dysregulation theory remains promising but inconclusive at this time.

Neuroanatomical and Neurophysiological Findings

Anatomical Findings

Although no single, reliable difference has been found in the anatomy of the brains of individuals with ADHD compared to those without the disorder, a number of brain regions and structures have been studied in individuals with ADHD. For example, in 1991, Dr. George Hynd from the University of Georgia Medical College conducted a landmark study. He examined the brains of seven children with ADHD compared to children without ADHD, using a technique known as magnetic resonance imaging (MRI). Hynd, Semrud-Clikeman, Lorys, Novey, Eliopulos, and Lyytinen (1991) found that the right frontal region of the brains of children with ADHD was smaller, as was the bundle of fibers that connected the right and left halves of the brain in these children (i.e., corpus callosum). Later, Hynd et al. (1993) found additional brain differences (i.e., asymmetry of the caudate nucleus) in individuals with and without ADHD. The authors speculated that these differences may be related to the attention and impulsivity problems characteristic of ADHD (Hynd & Willis, 1988). Berquin et al. (1998) reported that the cerebellum was significantly smaller in individuals with ADHD compared to those without the disorder. Giedd et al. (1994) also found that the corpus callosum was smaller in adolescent boys with ADHD. Similar anatomical differences between those with and without ADHD were reported by Filipeck (1999) and Tannock (1998). Using MRI, Semrud-Clikeman and colleagues (2000) found that boys with ADHD, compared to boys without the disorder, had structural brain differences in the caudate and frontal regions, consistent with previous research findings. This study also found that boys with ADHD performed more poorly on neuropsychological tasks compared to boys without ADHD, further supporting a relationship between brain anatomy and behavioral deficits.

With regard to overall brain size, Castellanos et al. (1994) was among the first to find that total brain volume was 5% smaller in boys with ADHD, and the normal asymmetrical size of the caudate nucleus was not found in boys with ADHD (caudate, see Figure 2.2). In other words, in boys without ADHD, the right side of the caudate is typically larger than the left, but this pattern was not found in those with ADHD. In addition, for boys without ADHD, the size of the caudate increases with age but in those with ADHD, no increase in size of this brain structure was observed. Other studies have supported these total brain volume and caudate findings (e.g., Castellanos et al., 2001; Hynd et al., 1993; Schrimsher, Billingsley, Jackson, & Moore, 2002; Semrud-Clikeman et al., 2000; Sowell et al., 2003). In 2002, Castellanos et al. studied 152 children and adolescents with ADHD and found that children with ADHD who had not received medication therapy had smaller brain volume, cerebellar volumes, and overall white matter compared to those who had received medication *and* compared to children without the disorder. More recently, Castellanos and colleagues (2003) investigated the size of the caudate in identical twin pairs in which one of the pair had ADHD and the other did not have the disorder. The results revealed that the twins with ADHD had significantly smaller caudate volumes than the twins without the disorder.

Although these studies indicate that anatomical differences often exist in the brains of individuals with and without ADHD, *the source of these differences* remains unclear (i.e., genetic or environmental). In addition, it is important to note that anatomical differences *are not necessarily related to or responsible for ADHD symptoms*. Additional research is needed to determine whether these anatomical differences are unique to individuals with ADHD, or whether they are directly related to the attention deficits and behavioral excesses associated with the disorder. However, when these anatomical findings are considered in conjunction with studies that assess brain functioning, they contribute an important piece to the ADHD physiology-puzzle.

Neurophysiological Findings

Techniques such as MRI measure allow researchers to examine brain structure, whereas techniques such as Functional Magnetic Resonance Imaging (fMRI) and Positron Emission Tomography (PET) allow researchers to measure brain function. Specifically, fMRI and PET enable researchers to measure changes in the brain's blood flow or use of glucose, the primary fuel for the brain (see Weyandt, 2006, *The Physiological Bases of Cognitive and Behavioral Disorders*, for a review of these and other brain imaging techniques). Hundreds of fMRI and PET studies have been conducted with children, adolescents, and adults with ADHD and overall support dysfunction of connections between the frontal regions of the brain and subcortical regions (i.e., frontal-striatal regions). The subcortical region most often implicated in ADHD is the striatum (see Figures 2.2 and 2.3) as described in the previous anatomical section. The striatum is a critical brain region to study in patients with ADHD as it is rich in the neurotransmitter dopamine and cells in this area project to other regions of the brain, including the frontal regions. As mentioned previously, stimulants are commonly used to treat ADHD and studies have found increased activation in the caudate and pathways to and from the frontal lobes following administration of stimulants. For example,

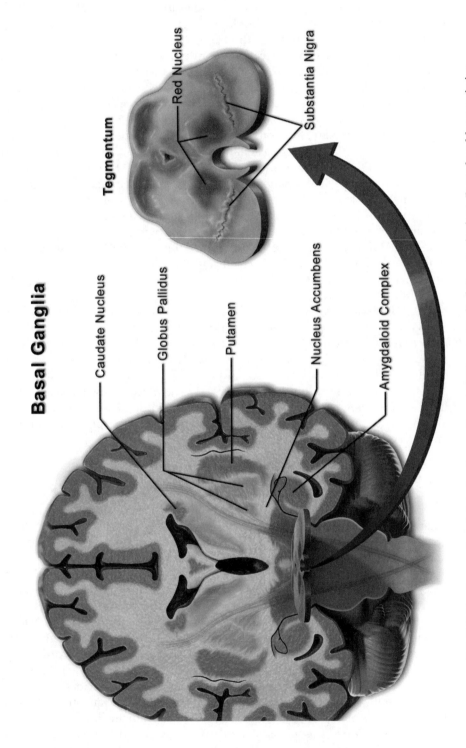

FIGURE 2.2. Image of caudate and putamen. Copyright Blausen Medical Communications. Reproduced by permission.

Vaidya et al. (1998) studied 10 boys with ADHD and 6 boys without ADHD (ages 8 to 13) using functional magnetic resonance imaging (fMRI) before and after taking stimulant medication (methylphenidate). The fMRI scans indicated that that the individuals with ADHD had less brain activity in the striatum compared to boys without ADHD. After taking the stimulant, this same area increased in activity for the boys with ADHD but much less so in the boys without the disorder. A recent study by Vaidya et al. (2005) found less activation in the striatal-frontal regions in children with ADHD relative to children without the disorder during a task that required inhibition of responses. When treated with stimulants, activation increased in these regions, which was related to improved task performance. Other studies have produced similar findings and collectively implicate abnormalities of the frontal-striatal regions in ADHD (Durston et al., 2003; Lou, Henriksen, Bruhn, Borner, & Nielsen, 1989; Rubia et al., 1999; Sieg, Gaffney, Preston, & Hellings, 1995; Zametkin et al., 1993).

As Seidman, Valera, and Makris (2005) recently noted, however, there are substantial problems with many of the studies that have examined brain anatomy and brain function in individuals with ADHD. For example, most of the students involve very few subjects (under 20) and do not control for factors such as co-existing disorders, influence of medications, family history, gender, subtypes of ADHD, or medical complications during pregnancy or childhood. Also, to be truly diagnostic, the brain imaging findings should be unique to ADHD and not simply a characteristic of many disorders.

In addition to brain imaging studies, researchers have explored whether individuals with ADHD have a nervous system that is under- or hyperaroused. Various techniques have been used to measure arousal including monitoring heart rate and galvanic skin responses, as well as electroencephalograms (EEGs) and quantitative electroencephalograms (QEEGs). Contrary to popular belief, these studies suggest that individuals with ADHD are not hyperaroused; rather, their nervous systems appear to be in a state of low arousal (Klove, 1989; Satterfield & Dawson, 1971). Chabot and Serfontein (1996), for example, using QEEG, found a different pattern of brain waves in individuals with and without ADHD (i.e., *cortical slowing*; and similar findings were recently reported by Monastra et al., 1999). Baving, Laucht, and Schmidt (1999) investigated brain activation patterns in unmedicated preschool and elementary age boys and girls with ADHD compared to children without the disorder. Using EEG recordings from various brain regions, the authors found that children with ADHD, compared to those without the disorder, had reduced brain activity in the right frontal region. This finding is consistent with previous anatomical and neurochemical studies that implicate the frontal regions in the underlying pathophysiology of ADHD. In addition, Borger and colleagues (1999) from The Netherlands reported differences in the heart rate variability of children with and without ADHD and speculated that the differences were due to regulatory systems stemming from the frontal lobes. In 2000, Borger and van der Meere found that children with ADHD had greater heart rate variability than children without the disorder. In a recent review of the literature, Willis and Weiler (2005) concluded that "EEG and MRI studies of childhood ADHD appear to support theories of the disorder that focus on frontal-striatal neurological substrates, but we have not reached a time when these procedures provide much diagnostic utility" (pp. 175–176).

Neuropsychological Factors

Prior to neuroimaging studies implicating frontal-striatal regions in ADHD, researchers had theorized that ADHD was due to a dysfunction of the frontal lobes (Figure 2.3). This theory arose mainly from neuropsychological studies of adults who had sustained damage to this area of the brain and subsequently displayed executive function deficits—attention, planning, self-regulation, and impulsivity problems, collectively known as the *frontal lobe syndrome* (Lezak, 1995). Given the similarity of symptoms in ADHD, researchers questioned whether children, adolescents, and adults with ADHD would perform poorly on tasks that are commonly used to measure neuropsychological deficits in patients who have sustained damage to the frontal lobes, so-called frontal lobe tasks. Numerous neuropsychological tasks exist and many have been used in the study of individuals with ADHD and a review of these studies is beyond the scope of this chapter. In general, however, research suggests that many of these "frontal lobe" tasks do not reliably discriminate between those with and without ADHD. For example, Barkley, Grodzinsky, and DuPaul (1992) reviewed 22 studies that used measures presumed to assess frontal lobe dysfunctions in children with ADHD and found that in general the tasks were not able to distinguish between children with and without ADHD. The authors concluded that "the pattern for other presumably frontal lobe tests is quite inconsistent and highly dependent on the measures used and age range of subjects" (pp. 183–184). More recently, Perugini et al. (2000) reviewed the usefulness of seven neuropsychological tasks in classifying children with ADHD and, similar to Barkley and colleagues, Perugini et al. found most tasks were not very accurate at identifying those with and without ADHD. Weyandt (2005b) came to a similar conclusion after reviewing neuropsychological studies with adults with ADHD, and noted that "adults with ADHD do not exhibit a unique neuropsychological profile" (p. 480).

In 1997, Dr. Russell Barkley (1997a) of the University of Massachusetts Medical Center proposed a unifying theory of ADHD. He posited that ADHD is due to a deficit in behavioral inhibition that is physiologically based and in turn results in executive function deficits in the areas of self-regulation, working memory, internalized speech, and motor control. Expanding on the frontal theory of ADHD, Barkley provided a comprehensive, testable, underlying model for ADHD. He argued that ADHD is primarily a disorder of behavioral disinhibition, that is, self-regulation. Self-regulation develops as a result of brain maturation and learning to control one's impulses. Deficits in this system lead to secondary impairments in executive functions such as the ability to plan, problem solve, and guide one's behavior through internal speech (i.e., self-talk). Deficits in executive functions can have profound negative effects on academic, social, and behavioral skills of both children and adults with ADHD. According to Barkley's theory, these executive function deficits are specific to ADHD and are not characteristic of other behavioral disorders such as oppositional defiant disorder or conduct disorder. A study by Klorman et al. (1999) provided preliminary support for Dr. Barkley's model, as they found that executive function deficits *were* characteristic of children and adolescents with ADHD but *were not* found in children and adolescents with reading or oppositional defiant disorders. Later studies found support for some aspects of Barkley's model, but not

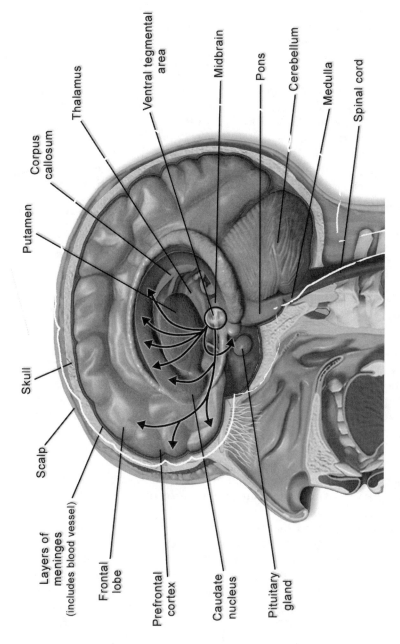

Layers of
meninges
(includes blood vessel)

Skull

Scalp

Frontal
lobe

Prefrontal
cortex

Caudate
nucleus

Pituitary
gland

Putamen

Corpus
callosum

Thalamus

Ventral tegmental
area

Midbrain

Pons

Cerebellum

Medulla

Spinal cord

FIGURE 2.3. Image of frontal-striatal pathways. Copyright Blausen Medical Communications. Reproduced by permission.

others. For example, Stevens, Quittner, Zukerman, and Moore (2002) studied 76 children with ADHD compared to control children and found those with ADHD exhibited deficits on some, but not all, executive function tasks.

Recent studies with preschoolers with ADHD have reported similar findings. For example, preschoolers with ADHD have been found to perform poorly on an auditory attention task that requires inhibitory control and sustained attention, compared to preschoolers without ADHD (Mariani & Barkley, 1997; Mahone et al., 2005). Studies with adolescents and young adults with ADHD have also reported impaired performance on some, but not all, executive function tasks (e.g., Fischer, Barkley, Smallish, & Fletcher, 2005; Seidman, Biederman, et al., 2001, 2005; Weyandt, Mitzloff, & Thomas, 2002; Weyandt, Rice, Linterman, et al., 1998). Collectively these neuropsychological studies suggest that executive function deficits, particularly response inhibition deficits, are often found in individuals with ADHD, however global executive function deficits do not appear to be characteristic of the disorder. As Willcutt, Pennington, Olson, et al. (2005) reported, "executive function weakness are neither necessary nor sufficient to cause most cases of ADHD" (p. 205). Similarly, Castellanos, Sonuga-Burke, Milham, and Tannock (in press) argue that executive function deficits may not be a primary characteristic of ADHD and propose newer etiologic models be developed.

Integration of Research Findings

Collectively, genetic, heritability, neuroanatomical, neuroimaging, and neuropsychological studies point to a neurobiological basis of ADHD. Various authors have attempted to integrate these findings and produce a neurobiological model of ADHD (Kirley et al., 2002). For example, Voeller (1991) was among the first to suggest that ADHD may be due to disturbances in several areas of the brain, particularly those that previously had been implicated in Parkinson's disease and Tourette's syndrome (i.e., basal ganglia, striatum). Castellanos (1999) advanced a more detailed neurobiological model of ADHD that integrated information from genetic, neurochemical, anatomical, neuropsychological, and neurodevelopmental areas of research. According to Castellanos' model, ADHD is a disorder of deficiencies in self-regulation influenced by genetic factors, brain maturation, and dysfunctional neurotransmitter systems. Pliszka (2003) offered an additional model that focused on the role of various brain regions and neurotransmitters found therein. Pliszka also suggested that genetic variations might alter normal functioning of the dopamine and norepinephrine systems and/or affect development of various brain structures and function. Other models have been advanced and current versions acknowledge the possible contribution of genetic, neurotransmitters, frontal-striatal pathways, as well as neurodevelopmental factors in the pathophysiology of ADHD (Biederman & Faraone, 2002). In a recent review of the literature, Barkley (2006) concluded that "heredity factors play the largest role in the occurrence of ADHD symptoms in children" (p. 236). Given that the brain is comprised of billions of cells and complex networks, a comprehensive model that takes into account total brain functioning as well as detailed interconnections is ultimately necessary to fully understand the biological underpinnings of ADHD. Unfortunately, until science gains a richer understanding of normal brain functioning, the explanations for pathological conditions such as ADHD will be limited.

Summary

Although a direct cause for ADHD has not been established, genetic, anatomical, neurotransmitter, neuroimaging, and neuropsychological studies collectively support a physiological basis for the disorder. Advances in technology and molecular genetics will continue to contribute to the understanding of the underlying neurobiological basis of ADHD. It is probable that ADHD does not result from a single factor but is due to interactions between physiological and environmental factors that affect central nervous system development and function. In summary, the research findings supporting a biological basis of ADHD are convincing but questions remain about the specific ways in which genetic and nongenetic factors interact to result in the collection of symptoms characteristic of ADHD.

CHAPTER

3

ADHD—How Is It Assessed?

It is critical that teachers, parents, physicians, employers, and others working with children, adolescents, or adults understand that simply because an individual is displaying attention, hyperactivity, and impulsivity problems, it does *not necessarily* mean that he or she has ADHD. These symptoms are not unique to ADHD and can be associated with numerous emotional medical, educational, or behavioral problems such as seizure disorders, learning disabilities, conduct disorder, anxiety disorders, substance use and abuse, or even boredom, as well as other problems. Difficulties with inattention, impulsivity, and hyperactivity are also present in normal children, as indicated by a 1971 study of a large number of school-age children (Werry & Quay, 1971). In this study, teachers rated 30% of boys and 12% of girls as overactive and 43% of the boys and 25% of the girls as having a short attention span. In a study by Weyandt, Rice, and Linterman (1995), 7% of college students reported having significant problems with attention, impulsivity, and attention. Hudziak, Wadsworth, Heath, and Achenbach (1999) found that parents rated 10% to 16% of normal boys and girls ages 4 to 18 as having moderate levels of attention problems. As Gordon and Barkley (1999) described, "inattention as a symptom resembles a fever or chest pains in that its presence alone does little to narrow the field of diagnostic possibilities" (p. 2). Moreover, many individuals with ADHD have coexisting problems such as learning disabilities, depression, anxiety, conduct and oppositional defiant disorders. Thus, the presence of attention or impulsivity symptoms is not sufficient for a diagnosis of ADHD. What is critical is that the symptoms are developmentally inappropriate and they cause impairment in daily functioning (Gordon et al., 2005). To accurately assess and diagnose ADHD, a thorough, *multimethod* approach is required. An accurate diagnosis of ADHD is crucial, as the disorder interferes with the daily lives of children with ADHD as well as the lives of their parents and families. As Escobar and colleagues (2005) recently noted, delays in recognizing, assessing, and managing ADHD can negatively affect the quality of life of these children.

Multimethod Assessment

Definition and Steps

To increase the accuracy of an ADHD diagnosis, a *multimethod assessment* approach has been advocated by many experts in the field, including the American Academy of Pediatrics (2000). A multimethod approach uses multiple assessment measures and multiple informants, and requires collaboration among medical and school personnel, and parents. Typically, information is provided by parents, teachers, and the individual under evaluation, although in the case of adult assessment, information may be provided by spouses, roommates, employers, and so on. Obtaining information from a variety of sources (e.g., parent *and* teacher) is critical, as research indicates that diagnoses based on a single informant are likely to be inaccurate (i.e., invalid) (Mitsis, McKay, Schulz, Newcorn, & Halperin, 2000). Recent research with school psychologists found that approximately 90% used rating scales to collect data from parents and more than 90% used rating scales to collect information from teachers when children were evaluated for ADHD (Demaray, Schaefer, & Delong, 2003). The steps and procedures for a multimethod ADHD assessment may vary depending on whether the evaluation is school or clinic based. For example, Foy and Earls (2005) published a 12-step protocol to increase the likelihood that children with ADHD in community settings will be assessed and managed according to the guidelines set forth by the American Academy of Pediatrics. In the USA, primary care physicians are often involved in the assessment, diagnosis, and treatment of ADHD, and Chan et al. found the majority spend 15–45 minutes and at least two office visits to confirm a diagnosis of ADHD. Eighty-three percent of the physicians surveyed in this study used information provided by the schools (e.g., rating scales, grades, report cards). Drs. George DuPaul and Gary Stoner, authors of *ADHD in the Schools: Assessment and Intervention Strategies* (2nd ed., DuPaul & Stoner, 2003), recommend a five-stage, school-based assessment process as depicted in Table 3.1.

Dr. Arthur Robin (1998) recommends a somewhat different sequence of steps for practitioners conducting assessments of *adolescents* suspected of having ADHD. Specifically, he recommends the following nine steps:

1. Collect, score rating scales.
2. Orient the family to the evaluation.
3. Interview the adolescent.
4. Administer IQ, achievement, and continuous performance tests.
5. Conduct direct observations.
6. Interview the parents.
7. Conduct medical evaluation.
8. Integrate all of the data.
9. Give feedback and recommendations.

Similar steps and procedures have been recommended for assessment of adults suspected of having ADHD (e.g., Barkley, 1998). Although the sequence of data collection may differ in schools, clinics, and private practice, similar information should be obtained when children, adolescents, or adults are evaluated for ADHD.

Components of a Multimethod Assessment

Based on decades of research, a thorough ADHD assessment should consist of interviews (parent, teacher, child/adolescent/adult); direct observations; behavior rating scales; self-report measures; record review; and possibly norm-

TABLE 3.1   Five Stages of the School-Based Assessment of ADHD

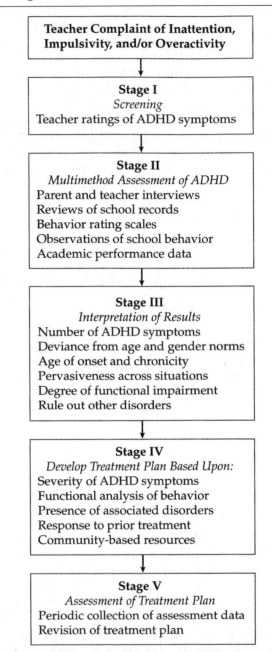

Teacher Complaint of Inattention, Impulsivity, and/or Overactivity

↓

Stage I
Screening
Teacher ratings of ADHD symptoms

↓

Stage II
Multimethod Assessment of ADHD
Parent and teacher interviews
Reviews of school records
Behavior rating scales
Observations of school behavior
Academic performance data

↓

Stage III
Interpretation of Results
Number of ADHD symptoms
Deviance from age and gender norms
Age of onset and chronicity
Pervasiveness across situations
Degree of functional impairment
Rule out other disorders

↓

Stage IV
Develop Treatment Plan Based Upon:
Severity of ADHD symptoms
Functional analysis of behavior
Presence of associated disorders
Response to prior treatment
Community-based resources

↓

Stage V
Assessment of Treatment Plan
Periodic collection of assessment data
Revision of treatment plan

Source: From *ADHD in the Schools: Assessment and Intervention Strategies* (p. 26), by G. J. DuPaul and G. Stoner, 2003, New York: Guilford Press. Adapted with permission.

referenced tests, laboratory measures, and a medical evaluation. Each measure yields a different type of information that is useful in determining whether an individual has ADHD and/or some other problem(s). As with most problems and disorders, careful consideration must be given to all of the factors that could be contributing to an individual's presenting symptoms, including historical as well as current factors. Use of an assessment framework such as the one presented in Table 3.2 will increase the likelihood that this information will be obtained. Of course, before the assessment process can begin, written informed consent must be obtained from the parents or, in the case of an adult, from the individual under evaluation.

TABLE 3.2   ADHD Assessment Framework

Information From Parent(s)*

- Background information
- Developmental history
- Medical history
- Academic history
- Social-emotional history
- Family history
- Previous evaluations

Current Information

- Medical status
- Academic status
- Social-emotional status
- Family functioning
- Parental concerns
- Perception of the problem(s)
- Available resources

Techniques to Gather Information From Parent

- Semistructured interview(s)
- Developmental and health questionnaires
- Behavioral rating scales
- Family functioning scales
- Medical, psychological, school records

Information From Teacher(s)

- Background information
- Academic history
- Social-emotional history
- Duration of problem(s)
- Tried interventions

Current Information

- Specific problem(s)
- Antecedents and consequences
- Frequency of problem(s)
- Situations in which problem occurs
- Situations in which problem does not occur

(Continued)

TABLE 3.2   (Continued)

Techniques to Gather Information From Teacher

- Semistructured interview(s)
- Behavioral rating scales
- Classroom observations
- Functional behavior analysis
- School records

Information From Individual Under Evaluation

- Current information
- Intellectual functioning
- Academic functioning
- Social-emotional functioning
- Presenting symptoms
- Perception of problem(s)

Techniques to Gather Information From Individual

- IQ testing
- Achievement testing
- Clinical interview
- Observations in multiple settings
- Self-report instruments
- Laboratory tests

*In the case of adult assessments, background information would most likely be obtained from the individual under evaluation.

Note: From Weyandt (2001).

Parent Interview

The main purposes of the parent interview are to

- Establish rapport
- Explain the evaluation procedures
- Address questions or concerns
- Obtain valid and reliable information about the child's, adolescent's, or adult's developmental, medical, cognitive, academic, behavioral, and social-emotional history, as well as current functioning
- Gather information about the family's history and current family functioning

Questionnaires

Different strategies may be used to gather this information. For example, some clinics and school districts mail a *health and developmental questionnaire* to parents and ask the parents to return the completed questionnaire before the first interview meeting. Examples of published questionnaires include the Background Information Questionnaire by Dr. Jerome Sattler (2006); the Childhood History Form for Attention Disorder–Revised (Goldstein & Goldstein, 1998) (see Appendix A); and the Developmental and Medical History Questionnaire published by Drs. Russell Barkley and Kevin Murphy (Barkley & Murphy, 1998). Dr. Sattler's Background Information Questionnaire is useful for ADHD, learning disabilities, and other types of evaluations; while the Developmental and Medical History Questionnaire and the Childhood History Form for Attention Disorder–Revised were developed specifically for ADHD evaluations. Additional questionnaires may also be mailed to the parents, such as behavioral rating scales, release of information forms, and the like. The information obtained from questionnaires is then reviewed by the clinician conducting the evaluation and any follow-up questions are presented during the initial interview with the parents. Other clinicians prefer to gather the background information during a semistructured interview with the parents.

Semistructured or Structured Interview

During a *semistructured interview*, the clinician asks the parent preplanned questions about the child's history and current functioning but does not generally follow a standard format. As an alternative, *structured interviews* can be included such as the Diagnostic Interview Schedule for Children and Adolescents (Costello, Edelbrock, & Costello, 1985). Regardless of which interview Format is used, it is important that questions representing *DSM-IV-TR* criteria for ADHD be addressed. To help assess parental perceptions of a child or adolescent's functioning, numerous behavioral rating scales are available and are discussed in the *Parental Perceptions* later in this chapter. For detailed information concerning interviewing, see Jerome Sattler's text, *Clinical and Forensic Interviewing of Children and Their Families* (1998).

Developmental History

As mentioned in chapter 1, *DSM-IV-TR* criteria require that ADHD symptoms are present before age seven. Additionally, research studies suggest that several early childhood behavioral characteristics are predictive of ADHD—a difficult temperament, accident proneness, excessive activity level, aggressiveness, fearlessness, noncompliance, and poor adaptation to environmental changes. A thorough review of the individual's developmental history will help to determine whether ADHD symptoms were *present early in life and have been of a chronic nature*. The developmental history also plays a crucial role in *differential diagnosis*, that is, determining whether the symptoms are associated with a disorder other than ADHD (e.g., pervasive developmental disorder, autism, or conduct disorder). As already mentioned, questionnaires are useful for obtaining this information from parents. For more information about the role of the developmental history in the ADHD evaluation, see Russell Barkley's text, *Attention-Deficit/Hyperactivity Disorder: A Handbook for Diagnosis and Treatment* (Barkley, 2006).

Medical History

A thorough review of the child, adolescent, or adult's medical history is also important in the ADHD assessment process. As mentioned in chapter 1, some research suggests that maternal health and prenatal complications are associated with the pregnancies of children with ADHD. Other research indicates that children with ADHD, compared to children without the disorder, are more likely to have medical problems such as asthma, allergies, enuresis, upper respiratory infections, ear infections, and accidental injuries (e.g., head injuries, broken bones, lacerations) (Gibbs & Cooper, 1989; Hartsough & Lambert, 1985; Stewart, Pitts, Craig, & Dieruf, 1966; Szatmari, Offord, & Boyle, 1989; Trites, Tryphonas, & Ferguson, 1980). Children with ADHD are also more likely to have minor physical anomalies, poor motor coordination, and sleep problems such as difficulty falling asleep, fewer total sleep hours, and problems with periodic limb movements (Barkley, DuPaul, & McMurray, 1990; Firestone, Lewy, & Douglas, 1976; Gaultney, Terrell, & Gingras, 2005; McLaughlin-Crabtree, Ivaneko, & Gonzal, 2003; Wilens, Biederman, & Spencer, 1994). It is important to note that *although these medical problems are commonly found in children with ADHD, not every individual with the disorder displays any or all of these problems.* The medical history also provides information that may be useful for differential diagnosis. For example, problems with inattention, impulsivity, and hyperactivity may be associated with other medical conditions such as seizure disorders, medication side effects, thyroid disorders, sleep apnea, lead poisoning, substance abuse, depression, and/or anxiety disorders. For more information about medical problems with symptoms associated with ADHD, see Barkley (2006), Cantwell and Baker (1987) and Goldstein and Goldstein (1998).

Social-Emotional History

The purpose of the social-emotional history is to gather information about the individual's interpersonal relationships and emotional functioning. For most individuals with ADHD, social problems emerge early in life.

Preschool Years. According to research, 60% to 70% of children later identified as having ADHD exhibited identifiable symptoms during their preschool years (Barkley, 1981). In general, studies suggest that preschoolers with ADHD are more inattentive, impulsive, and noncompliant than their non-ADHD peers. They also tend to be less cooperative in a group setting, often have communication skills deficits, and are disruptive in classroom and play settings (e.g., Alessandri, 1992; Ornoy, Uriel, & Tennenbaum, 1993). Several studies have found that preschool children with ADHD have social skill impairments relative to preschool children without the disorder (Tutty, Gephart, & Wurzbacher, 2003). Research also suggests that preschoolers with ADHD are often more aggressive than their same age peers (Lahey, Pelham, Loney, Lee, & Willcutt, 2005). Studies also indicate that preschoolers who have attention deficits and are highly aggressive tend to come from families that are dysfunctional and/or physically and verbally aggressive (Stormont-Spurgin & Zentall, 1995; Sukhodolsky et al., 2005).

Middle Childhood.   During middle childhood, children with ADHD continue to have academic and social problems; and emotional problems such as anger control and low frustration tolerance become more apparent. Peer rejection is a common problem experienced by children with ADHD. Research suggests that this problem is strongly related to the aggressive, noncompliant, and disruptive behaviors that are often displayed by children with ADHD (Bickett & Milich, 1990). These children (and their parents) are aware that they tend to have more behavioral and social problems, as found in a study by Hoza, Pelham, Milich, Pillow, and McBride (1993). Interestingly, children with ADHD tend to view their problematic behavior as less within their control compared to children without ADHD (Kaidar, Wiener, & Tannock, 2003). Kendall, Hatton, Beckett, and Leo (2003) interviewed 39 children and adolescents with ADHD regarding their perceptions and experiences of living with the disorder and found that 100% of the group reported difficulties related to what they saw as ADHD (e.g., difficulty following rules, difficulty getting along with others, feeing distracted). Most of the children and adolescents also reported frequent feelings of frustration, anger, and shame, and many viewed their ADHD as an illness.

With respect to play, research has found that children with ADHD tend to be more talkative, active, and off-task than their non-ADHD peers. They also tend to make more negative statements, are more boisterous and intrusive, and are less cooperative than children without the disorder (e.g., Landau & Moore, 1991; Swain & Zentall, 1990). Children with ADHD are also at greater risk for being rejected by their peers in naturalistic settings such as the playground, and tend to have fewer friends (Erhardt & Hinshaw, 1994; Hoza et al., 2005). Hodgens, Cole, and Boldizar (2000) found that boys with ADHD predominately inattentive type were more likely to display withdrawal in play sessions, while those with ADHD combined type were viewed by their peers as more likely to start fights and arguments. As mentioned in chapter 1, research has discovered that girls with ADHD are also more likely to display aggressive behaviors (compared to girls without the disorder), and have difficulty establishing and maintaining friendships (Blachman & Hinshaw, 2002). Clearly, both boys and girls with ADHD are at greater risk for social skill problems compared to children without ADHD. The Social Skills Assessment (Parent Form) developed by Goldstein and Goldstein (1988) may be useful in assessing the parent's perception of the child or adolescent's social skill functioning (see Appendix J).

Adolescence.   Research indicates that many of the problems that emerged in childhood continue or worsen into adolescence. Given their history of peer rejection and underachievement, it should be no surprise that adolescents with ADHD are more likely to have low self-esteem and depression and exhibit acting out behavior. Brooks and Boaz (2005) recently studied adolescents with ADHD and co-existing learning disabilities and found that most had comorbid depression, oppositional defiant disorder, problems with aggression and/or were using illegal substances. Based on research findings concerning the social-emotional risks of adolescents with ADHD, it is important that the professional conducting the evaluation ask the individual or the parent(s) in-depth questions about their child's interpersonal relationships, friendships, and social skills during their preschool, middle childhood, and adolescent years. Self-report instruments are available for adolescents, and behavioral rating scales are also invaluable in assessing a parent's perception of a child or adolescent's social-emotional functioning (see *Parental Perceptions* later in this chapter).

Academic History

One of the most common problems associated with ADHD is chronic under-achievement relative to intellectual abilities (Barkley, 1990). Problems may surface as early as preschool, as many children with ADHD may lack school readiness skills such as the ability to follow directions, remain seated and attentive, and to be nondisruptive. As mentioned in chapter 1, children with ADHD are more likely to fall behind academically in elementary school, being retained at least one grade before high school (Barkley, DuPaul, & McMurray, 1990); and at least 30% to 45% receive special educational services during the elementary school years (Barkley, 1998). Brooks and Boaz (2005b) recently reported that 94% of adolescents with ADHD in their study were diagnosed as having a learning disability. As adolescents, they are more likely to have behavioral problems that lead to detention and school suspensions. They are also more likely to drop out of high school, and relatively few pursue a college education (Mannuzza, Klein, Bessler, & Malloy, 1993). Given this body of information, it is often useful for clinicians to ask parents to provide a chronological account of the child's academic history beginning with preschool. Information concerning grades, attendance, standardized test scores, previous evaluations, special services, and teacher reports should be obtained during the interview. When possible, this information should be verified through school records and other such documentation. Goldstein and Goldstein's Childhood History Form in Appendix A may be useful in organizing the academic history information.

Family History

ADHD tends to run in families, and it has been established that the concordance rate for identical twins is higher than fraternal twins. Furthermore, biological parents of children with ADHD are more likely to have the disorder than adoptive parents (see chapter 2). Thus, the family history may provide useful information in the ADHD assessment process. Family history is also important for (a) differential diagnosis and (b) identifying areas of needed intervention. For example, research indicates that parents of children with ADHD, particularly those with coexisting aggression and conduct problems, are more likely to experience a variety of psychiatric problems such as alcoholism, stimulant/cocaine dependence, anxiety disorders, antisocial behavior, depression, and learning disabilities (Chronis et al., 2003; Faraone, Biederman, Mennin, Wozniak, & Spencer, 1997). It is important to note, however, that while a family history of psychiatric problems is strongly associated with ADHD not all children with the disorder come from families with such a history. Sattler's Background Information Questionnaire (2006) the Childhood History Form for Attention Disorder–Revised (Goldstein & Goldstein, 1998; see Appendix A) can be useful for obtaining family history information.

Family Functioning

In addition to family history, information about the family's current level of functioning is vital to the evaluation. A number of questionnaires are available to help assess family functioning and interactions, including the Parenting Stress Index (Abidin, 1983); the Parent-Adolescent Relationship Questionnaire (Robin, Koepke, & Moye, 1990); and the Personality Inventory for Children (Wirt, Lachar, Klinedinst, & Seat, 1990). For additional information concerning these instruments, see Barkley (1998) and Robin (1998). Information concerning family functioning assists in differential diagnosis as well as the development of appropriate treatment recommendations.

Parental Perceptions of Current Behavior

With respect to parental perceptions of the referred child's behavior and social-emotional functioning, numerous behavioral rating scales are available. In general, the scales are of two categories: those that assess a broad range of symptoms and behavior, and those that assess symptoms and behaviors specifically associated with ADHD.

Parent Rating Scales.   For ADHD assessments, behavioral rating scales that assess both broad and narrow ranges of behaviors should be included in the evaluation process. One of the most widely used and researched broad-range scales is the Child Behavior Checklist (CBCL) (Achenbach, 1991). The CBCL (preschool and school age scales) is appropriate for ages 1;5 to 5 years and 6 to 18 years. The scales include more than 100 questions that measure social competence (activities, social, and school competencies) and behavior problems (withdrawal, somatic complaints, anxious/depressed, social problems, thought problems, attention problems, delinquent behavior, and aggressive behavior). Research has demonstrated that the CBCL is an excellent tool for screening (a) children with and without ADHD and (b) children with ADHD who have coexisting problems (Anastopoulos, 1993; Biederman, Monuteaux, Kendrick, Klein, & Faraone, 2005; Chen, Faraone, Biederman, & Tsuang, 1994). Teacher and adolescent versions are also available (i.e., Teacher Report Form and the Youth Self Report).

The Behavior Assessment System (BASC, Reynolds & Kamphaus, 1992) is a comprehensive set of rating scales for parents and teachers (BASC–PRS and BASC–TRS). The BASC also offers a student observation system and a structured developmental history form. The BASC assesses a wide range of adaptive and problem behaviors, and is appropriate for ages 2 through 21 years. The BASC parent and teacher forms consist of more than 100 items that provides information concerning externalizing (e.g., acting out) and internalizing problems (e.g., depression, anxiety), attention and learning problems, withdrawal problems, and adaptive behavior. Several studies have found that the BASC can reliably differentiate individuals with and without ADHD (e.g., Jarratt, Riccio, & Siekierski, 2005).

ADHD Scales.   Numerous ADHD behavioral rating scales are available for evaluating children and adolescents suspected of having ADHD. Four commonly used scales include the ADHD Rating Scale–IV (DuPaul, Power,

Anastopoulos, & Reid, 1998; Appendix B); Attention Deficit Disorders Evaluation Scale (ADDES; McCarney, 1995); Conners Parent Rating Scale–Revised
(Conners, 1997); and the Home Situations Questionnaire (Barkley & Murphy,
1998). A 40-item Diagnostic Rating Scale (DRS) for parents and teachers is also
available, which the authors recommend be used for screening purposes in settings in which extensive ADHD evaluations are infeasible (Weiler, Bellinger,
Marmor, Rancier, & Waber, 1999). Follow-ups and more resource-intensive
diagnostic procedures could then be administered to individuals who met
DSM-IV criteria for ADHD. In 2003, Angello et al. evaluated the strengths and
limitations of several ADHD rating scales with regard to purpose, content, stan-
dardization, and technical properties and concluded that the ADHD Rating
Scale IV (DuPaul et al., 1998) and the Conners Parent Rating Scale–Revised
(Conners, 1997) were the most psychometrically sound and appropriate for diagnostic assessment. Concerns were raised, however, about the use of these and
other ADHD instruments with minority students as little empirical information
is available about these groups. A relatively new ADHD instrument with both
parent and teacher versions, is the Vanderbilt ADHD rating scale developed by
Dr. Mark Wolraich and colleagues at the Child Study Center in Oklahoma City,
Oklahoma. Preliminary research suggests that these scales are psychometrically sound and useful in the assessment of ADHD in children (Wolraich et al.,
2003). See Sattler (2006) for additional information about ADHD Rating Scales
for children.

ADHD scales are also available for adult assessments, however less empirical information is available for these scales compared to the childhood scales.
In addition, most adult scales rely on self-report information which may not
be as accurate as information provided by a parent or significant other. Several scales that are available include the Adult Rating Scale (Weyandt, Rice, &
Linterman, 1995); Brown ADD Scales (Brown, 1996); Conners Adult ADHD
Rating Scales (CAARS; Conners, 1999a); the Current Symptoms and Childhood Symptoms Scales (Barkley & Murphy, 1998); and the Wender Utah Rating Scale (Ward, Wender, & Reimher, 1993). It is important to note that assessment of ADHD in adults is a relatively new area and limited information is
available concerning the technical properties of the scales that are available.
For example, the ARS (Weyandt et al., 1995; Appendix E) is primarily a research instrument, while more information is available concerning the use of
the CAARS (Conners, 1999a) in clinical evaluations of adults suspected of
having ADHD. Several studies have reported low agreement between parent
and teachers concerning ADHD symptoms (e.g., Wolraich, Lambert, Bickman,
et al., 2004) and most studies report found that a combination of parent and
teacher ratings was superior to parent ratings alone in identifying ADHD
(Owens & Hoza, 2003). Murphy and Gordon (2006) and Barkley (2006) offer a
detailed protocol for adult ADHD evaluations and recommend use of several
ADHD rating scales as well as medical, developmental, employment, and social history questionnaires.

In summary, the use of broad-range scales (e.g., CBCL) and narrow-range
scales (e.g., the ADHD Rating Scale IV) are essential in the ADHD assessment
process. Many of the instruments developed for children and adolescents have
excellent psychometric properties (i.e., validity and reliability); and an individ-

ual's ratings can be compared to the ratings of a large group of individuals of the same age, gender, and, in some cases, ethnicity. In other words, the scores on these scales help to determine how deviant an individual's behavior or symptoms may be, at least from the parent's (or teacher's) perspective. This information can then be compared to information gathered from teachers and the individual under evaluation.

Teacher Interview

The main purpose of the *teacher interview* is to gather valid and reliable information about the child or adolescent's

- Academic achievement
- Behavior problems
- Interpersonal skills

Given that most children spend the majority of their day in the classroom, teachers can provide invaluable input about a student's academic and interpersonal skills. Teachers are also in an ideal position to observe a child's attention and behavior and to compare his or her behavior to similar-aged peers. Since the demands of the classroom and learning process require an ability to sustain attention, remain on task, and to be nondisruptive, teachers are often the first to refer a child for an evaluation. With regard to ADHD, research indicates that *diagnostic certainty increases with the number of informants*; hence, information from teachers is critical to the evaluation process. Studies have also found that teachers ratings on behavioral rating scales relate moderately to ratings provided by parents (e.g., Biederman, Faraone, Milberger, & Doyle, 1993; DuPaul, 1991). Teachers are also in the position to provide critical information about the child's academic performance in addition to his or her behavior. As Pelham, Fabiano, and Massetti (2005) recently noted the most efficient ADHD assessment method is obtaining information from teacher and parent rating scales and by using both sources of information the accuracy of an ADHD diagnosis is enhanced.

Semistructured Interview

As in the parent interview, different strategies can be used to obtain teacher information. For example, if the evaluation is school-based, the school psychologist will likely meet with and interview the teacher(s) on one or more occasions. A semistructured interview is typically used, and questions are designed to fit the student's academic skill level, strengths and needs, and behavioral and interpersonal skills. During the interview, teachers should be asked to identify a student's specific problems, and a method known as *functional assessment* is recommended to facilitate this process. According to IDEA (2004) a functional behavior assessment should be part of the evaluation process for children with disabilities whose behavior is interfering with their education or that of others.

Functional Behavior Assessment

Functional behavior assessment refers to the use of multiple assessment strategies in order to delineate specific events that are happening immediately before and after the student's problem behavior (i.e., antecedents and consequences) that set the occasion for and/or maintain a target behavior (Horner, 1994). The goals of functional assessment are to determine (a) what purpose the problem behavior is serving for the student, and (b) what environmental events increase the likelihood that the behavior will occur (DuPaul & Ervin, 1996). In addition to the teacher interview, interviews with the parents and the student, as well as direct classroom observations, will help to identify antecedent and consequent events. Functional assessment studies with students with ADHD have identified several problem behaviors that commonly occur in these students

- vocalizations
- out-of-seat behavior
- disruptive behavior
- off-task behavior

Furthermore, functional analysis studies (e.g., Northup, Broussard, Jones, & George, 1995; Northrup et al., 1997; Umbreit, 1995) have revealed that the primary functions of these behaviors are to

- Escape tasks
- Gain peer attention
- Gain teacher attention
- Gain access to tangible objects
- Achieve self-stimulation purposes (e.g., daydreaming)

Obtaining this type of information during the assessment process is important not only for diagnostic purposes but also for intervention and treatment purposes. Ultimately, diagnoses are made so that appropriate treatments can be rendered. In the case of functional behavior assessment, the interventions will vary depending on the student's specific ADHD-related problems and the antecedents and consequences that may be maintaining these behaviors. For example, Boyajian et al. (2001) found that aggressive behavior in boys with ADHD served different functions (i.e., to gain attention or to escape an assignment) and classroom interventions designed to address these specific functions greatly reduced the aggressive behavior. The Functional Behavior Analysis Worksheet in Appendix I may be useful for identifying specific behaviors and factors that maintain these behaviors. For more information about functional behavior assessment for ADHD, see DuPaul and Ervin (1996) and Nelson, Roberts, and Smith (1998) for assessment forms and information.

Teacher Rating Scales

In addition to interviews, teachers should complete broad-range behavioral rating scales such as the Teacher Report Form (TRF; Achenbach, 1991) and the BASC–TRF (Reynolds & Kamphaus, 1992), as well as more specific ADHD rating scales such as the ADHD Rating Scale–IV (DuPaul, 1991), the School Situations Questionnaire (Barkley & Murphy, 1998), or the Conners Teacher Rating Scale (Conners, 1997). The Social Skills Assessment Teacher Form (Goldstein, 1988) or the Walker–McConnell Scale of Social Competence and School Adjustment (Walker & McConnell, 1988) may be useful for gathering information about the student's social interactions with classmates. Similar to the parent versions, these rating scales will help to identify the student's specific strengths and problem areas. They are also extremely useful for determining whether a student meets the criteria for ADHD and in diagnosing co-existing social, behavioral, and/or emotional problems. The scales can be used to monitor the effectiveness of interventions such as medication or a behavior management program. See Frauenglass and Routh (1999), Collet, Ohan, and Myers (2003), or Demaray, Elting, and Schaefer (2003) for a review of ADHD instruments appropriate for teachers.

Academic Skills and Information

In addition to obtaining information from behavior rating scales, it is important that information be obtained about the student's academic skills, grades, standardized test scores, school attendance, and deportment. This information can be gathered during the teacher interview and from the student's school record. Based on research, students with ADHD tend to have more disciplinary problems and earn lower grades than would be expected based on their capability level. The school record may also contain teacher comments about the student such as inconsistent work performance, disorganization, attention problems, behavior problems, distractibility, impulsivity, and failure to follow through on tasks. A teacher rating scale such as the Academic Performance Rating Scale (DuPaul, Rapport, & Perriello, 1991; Appendix C) can also be useful for gathering information about the student's classroom performance.

Child, Adolescent, or Adult Observations and Interview

The main purposes of the observations and interview components of the ADHD assessment process are to

- Gather objective information about the individual's behavior relative to his or her peers

- Become acquainted and develop rapport with the individual under evaluation
- Gather information about the individual's perspective regarding his or her problem behavior
- Gather information about the individual's interpersonal relationships and social-emotional functioning
- Observe the individual's appearance, behavior, problem-solving, and language skills

Observations

Two types of observations are important in the assessment process: (a) those conducted by the clinician during the interview and testing procedures and (b) direct observations of the individual in the school (or work) setting. During the initial interview and testing procedures, individuals with ADHD may exhibit inattentive, impulsive behavior; or, if the situation and setting are novel, they may *not* display symptoms associated with ADHD (Barkley, 1990). For example, during an office visit or when working one on one with the referred individual, the child, adolescent, or adult may appear on task and attentive. Parents, teachers, and spouses may complain that "since they can play a video game for hours" or "become engrossed in a book" or "play cards for hours," they could be attentive to their schoolwork or job if they "just tried harder." This notion that individuals with ADHD are simply lazy or selectively inattentive is a common misconception. In fact, research indicates that variability and inconsistency in performance are characteristic of the disorder. When an individual with ADHD is playing a video game or reading an intriguing book, he or she is receiving immediate, positive feedback, which serves to maintain his or her attention. When working on a dull or protracted task such as a homework or job assignment, the individual may not receive any feedback, or, worse, the task may be boring and a struggle to complete. It is in these situations that individuals with ADHD are predictably inattentive and off-task, while a person without the disorder can remain focused until the task is completed. Thus, this information should be kept in mind when evaluating and observing an individual referred for an ADHD assessment. In addition, the examiner should note the individual's attention and physical activity levels, response style, ability to follow instructions, problem-solving style, frustration level, and degree of cooperation. Ideally, direct observations in the school setting would be (a) conducted without the child or adolescent's knowledge to avoid influencing his or her behavior; (b) across multiple settings (e.g., math class, history class, playground, cafeteria) and times (e.g., morning, afternoon); and (c) during independent seat work. Typically, observations should last 20 to 30 minutes, and it is often useful to observe the individual under evaluation and an "average" student for comparison purposes.

Observation Methods. Numerous direct behavior observation systems are available; see DuPaul and Stoner (2003), Merrell (1999) or Platzman and colleagues (1992) for a review of these systems. In general, research indicates that observation systems that include measures of off-task behavior, motor activity, and negative vocalizations, such as verbally refusing to obey teacher commands, are the best at discriminating students with and without ADHD (DuPaul & Stoner, 2003). One such system known as the TOAD (Talking out, Out of seat, Attention problem, Disruption) was developed by Goldstein and Goldstein (1998) and appears in Appendix D. This system is very useful for collecting data for the individual under evaluation and for collecting data on a comparison student.

It is interesting to note that according to Platzman's research, observations conducted in the classroom are *superior* to observations conducted in clinic settings in terms of discriminating individuals with and without ADHD. Classroom observations can also provide insightful information about a child or an adolescent's interactions with his or her teachers and peers. Recent research by Antrop, Buysse, Roeyers, and Van Oost (2005) found that children with ADHD displayed more motor activity and more noises in the classroom when they were in a waiting situation versus a nonwaiting situation.

Obviously, this step of the assessment process does not apply to adults, and clinicians must rely on interviews and self-report instruments discussed in the following sections.

Child, Adolescent, or Adult Interview

The interview with a child, an adolescent, or an adult is an important component of the ADHD assessment process. Observations during the interview can be a rich source of information; however, as mentioned previously, research indicates that children with ADHD may not show attention, impulsivity, or hyperactivity problems when working one on one with a clinician or in the physician's office (Sleator & Ullmann, 1981). Additionally, according to Barkley (1998), children less than 9 to 12 years of age are not reliable reporters of their own behavior. For example, they may deny that they have any problems and report that they are doing well at school and have many friends, despite teacher and parent reports to the contrary. Adolescents may be more reliable reporters of their own behavior as found in studies by Schaughency and colleagues (1994) and Cantwell, Lewinsohn, Rhode, and Seeley (1997). Information concerning the reliability of behavioral symptoms reported by adults is sparse, but preliminary findings suggest that adults can provide an accurate account of their childhood and current behavior (Murphy & Schachar, 2000). Thus, the age of the individual being evaluated must be taken into consideration when drawing inferences from interviews.

Interview Methods.   Similar to parent interviews, interviews with children can follow a structured format, such as the Kiddie SADS-E (Orvaschel, 1985), or a semistructured format such as the Social Adjustment Inventory for Children and Adolescents (SAICA; Orvaschel & Walsh, 1984). According to a study by Biederman, Faraone, and Chen (1993), the SAICA is a very useful interview method for measuring an individual's functioning in school, spare-time activities, peer relations, and home life. Furthermore, the SAICA is able to discriminate children and adolescents with and without ADHD and can also identify coexisting problems such as depression, anxiety, and conduct disorders. For more information about interviewing, see Dr. Jerome Sattler's texts, *Clinical and*

Forensic Interviewing of Children and Their Families (1998) or *Assessment of Children*, 5th edition (2006).

Self-Report Rating Scales

Similar to the parent interview, children, adolescents, or adults should be asked to complete behavior rating scales either before or during the initial interview. Several self-report, behavior rating scales are available for adolescents and adults, but because of the reading and cognitive skills required to complete these scales, fewer are available for children. Two broad-range, self-report scales that are available for children include the Youth Self Report (YSR; Achenbach, 1991) for ages 11 to 18 and the BASC (Reynolds & Kamphaus, 1992) for ages 12 through adulthood.

The data obtained from these scales should be interpreted cautiously, however, given the previous discussion about the reliability and validity of children's reporting. Nevertheless, these instruments can be extremely useful in identifying ADHD symptoms as well as other problems such as depression, anxiety, antisocial behavior, and so on. Additional ADHD scales that are available for adolescents include the Conners–Wells Adolescent Self-Report Scale (CASS; Conners & Wells, 1997) and the Brown Adolescent (and Adult) Attention Deficit Disorder Scales (Brown, 1996). For adults, the Brown (1996) scale is available, as is the Wender Utah Rating Scale (WURS; Ward et al., 1993); the Current Symptoms Scale and Childhood Symptoms Scale (Barkley & Murphy, 1998); the Work Performance Rating Scale (Barkley & Murphy, 1998); the Adult Rating Scale (Weyandt et al., 1995, Appendix E); and the Internal Restlessness Scale (Weyandt et al., 2003). As mentioned previously, it is important to note that relative to the child behavior rating scales, little research information is available for the adult ADHD instruments. For example, the Adult Rating Scale and the Internal Restlessness Scale have been found to discriminate between adults with and without ADHD; however, information concerning the performance of other clinical groups (e.g., depression) on this scale is lacking. Relatively more scientific information is available for the WURS; however, this scale relies on an adult's recollection of his or her childhood and should be used in conjunction with a rating scale that assesses current functioning. Gordon and Barkley (1999) have expressed concern with the Brown scales, stating that the scales are not empirically based and result in overidentification of ADHD in adults. Brown (1999), however, defends the scales, arguing that they are useful in assessing inattention and other cognitive symptoms in adolescents and adults. Clearly, more research is needed on all of the adult instruments that are currently available, and, as with any rating scale, the information obtained from self-report instruments should be interpreted cautiously and used as only one part of the ADHD assessment process.

Social-Emotional Rating Scales.   A multitude of rating scales are available to help measure additional aspects of an individual's social-emotional functioning (e.g., self-esteem, social skills, anxiety, depression); see Dr. Kenneth Merrell's text, *Behavioral, Social, and Emotional Assessment of Children and Adolescents* (1999) or Sattler (2006) for a review of these instruments. In addition, projective instruments such as the Rorschach, sentence completion, and storytelling techniques have been used to help assess social-emotional functioning in children, adolescents, and adults. The validity and reliability of these tools have been questioned by many; see Merrell for additional information. With respect to ADHD assessment, a few studies have been published using the Rorschach and storytelling techniques (e.g., Bartell & Solanto, 1995; Costantino, Colon-Malgady, Malgady, & Perez, 1991) with mixed results. Given the availability of more objective and psychometrically sound instruments and the concerns raised about projective techniques, authors such as DuPaul and Stoner (1994; 2003) have *strongly discouraged* the use of projective techniques in ADHD evaluations and consequently they should not be used as diagnostic tools in the ADHD assessment process.

Standardized, Norm-Referenced Tests

Standardized, norm-referenced tests that may be used in an ADHD evaluation include intelligence tests and achievement tests. Standardized means that the tests have specific procedures for administration and scoring, and norm-referenced means that the tests results can be compared to a larger group based on age, ethnicity, sex, geographic location, and so on. The primary purpose of administering these tests is to assess an individual's intellectual functioning as well as his or her achievement skills relative to others his or her age. Although research does *not* support the use of these tests as ADHD diagnostic measures, they are useful for (a) understanding an individual's cognitive and academic strengths and weaknesses and (b) differential diagnoses.

IQ Tests

Several traditional IQ tests are available for school-age children, and the Wechsler scales are the most frequently used IQ tests in the public school systems. The Wechsler scales (i.e., Wechsler Adult Intelligence Scale–Third Edition, the Wechsler Intelligence Scale for Children–Third Edition, and the Wechsler Preschool and Primary Scale of Intelligence–Revised) have also received the most attention with respect to ADHD assessment. In particular, researchers have focused on subtests—coding, arithmetic, and digit span—that collectively form an index called the *freedom from distractibility factor*.

Freedom From Distractibility Factor

Numerous studies have investigated whether children with ADHD perform more poorly on the freedom from distractibility factor, and the results have been inconsistent. For example, Prifitera and Dersch (1993) reported differences between groups of children with and without ADHD, while others have not found these differences (e.g., Anastopolous, Spisto, & Maher, 1994). Cohen, Becker, and Campbell (1990) investigated whether parent and teacher ratings on a popular ADHD rating scale were related to children's scores on the freedom from distractibility factor. Based on their findings, the authors concluded that the freedom from distractibility factor is *not* a reliable measure of ADHD. Weyandt, Mitzlaff, and Thomas (2002) also found that this factor did not distinguish college students with and without ADHD. After reviewing a large number of studies investigating the Wechsler tests and freedom from distractibility factor, Dr. Russell Barkley, perhaps the world's leading authority on ADHD, concluded that, "these tests have not been shown to be of value in detecting ADHD characteristics. In other words, no subtest or configuration of subtests is sensitive or specific to the disorder" (Barkley, 1998, p. 297). Thus, the most appropriate use of IQ tests in the ADHD assessment process is to measure an individual's intelligence—the purpose for which the tests were designed.

A different type of intelligence measure, the Das–Naglieri Cognitive Assessment System (CAS; Naglieri & Das, 1997), assesses attention, planning and, problem-solving processes, features that are not available on other IQ tests. Some studies have found that children with ADHD perform more poorly on aspects of this test that are designed to measure attention and planning processes (Paolitto, 1999; Naglieri, Goldstein, Delauder, & Schwebach, 2005). Although additional studies need to be conducted, preliminary results suggest that the CAS may be useful in the identification and diagnosis of children with ADHD. Woods and colleagues (2002) examined a discrepancy formula involving intelligence test performance and executive function test performance in adults with ADHD and concluded that this method was sensitive at identifying ADHD. Like the CAS, more studies are needed to explore the usefulness of neuropsychological discrepancy analysis in the assessment of ADHD.

Achievement Tests and Curriculum-Based Measurement

Similar to the IQ tests, numerous standardized, norm-referenced achievement tests are available to assess an individual's academic skills in a variety of subject areas. For example, the Woodcock–Johnson Psychoeducational Battery–3rd edition (WJIII; Woodcock & Johnson, 1987) is one of the most valid and reliable achievement tests and is appropriate for children and adults. Although the WJ is not useful for ADHD diagnostic purposes, it is valuable in identifying an individual's academic strengths and needs. This information is useful for differential diagnosis (e.g., learning disability assessment) and also for designing interventions. For more information concerning achievement and intelligence tests, see Sattler (2006). Information concerning the role of curriculum-based measurement techniques in the assessment of ADHD is limited, although these techniques can certainly be used in designing interventions for promoting desired classroom behavior and skills. Curriculum-based measurement has also been used in evaluating medication effects for students with ADHD (Roberts & DuPaul, (2005).

Laboratory Measures

Laboratory measures in ADHD assessments typically include neuropsychological tests and continuous performance tests.

Neuropsychological Tests

As discussed in chapter 2, numerous neuropsychological tests have been used in research with individuals with ADHD, including various cancellation tests, the Matching Familiar Figures Test, Stroop Word-Color Test, Wisconsin Card Sort Test, Trail Making Test, Tower of Hanoi, and various verbal fluency and visual search tasks, to name a few. For more information about these tests, see Lezak (1995). Similar to the freedom from distractibility research, the findings have been highly inconsistent from study to study (e.g., Barkley, Grodzinsky, & DuPaul, 1992; Boucugnani & Jones, 1989; Rice & Weyandt, 2000; Weyandt, 2005; Weyandt & Willis, 1994) and consequently research does not support their use as diagnostic tools for ADHD. For more information, see Barkley (1998) and Weyandt (2005a, 2005b).

Continuous Performance Tests

Continuous performance tests (CPTs) are computerized tests designed to measure attention, impulsivity, and reaction time. Numerous CPTs are available, for example, the Conners Continuous Performance Test II (Conners, 1995), the Gordon Diagnostic System (Gordon, 1988), and the Tests of Variables of Attention (TOVA; Greenberg, 1990). Although differences exist among these tasks, they generally involve the presentation of a target stimulus (e.g., a number or a figure) on the computer screen followed by similar but different stimuli. Some CPTs (e.g., TOVA) also have an auditory component, and the target stimulus is a sound. The individual taking the task is instructed to press a button each time the target stimulus appears and to refrain from pressing the button when a nontarget stimulus appears. The scores produced vary among the CPTs, but, in general, the number of correct responses, incorrect responses (commission errors), and missed responses (omission errors), and possibly reaction time are recorded. The commission errors (and reaction time) are thought to be a measure of impulsivity, while the omission errors and correct responses are thought to measure ability to sustain attention. Lin, Hsiao, and Chen (1999) investigated the normal development of sustained attention using a CPT in children ages 6 to 15 years and reported that sustained attention, as reflected by CPT scores, develops gradually during the primary school ages.

CPT and Movement Studies and ADHD.   Many CPT studies have been conducted with individuals with ADHD; see Corkum and Siegel (1993) and Epstein et al. (2003) for a review of this literature. In general, research suggests that CPTs can discriminate groups of children and young adults with and without ADHD and may even be helpful in diagnosing subtypes of ADHD (Fischer, Barkley, Smallish, & Fletcher, 2005; Marks, Himelstein, Newcorn, & Halperin, 1999). CPTs can also useful for measuring stimulant drug effects (e.g., Berman, Douglas, & Barr, 1999; Boonstra, Kooij, Oosterlaan, Sergeant, & Buitelaar, 2005; Rapport, Tucker, DuPaul, Merlo, & Stoner, 1986). Shaw, Grayson, and Lewis (2005) found that children with ADHD performed better on a game-like version of the Conners' CPT relative to their performance on the traditional version. Interestingly, Teicher, Ito, Glod, and Barber (1996) found that the movement patterns of boys with and without ADHD differed significantly while they were engaged in a continuous performance test. Specifically, they found that boys with ADHD moved their heads more often and displayed more frequent and larger body movements than children without ADHD. These findings are consistent with previous studies that have reported that individuals with ADHD, compared to individuals without the disorder, have higher activity levels at all times of the day, including during sleep. With regard to movement, Dane, Schachar, and Tannock (2000) found children with ADHD were significantly more active during the afternoon compared to those without ADHD, however no difference was found between the children during the morning session. This information is consistent with teacher reports that the activity level of children with ADHD becomes progressively worse throughout the day.

Concerns About CPTs.   Concerns have been raised about cases in which individuals with ADHD perform normally (*false negatives*) and individuals without ADHD perform poorly (*false positives*). According to Goldstein and Goldstein (1998), approximately one third of individuals with ADHD are not identified as such with current CPTs. A second concern is that relatively little information is available concerning CPT performance in adults with ADHD and in individuals with other types of problems such as depression, learning disabilities, or anxiety disorders. For example, McGee, Clark, and Symons (2000) found that children with reading disabilities performed more poorly than children with ADHD on the Conners' CPT. Recently, Najt et al. (2005) found that individuals with bipolar disorder displayed substantial impairments on a CPT measure. Rovet and Hepworth (2001) found that both children with ADHD and children with congenital hypothyroidism performed poorly on a CPT. Collectively, these studies suggest that CPT performance can sometimes distinguish those with and without ADHD but cannot necessarily distinguish clinical groups (Epstein et al., 2003).

A third concern, as noted by van der Meere, Vreeling, and Sergeant (1992), is that certain task parameters such as the duration of the CPT, rate of stimulus presentation, sensory modality, and stimulus complexity can influence performance. In other words, the length of the task, how quickly the objects are presented on the screen, whether the task is visual or auditory, and whether the task requires one or more responses from the individual under evaluation could all affect an individual's performance on the CPT. A final concern is that CPT performance does not always correlate with classroom measures such as cognitive, behavior, or academic performance. Dr. Paul Chae (1999) investigated the relationship between intelligence test scores and CPT (TOVA) scores in a group of 40 children with ADHD and found that the scores were poorly related. Weyandt, Mitzlaff, and Thomas (2003) found similar results with college students with ADHD. In other words, intelligence and CPT tests appear to be measuring different cognitive abilities, and performance on one test is not related to performance on the other. Thus, CPTs should *not* be used as a sole diagnostic test for ADHD but rather as part of a comprehensive assessment battery.

Medical Evaluation

As mentioned at the beginning of this chapter, problems with attention, impulsivity, and hyperactivity can be associated with various social or emotional problems but can also be indicative of medical disorders such as thyroid malfunction, seizures, sleep apnea, lead poisoning, allergies, reactions to medication, and other medical conditions. As a result, it is often beneficial for an individual to have a medical evaluation, particularly if an ADHD assessment is conducted by someone other than a physician. Furthermore, in order for a student to receive special educational services under the IDEA "health impaired" category, the law requires that student to be evaluated by a medical provider. It is important to note that there are currently no medical tests for ADHD, although a number have been used in experimental studies, such as those that measure "neurological soft signs" (clumsiness, reflexes, hand sequencing, motor flexibility problems), as well as EEG, CT, MRI, and neuroimaging techniques. Some studies have found differences on these tests in groups of individuals with ADHD, while others have not (e.g., Slatts-Willemse, de Sonneville, Swaab-Barneveld, & Buitelaar, 2005; see Goldstein & Goldstein, 1998, for a summary of these findings). These tests are useful, however, for diagnosing seizure disorders and other brain or central nervous system anomalies and may be appropriate in select cases. More recently, research studies have incorporated the use of more sophisticated technology such as fMRI, PET, and transcranial magnetic stimulation in the study of ADHD. As discussed in chapter 2, several studies using brain imaging techniques such as fMRI and PET have reported blood flow and glucose metabolism differences between children, adolescents, and adults with ADHD compared to those without the disorder. These results have *not* been found consistently in individuals with ADHD and are not necessarily unique to ADHD, and therefore these techniques should be regarded as research, *not diagnostic instruments* for ADHD. Unfortunately misinformation about the use of fMRI and PET abounds in the media and on the Internet and several businesses now offer, for a substantial cost, brain imaging as part of an assessment for ADHD. Again, to date, there is no specific fMRI or PET finding that is a conclusive diagnostic marker for ADHD, although these tools one day may be useful in the diagnosis of ADHD. In summary, although a medical evaluation may not be able to conclusively rule in ADHD, it is useful for eliminating conditions that may produce ADHD symptoms.

Integration of Information

Making sense of all of the information gathered from multiple methods and multiple informants during an ADHD assessment can be a daunting process. To guide the interpretation process, Schaughency and Rothlind (1991) recommended that four key questions be answered

- Does the individual meet *DSM-IV-TR* criteria?
- Does an alternative educational diagnosis or medical condition account for the attention difficulties?

TABLE 3.3   *DSM-IV-TR* Criteria for ADHD and Assessment Techniques

■ **Does the individual meet *DSM-IV* criteria?**
Answer: Parent, teacher, individual interviews
            Developmental, social, academic histories
            Rating scales
            Observations
            School records

■ **Does an alternative educational diagnosis or medical condition account for the attention difficulties?**
Answer: IQ and achievement results
            School records
            Interviews
            Rating scales
            Medical evaluation

■ **Are the behaviors displayed by the child developmentally appropriate?**
Answer: Rating scales
            Observations

■ **Do these behaviors impair the child's functioning in home, school, or social relations situations?**
Answer: Interviews
            Rating scales
            Observations
            Testing
            School records

Note: From Weyandt (2001).

■ Are the behaviors displayed by the child developmentally appropriate?
■ Do these behaviors impair the child's functioning in home, school, or social relations situations?

Table 3.3 summarizes how each of these four questions can be addressed by various assessment procedures.

Subtyping

Lastly, three subtypes of ADHD currently exist:

■ ADHD, combined type
■ ADHD, predominately inattentive type
■ ADHD, predominately hyperactive-impulsive type

Based on *DSM-IV-TR* criteria and the data collected from the entire assessment process, the clinician must determine whether the evidence supports the presence of inattention, hyperactivity and impulse problems, or a combination of only a few of these core symptoms. Problems in all three areas are consistent with ADHD, combined type; whereas attention problems but not problems with hyperactivity and impulsivity are consistent with ADHD, predominately inattentive type. Lastly, if the child is of preschool age and attention and academic work cannot adequately be measured, then a diagnosis of ADHD, predominately hyperactive-impulsive type, might be appropriate. For numerous case study examples of these subtypes as well as ADHD plus coexisting problems in children, see Barkley (2006), and Goldstein and Teeter-Ellison (2002) for information concerning assessment of ADHD in adults.

Differential Diagnosis

To complicate matters, ADHD is frequently accompanied by coexisting problems; it is therefore essential that clinicians address whether symptoms associated with other disorders are also present. The same assessment procedures discussed in this chapter can be used for differential diagnoses, and, when appropriate, additional interviews, tests, or rating scales may be incorporated (e.g., personality inventories or depression or anxiety scales). Barkley and Murphy (1998) have published an excellent, comprehensive, structured clinical interview for parents that is ideal for differential assessment. Robin (1998) has created a series of questions that are highly useful in assessing coexisting problems in adolescents (Appendix F).

Problems that most frequently coexist with ADHD include

- Learning disabilities
- Mood disorders
- Conduct disorder
- Oppositional defiant disorder
- Anxiety disorders
- Substance use/abuse disorders

Additional problems may include language, tic, auditory processing, and sleep disorders. Of course, depending on the individual, other disorders may also be present.

Learning Disabilities

Depending on which study is read, 8% to 75% of children with ADHD have a coexisting learning disability (LD), usually a reading disability. In 2005, the Centers for Disease Control and Prevention (CDC) reported that 4.4 million children in the United States ages 4 to 17 had been diagnosed with ADHD, and in 2002 the CDC reported that 4% of children ages 6 to 11 had been diagnosed with ADHD and LD (Pastor & Reuben, 2002). Although state requirements for learning disability assessments vary, a learning disability is characterized by a significant discrepancy between an individual's intellectual capacity and his or her achievement. According to the federal definition, there are seven areas in which learning disabilities can occur: reading comprehension, basic reading, written expression, oral expression, listening comprehension, math calculation, and mathematical reasoning. By this definition, the discrepancy between an individual's intelligence (i.e., IQ score) and his or her achievement is not due to mental retardation, medical, emotional, cultural, or environmental factors.

Many children with learning disabilities have significant problems with attention, behavior, and organization; therefore, it is imperative that the clinician determine whether (a) the learning disability accounts for the ADHD-like symptoms, or (b) the learning disability is secondary to ADHD. This issue is a matter of debate within the literature, and some researchers such as Shaywitz, Fletcher, and Shaywitz (1995) argue that there are many overlapping characteristics of ADHD and reading disability, while others such as Pennington, Groisser, and Welsh (1993) argue that they are distinguishable disorders but often coexist. Recently, Willcutt, Pennington, Olson, et al. (2005) found distinct neuropsychological differences between subjects with ADHD only, reading disability only, and those with ADHD and co-existing reading disability. Preliminary genetic studies suggest that certain genes (or regions on genes) may uniquely influence the development of ADHD or reading disability, while other genes may be linked to the development of both disorders (Gayan et al., 2005; Stevenson, Asherson, et al., 2005; Stevenson, Langley, et al., 2005). What ever the cause, it is clear that many individuals with ADHD have the compounded problem of reading disability, which places them at even greater risk for academic difficulties.

Behavior Disorders

Depending on the study that is reviewed, acting out disorders such as conduct disorder (CD) and oppositional defiant disorder (ODD) may occur in 60% to 65% of children and adolescents with ADHD and are more common in boys (Klassen, Miller, & Fine, 2004). Conduct disorder is a persistent pattern of behavior (for at least 6 months) in which the basic rights of others or age-appropriate societal rules are violated by the child or adolescent (American Psychiatric Association, 2000). Such behaviors may include cruelty to animals, theft, lying, physical aggression, or destruction of property and are not characteristic of ADHD. Oppositional defiant disorder is a persistent (for at least 6 months) pattern of hostile, argumentative, negativistic, defiant behavior that causes impairment in the child or adolescent's social, academic, or occupational functioning (American Psychiatric Association, 2000). Similar to CD, ODD symptoms are *not* inherently characteristic of ADHD. Essentially, ODD and CD differ from ADHD with regard to core symptoms (inattention, hyperactivity, impulsivity vs. antisocial/defiant behavior), age of onset, and presumed underlying cause. ADHD is believed to be physiologically based, while CD and ODD are strongly related to family functioning and environmental factors. Recent genetic studies, however, suggest that CD and ODD, like ADHD many have a genetic component (Dick, Viken, Kaprio, Pulkkinen, & Rose, 2005).

Depression and Anxiety

Klassen, Miller, and Fine (2004) found that 68.7% of children with ADHD had a co-existing disorder, including mood disorders such as major depression and bipolar disorder. Major depression and bipolar disorder sometimes occur more frequently in females with ADHD than in males but recent research suggests that both sexes are at risk for co-existing clinical disorders (Biederman, Faraone, Mick, Williamson, et al., 1999; Biederman et al., 2005; McGough, Smalley, et al., 2005). Depression is characterized by a depressed, irritable mood; diminished interest or pleasure in activities; insomnia; fatigue; and feelings of worthlessness; as well as other symptoms (American Psychiatric Association, 2000). Findings from studies differ, but it is estimated that 9% to 32% of children with ADHD have co-existing depression, and approximately 17% of adolescent females with ADHD also suffer from depression (Biederman, Faraone, Mick, Williamson, et al., 1999). Bipolar disorder is characterized by intermittent periods of depression and periods of elated, expansive mood. Although precise numbers are unknown, it has been estimated that approximately 11% of children with ADHD also suffer from bipolar disorder (e.g., Biederman et al., 1999; Biederman et al., 2005; Milberger et al., 1996). Anxiety disorders occur more frequently than mood disorders in children and adolescents with ADHD, with estimates ranging from 25% to 40% (Geller et al., 2004; Jensen, Shervette, Xenakis, & Richters, 1993). Anxiety disorders are characterized by excessive, unrealistic fears and worries that interfere with an individual's social, academic, or occupational functioning. Various types of anxiety disorders exist including panic disorder, obsessive–compulsive disorder, separation anxiety disorder, and posttraumatic stress disorder, to name a

TABLE 3.4   Differential Diagnosis

Rule In
- Early pattern of symptoms
- Pervasiveness of symptoms
- Documented impairment
- Advantageous to label
- *DSM-IV-TR* subtype

Rule Out
- Unrealistic expectations
- Mood disorders
- Anxiety disorders
- Medical problems
- Conduct or oppositional disorders
- Substance use/abuse
- Parent-child personality conflict
- Teacher-child personality conflict
- Parent/teacher skill deficits
- Gifted and bored
- Educational disorders (LD, MR)

Note: From Weyandt (2001).

few. Recent research has found that the majority of adults with panic disorder had a childhood history of disruptive behavior disorders such as ADHD or anxiety (Biederman et al., 2005). It is important to note that not all children with ADHD suffer from anxiety disorders and most children with anxiety disorders do not have ADHD (Masi et al., 2004). Nevertheless, these findings underscore the importance of differential diagnosis as a crucial component of ADHD evaluations. Differential diagnosis helps to (a) increase the accuracy of an ADHD diagnosis, (b) identify co-existing problems and disorders, and (c) identify areas of needed remediation and treatment. Table 3.4 may be useful in the differential diagnosis process.

Summary

Identification and diagnosis of ADHD require a comprehensive evaluation using multiple assessment methods and multiple informants. The mere presence of *DSM-IV-TR* symptoms does *not* warrant a diagnosis of ADHD, as these symptoms can be present in a variety of educational, medical, or behavior disorders. In addition, many individuals with ADHD have co-existing behavior or emotional problems that require a thorough differential diagnosis. No single source of information is conclusive, and a careful analysis of all the information is essential to reach an accurate diagnosis. The reader should be skeptical and critical of any claims that ADHD can be assessed simply and quickly or by any single test.

4 ADHD—How Is It Treated? School- and Home-Based Approaches

As with weight-loss programs, there are numerous interventions promoted for ADHD. Also similar to weight-loss programs is the fact that some of these interventions are well studied, safe, and reliable, while others are costly, have no scientific basis, and are ineffective. Like weight problems, there is no magic cure for ADHD and treatment typically requires a multimethod approach. Although questions remain, decades of research indicate that the most effective treatment approach for ADHD is

- Designed for the specific needs of the individual
- Multidimensional
- Monitored and evaluated regularly
- Data based
- Modified as needed

The following interventions are organized as school- and home-based interventions. Be aware that behavioral support and medication approaches have been researched most extensively, while many of the other interventions are less well studied. It is also important to recognize that there is nothing *magical* about these interventions; they are manageable, usable, and beneficial for *all* students—not only those with ADHD.

School-Based Interventions

Schools play a vital role in early identification of children with ADHD and, in many cases, school personnel coordinate efforts among teachers, parents, physicians, and community resources with regard to the assessment and treatment of children and adolescents with ADHD (Sloan, Jensen, & Hoagwood, 1999). In the United States, primary care physicians are often involved in the assessment, diagnosis, and treatment of ADHD, and Chan et al. (2005) found 83% of the physicians surveyed in this study used information provided by the schools (e.g., rating scales, grades, report cards). Obviously, if physicians are requesting school information for their assessments, a coordinated effort is required between home, school, and physicians. Unfortunately, less than 50% of children with ADHD receive the appropriate care and treatment as recommended by the

American Academy of Child and Adolescent Psychiatry, and only 24% of children with ADHD receive necessary school services such as special instructional help or counseling (Hoagwood, Kelleher, Feil, & Comer, 2000; Jensen et al., 1999). Given this information, the following suggestions can help educators better meet the needs of children and adolescents with ADHD.

Teacher Preparation

The majority of individuals with ADHD receive their education in a regular classroom setting; meeting the needs of these students is often challenging for teachers. However, according to a study conducted by CH.A.D.D. (Children and Adults with Attention Deficit Disorders), 89% of the teachers surveyed had not received training in ADHD, yet 98% felt that they needed this training (CH.A.D.D., 1992). Similar findings were reported by Yasutake, Lerner, and Ward (1994), who surveyed teachers in the Chicago metropolitan area. In Houston, Texas, researchers found that 46% of teachers surveyed had received previous training regarding ADHD but 95% thought additional training would be beneficial (Pisecco, Huzinec, & Curtis, 2001). With regard to teacher knowledge, most studies have found that teachers are not very knowledgeable about ADHD, despite the likelihood that 1 to 2 students in their classroom will have the disorder. For example, Sciutto, Terjesen, and Bender-Frank (2000) surveyed teachers in the United States concerning their knowledge about ADHD and discovered their average knowledge was only 47.8% based on a questionnaire about the disorder. Recently, Kos, Richdale, and Jackson (2004) surveyed 120 teachers in Australia and found they were able to correctly answer 60.7% of items on an ADHD knowledge questionnaire. Similar findings concerning teacher knowledge of ADHD have been reported in Israel (Brook, Watemberg, & Geva, 2000) and Canada (Jerome, Gordon, & Hustler, 1994). Collectively these studies suggest that teachers could benefit from additional information and training about the etiology, assessment, and treatment approaches for students with ADHD.

The issue of training and experience with ADHD is strongly related to a teacher's confidence in working with these children, as indicated by a study done by Reid, Vasa, Maag, and Wright in 1994. Specifically, this study compared the perceptions of elementary school teachers with and without ADHD training and experience and found that those teachers without training expressed a lack of confidence in their ability (a) to effectively teach students with ADHD and (b) to create and develop effective behavioral interventions for these students. Interestingly, greater years of teaching experience are not necessarily associated with increased knowledge about ADHD. For example, Bekle (2004) and Sciutto et al. (2000) found higher knowledge scores among teachers with greater years of teaching experience (compared to fewer years of teaching experience) but other studies have not supported this finding (e.g., Jerome, Gordon, & Hustler, 1994; Kos, Richdale, & Jackson, 2004). Education about ADHD is vital, since the classroom teacher is viewed as a major determining factor in whether a student with ADHD succeeds or fails in the classroom (Satterfield, Satterfield, & Cantwell, 1981).

In-Service Training.   Training information about ADHD would ideally include information about characteristics, assessment and diagnosis, etiological theories, and, perhaps most importantly, information concerning educational practices and interventions that can help address the academic, social–emotional, and behavioral needs of students with ADHD. Preliminary studies suggest that ADHD educational programs for teachers *are* associated with improved teacher knowledge and decreased teacher stress related to behaviors associated with ADHD (Barbaresi & Olsen, 1998; Kotkin, 1998). For example, Barbaresi and Olsen (1998) found that at pretraining, 41% of teachers thought ADHD could be caused by poor parenting and 41% thought it could be caused by food additives or sugar. Postintervention percentages of teachers reporting these beliefs dropped to 7% and 5% respectively. The purpose of this chapter is to review interventions that can be useful in addressing the academic, social–emotional, and behavioral needs of individuals with ADHD. The reader is encouraged to seek additional information as needed and to refer to the resources provided in Appendix G. An in-service training outline is provided in Appendix H.

Attention and Academic Issues

Children and adolescents with ADHD frequently have difficulty with sustaining attention, impulsivity, following instructions, solving problems, and completing assignments. Given these issues, it is not surprising that nearly 80% of individuals with ADHD struggle academically (Cantwell & Baker, 1991). Unfortunately, research has focused primarily on intervention strategies to manage social behavior and deportment in the classroom, and relatively less attention has been given to strategies designed to optimize academic achievement and performance (DuPaul & Eckert, 1998). Of those studies that have been done, many have been conducted in lab settings; thus, the generalization to the classroom is questionable (DuPaul & Weyandt, 2006a, 2006b). Also, when research is conducted in the classroom, it frequently focuses on the problem student (i.e., single subject) and it is unknown whether other students with ADHD would respond similarly. Furthermore, in many classrooms it is not always possible to control for factors other than the intended instructional intervention that might affect the outcome of the study (e.g., whether the child is receiving tutoring at home, taking medication, academic skill level or intelligence of students, etc.). Therefore, most of the following interventions should be considered as *suggestions* and not necessarily as valid and reliable interventions. A summary of the following recommendations appears in Table 4.1.

Acceptability of Interventions.   The acceptability of behavioral and other interventions for children with ADHD appears to differ among teachers. For example, Power, Hess, and Bennett (1995) found that elementary and middle school teachers rated daily report cards as more acceptable than punishment (response cost) and stimulant medication. If medication was used, teachers preferred that it be used in conjunction with behavior management rather than in isolation. Other studies have also found that teachers preferred use of a daily report card or positive reinforcement compared to punishment or medication

TABLE 4.1 Suggestions for Increasing Attention and Academic Productivity in Students With ADHD

- Use a multimethod, multisensory teaching approach.
- Maintain a regular classroom routine.
- Try to offer more complex assignments in the morning hours.
- Design academic tasks that require active responses.
- Provide frequent and immediate feedback.
- Provide explicit, highly structured instructions.
- Add color to relevant aspects of assignments.
- Reduce lengthier assignments to several, smaller units.
- Allow students to read aloud to enhance comprehension.
- Allow students extra time to complete assignments.
- Supplement orally presented information with visual cues.
- Minimize classroom background noise and conversation.
- Encourage computer use for academic assignments.
- Encourage note taking.
- Teach organizational skills and techniques.
- Implement a study-skills training program.
- Increase work completion with reinforcement programs.
- Provide extra supervision during unstructured activities.
- Implement a classwide peer tutoring program.
- Provide test-taking accommodations.
- Allow class time for organizing assignment and homework materials.

Note: From Weyandt (2001).

in the treatment of students with ADHD (Nietfeld & Hunt, 2005; Pisecco, Huzinec, & Curtis, 2001).

Designing, Implementing, and Monitoring Interventions. Increasingly, general education teachers, in collaboration with specialists such as school psychologists and special education teachers, are expected to develop, implement, and evaluate classroom interventions for children who are experiencing academic performance deficits. Research suggests, however, that teachers frequently do not follow through with intervention programs after several days. Noell, Witt, Gilbertson, Ranier, and Freeland (1997) found that feedback (i.e., 3 to 5 minutes daily) from a consultant (e.g., behavior specialist, school psychologist) significantly increased the likelihood that teachers would adhere to intervention programs implemented in the classroom. Noell and colleagues (2000) reported similar findings in a more recent study, and other studies have found that collaboration among teachers, administrators, and researchers increases the likelihood of successful outcomes for student intervention programs (Weinstein et al., 1991). Programs that are less demanding of the teacher's time and resources are also more likely to be followed. It is important to note that these studies have been conducted with regular education students and presumably apply to students with ADHD but additional studies are needed. Miranda, Presentacion, and Soriano (2002) studied the effects of a multicomponent program on the behavior of children with ADHD, and the program included teacher training in the use of behavior modification, cognitive-behavior strategies, and instructional management strategies. Based on teacher and parent ratings, improvements were found in inattention, disorganization, and hyperactivity–impulsivity symptoms of students with ADHD. Improvements were also found in the children's academic performance. Unfortunately, based on the design of the study it was difficult to determine which aspect of the program was associated with student behavioral and academic improvement.

When intervention programs are implemented, it is important that teachers monitor and evaluate the effectiveness of instructional strategies so that decisions about the program are based on data and not simply impressions or opinions. There are numerous methods that can be used to design, implement, and collect data and evaluate instructional programs or interventions, though a summary of these methods is beyond the scope of this primer. At minimum, however, teachers should

- Systematically collect data concerning the student's academic problem(s) before implementing the intervention (i.e., *baseline data*)
- Systematically collect data during the intervention
- In cases in which the intervention is withdrawn, continue to collect data concerning the student's academic performance

When these procedures are followed, teachers can make well-informed decisions about the effectiveness, need to modify, or need to discontinue an intervention program. When designing, implementing, and evaluating interventions for students with ADHD, DuPaul and Stoner (2003) recommend the five guidelines that appear in Table 4.2.

Instructional Strategies.   Various instructional strategies have been recommended for students with ADHD, some of which have been supported by research with students with ADHD and others are based on studies with students without the disorder. Most of the research has been conducted with elementary students. There is an obvious need for additional research with preschool, middle, high school, and college students with ADHD. A summary of instructional strategies follows, and many of the suggestions can be modified to meet the needs of elementary and secondary students. Scientific studies with groups and

TABLE 4.2   Guidelines for the Design, Implementation, and Evaluation of Interventions for Learning and Behavior Problems

1. Intervention development, evaluation, and revision are *data-based* activities.
2. Intervention development, evaluation, and revision are driven by *child advocacy* and focus on attainment of clearly identified, socially valid *child outcomes.*
3. Intervention procedures must be thoroughly identified and defined, as well as implemented with integrity by persons with clearly delineated responsibilities.
4. Effective interventions produce or lead to increased rates of appropriate behavior and/or improved rates of learning, not solely decreases in undesirable or disturbing behavior.
5. Prior to its implementation, an intervention's effects on the behaviors of the identified child, the teacher, and on the classroom are unknown.

Source: From *ADHD in the Schools: Assessment and Intervention Strategies* (p. 99), by G. J. DuPaul and G. Stoner, 2003, New York: Guilford Press. Reprinted with permission.

individuals are needed to further explore the effectiveness of these strategies across all age levels.

Teacher and Student Education About ADHD.   According to Hall, Marshall, Vaughn, Hynd, and Riccio (1997), teacher education about ADHD is "paramount to the establishment of productive corrective techniques" (p. 135). As mentioned previously, most teachers do not receive adequate training about ADHD and according to a recent study by Havey et al. (2005) out of 121 students, nearly 24% were identified by teachers as meeting *DSM-IV* criteria for ADHD. Obviously, this rate does not accurately reflect the prevalence of ADHD, and education about ADHD at building or district levels would likely be beneficial for teachers. A suggested outline for an in-service training program on ADHD is offered in Appendix H. To increase the likelihood that a child with ADHD will succeed academically and socially, Barkley (1994) recommends that parents take an active role in choosing an optimum classroom and teacher for their child with ADHD. Specifically, he suggests that parents consider three compatibility issues—(a) philosophical compatibility, (b) personality compatibility, and (c) resource compatibility—as well as the teacher's instructional competence. It is also important that individuals with ADHD become educated about the disorder. A large number of resources are available such as books, research articles, Web sites, and national organizations. Resource information for children, adolescents, adults, and parents is provided in Appendix G.

Action-Oriented Tasks.   According to work by Zentall and Meyer (1987), children with ADHD perform better on academic tasks that require *active responses* to the material. For example, tasks that require manipulation of materials, hands-on activities, physical movement, and verbal interactions will likely maintain the attention of students with ADHD, as opposed to rote tasks. Alberts and van der Meere (1992) found that children with ADHD displayed more body movements during a visual task compared to those without the disorder, however their visual attention to the task was just as good as those without ADHD. The authors suggested that motor activity may be a form of self-stimulation that helps to prevent deterioration of task performance for children with ADHD. Based on these findings, teachers should expect greater body movement from children with ADHD and understand that it may facilitate (not interfere with) their attention to tasks.

Frequent Feedback.   Children with ADHD are likely to be more productive when they are given individual and immediate feedback. Rapport, Tucker, and colleagues (1986) found that children with ADHD preferred a smaller, more immediate reward (e.g., one toy) over a larger, delayed reward (e.g., three to four toys) upon completion of an academic assignment. The researchers interpreted the behavior of the students with ADHD as a *grab-and-run* style—choosing the greatest reward possible in a relative brief period of time. In a related study, Slusarek, Velling, Bunk, and Eggers (2001) found that children with ADHD were able to perform similar to children without ADHD on a task that required inhibition of responses when the incentives were high. In a recent review of the literature concerning this topic, Luman, Oosterlaan, and Sergeant (2005) concluded that children with ADHD prefer immediate over delayed rewards and a high intensity rather than a low intensity of reinforcement. The implications for the classroom are that students with ADHD, compared to those without the disorder, have great difficulty delaying gratification and will require more consistent and immediate feedback.

Instructions.   Instructions should be explicit, and academic tasks should be highly structured. Zentall (1993) reported that students with ADHD were more on task and less active when assignments were accompanied by explicit instructions and structured task materials (i.e., art materials) compared to nonspecific instructions and no task materials. In other words, teachers should not assume that students with ADHD can organize themselves and their activities even if their peers are capable of doing so. It is important for teachers to remember that disorganization and difficulty following through on tasks are characteristic of the disorder. Instructions should also be simple. Mithaug and Mithaug (2003) found that students with disabilities who were taught self-management skills were better able to manage and complete independent work compared to those who were instructed by teachers. Additional research is needed to explore whether these findings apply to students with ADHD as well. According to DuPaul and Stoner (2003) a student with ADHD should be asked to repeat the directions to the teacher to be sure he/she understood correctly. Neef and colleagues (2004) recently found that instructions in the form of being told what to do and instructions in the form of showing students what to do were equally effective with children with ADHD.

Stimulating Materials.   Research indicates that students with ADHD often fail to focus on relevant academic information when it is subtle, less salient, or embedded in a task (e.g., a lengthy, detailed story). However, these students do appear to attend to important information and relevant aspects of assignments when an attention enhancer such as color is added (Belfiore, Grskovic, Murphy, & Zentall, 1996; Zentall, 1989). Thus, use of color can be added to assignments to help increase attention to important details and increase academic performance of students with ADHD. Iovino, Fletcher, Breitmeyer, and Foorman (1998) found that blue overlays (compared to a red or no overlay) significantly improved reading comprehension performance in children with ADHD. Teachers must be careful not to add color to irrelevant aspects of assignments, however, as Zentall found that this actually *decreased* academic performance of children with ADHD on a spelling task. Presumably, when irrelevant details of an assignment are highlighted, students with ADHD become distracted and their performance suffers.

Length of Assignments.   Research indicates that students with ADHD are less able to sustain their attention as length of assignments increases, repetition and rehearsal increase, and novelty decreases (Zentall, 1993). Thus, to help maintain attention and prevent boredom in students with ADHD, it may be helpful to reduce lengthier assignments to several, smaller units, and students should be reinforced for completing each smaller unit. According to DuPaul and Stoner (2003) the length of the assignments can be gradually increased, followed by reinforcement. It should be noted that although most books concerning ADHD recommend breaking lengthier assignments into smaller units, there is a lack of empirical studies to substantiate that this is actually an effective intervention for students with ADHD.

Multisensory Teaching.   Because children and adolescents with ADHD become bored more quickly than individuals without the disorder, repetition of tasks should be avoided and novelty should be incorporated into tasks as much as possible. Sosne (1988), for example, recommends using a multimodal (e.g., blackboard and handouts), multisensory (verbal and written instructions) approach in teaching. Similarly, Fiore and Becker (1993) suggest that teachers vary the presentation rate at which they cover information to find the optimal rate that maintains the attention of students with ADHD. Sandra Rief (1993), in her book, *How to Reach and Teach ADD/ADHD Children*, recommends using visual aids, games, colorful flashcards, and various types of hands-on activities to learn concepts that are traditionally learned via rote methods (i.e., math). Adaptive technological computer programs such as Dragon Speaking Naturally, incorporate the use of color, voices, and other strategies to enhance learning for students with disabilities including ADHD.

Computer Use and Adaptive Technology.   Allowing students with ADHD to complete written assignments on the computer rather than by hand may increase their attention and productivity (DuPaul & Eckert, 1998). Similarly, permitting students to complete math assignments on the computer can increase the number of problems that they solve (Kleiman, Humphrey, & Lindsay, 1981). Presumably, computers, compared to the traditional paper–pencil format, increase attention and performance as they provide immediate feedback, highlight essential material, and require multisensory involvement (i.e., vision and finger movement). As mentioned previously, several computer adaptive technology programs are now available (e.g., Dragon Speaking Naturally) that allow students to scan reading materials into the computer which is then read aloud by a computer activated voice, highlight reading material in a variety of colors, locate the meaning of words with a simple click of the mouse, and so on. Research is needed to determine whether these programs can truly improve the attention and academic performance of students with ADHD.

Note Taking.   Encouraging students to take notes during lectures (rather than sitting passively) may increase on-task behavior. Due to their attention problems, poor organizational skills, and difficulty deducing the important points when listening to a lecture, many students with ADHD are poor note takers (e.g., Evans et al., 2001). Consequently, these students may require training in how to listen for and record main ideas, details, and essential information presented in lectures. Evans, Pelham, and Grudber (1995) found that adolescents with ADHD who had poor note-taking skills were able to acquire good note-taking skills with teacher instruction. Furthermore, the researchers found that the adolescents' comprehension of the material increased as did their on-task behavior.

Listening and Reading Comprehension.   When listening to lectures or instructions, students with ADHD are more likely to have difficulty comprehending the material if it is highly detailed or descriptive (Shroyer & Zentall, 1986).

Children with ADHD are also less likely to recall what they have just heard if they are required to rely on auditory memory (Hamlett, Pellegrini, & Conners, 1987). Their recall improves significantly, however, if visual cues are provided along with the orally presented information. Thus, to help improve the listening comprehension skills of students with ADHD, it may be helpful to supplement orally presented information with visual cues such as handouts, outlines, photographs, pictures, and flowcharts. Some research suggests that, when completing reading assignments, students with ADHD make fewer errors and have better reading comprehension when reading aloud versus reading silently (Dubey & O'Leary, 1975). Semrud-Clikeman and colleagues (1999) found that children with ADHD had poorer visual and auditory attention skills compared to children without the disorder, and following an 18-week intervention program, children with ADHD showed enhanced visual and auditory attending skills. Similar to other academic assignments, studies indicate that the reading comprehension of students with ADHD is better with short versus long passages. Interestingly, Nussbaum, Grant, Roman, Poole, and Bigler (1990) suggest that the vocabulary skills of children with ADHD are likely to be within the average range as vocabulary acquisition does not necessarily require sustained attention. It is important to note that many children and adolescents with ADHD also have a reading disability and special education may be needed to meet the needs of these individuals (Purvis & Tannock, 2000).

Study Skills.   According to Dowdy, Patton, Smith, and Polloway (1998), "one of the most important areas in which students with ADHD need to achieve competence is study skills" (p. 105). Although numerous study skill programs are available for students in general, the use of these programs with students with ADHD needs to be investigated scientifically. Nevertheless, given that most students benefit from good study skills and habits, it makes common sense that students with ADHD would benefit from these skills as well (Hoover & Patton, 1995). The specific components of study skill programs vary; however, most programs teach students (a) organizational skills, (b) strategies for identifying main topics and meanings, (c) strategies for improving comprehension, (d) review strategies, and (e) techniques to improve test-taking performance.

Work Completion.   Academic work completion can also be increased by use of reinforcement programs. It is vital that the teacher not make assumptions about the student before beginning a reinforcement program but instead discuss with the student the types of things that he or she finds rewarding. A reinforcement list can then be created and reviewed with the student prior to the beginning of the assignment (see Table 4.3). According to Rapport and Gordon (1987), the student should be permitted to choose the reinforcement (i.e., "prime" the student), which enhances the student's incentive to complete the academic assignment. Depending on the complexity and length of the task, reinforcement can be applied after part or completion of an assignment.

Positive Reinforcement.   *Reinforcement* involves the delivery of a consequence, after a behavior has occurred, to increase the likelihood that the behavior will re-occur in the future. In other words, the purpose of positive reinforcement is to strengthen a particular, desirable behavior. *Positive reinforcement* involves the

TABLE 4.3   Reinforcement List*

- Computer time
- Decorating the classroom
- Educational game
- Educational video game
- Errands for teacher
- Erasing black/white board
- Free choice activity
- Internet access
- Listening to music
- Reading a book
- Reading announcements over loud speaker
- Small group activity
- Shooting basketball
- Stickers
- Tangible items
- Others chosen by student (list):

*It is crucial that students choose the reinforcers, as what may be rewarding to one student may be aversive to another! Remember to review the reinforcers prior to the academic activity to provide more incentive to the student for completion of his or her work.

Note: From Weyandt (2001).

delivery of a consequence that a student finds rewarding and may include tangible objects such as pencils, erasers, stickers, and so on; however positive reinforcement also can be in the form of a *token*. A token is an object such as a poker chip that can later be exchanged for a tangible reward. Positive reinforcement may also involve intangible objects such as verbal praise, free time, or other social reinforcers. The goal of positive-reinforcement programs should be to gradually move from the use of tangible reinforcers to social reinforcers, and ultimately to intrinsic rewards, for a behavior or task well done. A multitude of positive-reinforcement programs are available for a classroom setting; ideally, all students would benefit from such a program (see *Classroom-Wide Reinforcement Programs* later in this chapter). Use of positive reinforcement should be the primary means of encouraging appropriate behavior in students with and without ADHD. Wigal and colleagues (1998) found that children with ADHD required more frequent reinforcement than classmates without the disorder and that inconsistent reinforcement was associated with higher frustration levels in children with ADHD. Slusarek et al. (2001) also found that the performance of children with ADHD was significantly better when they were provided with consistent feedback and high incentives. Some research, however, suggests that children with ADHD may become distracted by the reinforcement and consequently become off task. In this situation, work by Abramowitz, O'Leary, and Rosen (1987) suggests that use of a *mild* form of punishment (e.g., reprimand or loss of tokens) may help to redirect the child to the academic assignment. Carlson and Tamm (2000) also found that response cost improved task performance of children with ADHD, and Kelley and McCain (1995) found that the effectiveness of home–school notes was improved when response cost was a component of the home–school note system. Oosterlaan and Sergeant (1998) however, reported that response cost did not improve the ability of children with ADHD to inhibit impulsive responding. With regard to classroom reprimands, Acker and O'Leary (1987) found that reprimands were associated with higher levels of on-task behavior and withdrawal of all reprimands caused significant increases in off-task behavior and decreases in academic productivity. It is important to remember, however, that reprimands are more effective if delivered while in close proximity to the student, while maintaining eye contact, and immediately after the behavior has occurred. The length of the reprimand is also significant, as short reprimands can improve on-task behavior, whereas lengthy reprimands have been found to *increase* off-task behavior in students with ADHD (Abramowitz, O'Leary, & Futtersak, 1988).

Extra Supervision.   Providing extra supervision, particularly during unstructured activities, may help students to remain on task and complete assignments (Waddell, 1991). As mentioned previously, students with ADHD tend to remain on task and have a higher level of productivity when they receive consistent and immediate feedback. Such feedback is provided when students are working one on one with the teacher or teacher's aid. Strayhorn and Bickel (2002) recently studied teacher ratings of students with ADHD before and after individual tutoring and found substantial decreases in ADHD as well as oppositional behaviors of children who participated in the tutoring.

Organizational Skills.   To assist with organizational strategies, a common recommendation is that teachers use checklists outlining assignments and that students with ADHD use assignment organizers and dividing notebooks. Other recommendations include establishing cooperative homework teams, encouraging students with ADHD to keep a *to do list* (see Table 4.4 for an example), encouraging the use of a daily planner, and encouraging collaboration between home and school (Stormont-Spurgin, 1997).

For example, teachers could sign and date the student's homework list and parents could initial the list after the assignments are completed. Zentall (1993) recommends that, before beginning a project, students create an outline of the steps required to complete the project. All of these organizational suggestions are based on the premise that students who are organized are more likely to succeed on academic assignments.

Noise Level.   Background classroom conversations and high-noise environments have been found to impair the academic performance of students with ADHD and lead to increased off-task behavior. Furthermore, when asked if they preferred background noise when working on assignments, students with ADHD reported that they did *not* prefer background noise (Zentall & Shaw, 1980). Abikoff, Courtney, Szeibel, and Koplewicz (1996), however, found that children with ADHD performed significantly better on a math assignment when music was playing in the background compared to voices or silence. The type and level of noise may be important for teachers to consider, however, as Lucker, Geffner, and Koch (1996) found that children with ADHD had a lower tolerance for noise level than those without the disorder. Thus, based on these few studies, research suggests that teachers should attempt to minimize noise level for students with ADHD when they are completing academic assign-

TABLE 4.4 To Do List

Name: _____

I. Homework

Subject	Assignment	Initials (T/P/S)*
1.		
2.		
3.		
4.		
5.		
6.		
7.		
8. Other:		

II. Things to Remember to Do:

1. _____
2. _____
3. _____
4. _____
5. _____

*T/P/S = Teacher, parent, student

Note: From Weyandt (2001).

ments. More research is needed to explore whether certain types of background noise (i.e., music) might enhance attention and academic productivity.

Test-Taking Accommodations.   For students with ADHD who qualify for special educational services, test-taking accommodations may be beneficial. Based on the particular needs of the student, teachers may allow for

- Extra time to complete exams
- Open-book exams
- Take-home exams
- Dictionary
- Verbal responses on exams rather than written (or vice versa)
- Computer use for written exams
- Exams on tape
- Frequent breaks during exams

- Books on tape
- Headphones for individual seat-work
- Note takers for class lectures

Although these accommodations may make common sense, very little research information is available concerning their effectiveness.

Peer Tutoring.   Peer tutoring involves the pairing of students to work together on an academic task, with one of the students providing assistance and immediate feedback to the other. Research investigating the effectiveness of peer tutoring on enhancing attention, accuracy, and work productivity of students with ADHD has been favorable (e.g., DuPaul, Ervin, Hook, & McGoey, 1998; DuPaul & Henningson, 1993; Robinson, Newby, & Ganzell, 1981). Peer-tutoring arrangements may include

1. A student with ADHD with a student who is not disabled
2. Two students with ADHD
3. A student with ADHD with another student who is disabled (e.g., LD)

DuPaul, Bankert, and Ervin (1994), for example, studied the effects of a classwide peer-tutoring program in 14 classrooms in two school districts. Fifteen students with ADHD (ages 6 to 11 years) were included in the study, and none of the students were taking medication for the disorder. Results indicated that on-task behavior of students with ADHD increased, as well as their academic performance. DuPaul, Ervin, Hook, and McGoey (1998) found that peer tutoring resulted in improvements in math and spelling performance for 50% of the students with ADHD. For more information about peer tutoring, see DuPaul and Eckert (1998). More recently Flood, Wilder, Flood, and Masuda (2002) found that attention from peers maintained off-task behavior in students with ADHD and peer-mediated reinforcement improved on-task behavior. Peer tutoring is recommended with students with ADHD, as it

- Is an efficient use of teacher time and resources
- Is highly acceptable among teachers and students
- Does not single out or stigmatize students with ADHD
- Is effective at increasing academic growth of students with and without ADHD

Specific Academic Subjects.   Numerous studies have found that individuals with ADHD are at greater risk for academic underachievement in many subject areas, especially reading and math. As discussed in chapter 1, research indicates that many students with ADHD have co-existing reading problems (Bonafina, Newcorn, McKay, Koda, & Halperin, 2000; Willcutt, Pennington, & DeFries, 2000). Jitendra et al. (2004) recently studied the effects of a tutoring intervention program for children with ADHD and other disabilities and found substantial growths in reading, spelling, and reading comprehension skills. With regard to math, Marshall, Hynd, Handwerk, and Hall (1997) found that children with ADHD performed significantly more poorly in math compared to students without ADHD. Marshall et al. suggested that attention problems interfere with students' ability to master abstract symbol systems, especially in the acquisition of basic arithmetic skills in the primary grades. Therefore, specific intervention approaches that focus on the acquisition of these skills might be particularly beneficial for students with ADHD. However, techniques to enhance academic skills in specific subject areas vary depending on the needs of the individual. For example, see Tilson and Bender (1997) for suggestions for improving math, spelling, and reading skills of secondary students with ADHD.

Behavioral Issues

Classroom Management.   Teachers report that a major concern facing them in the classroom is misbehavior of all students, not only students with ADHD. Research by Martin, Linfoot, and Stephenson (1999) indicates that the greater the teacher's concern about misbehavior, the less confident they are in dealing with the behavior and the more likely they are to refer the child to other school personnel or to use nonphysical punishment. Many behavioral problems can be avoided in children with and without ADHD by the use of basic classroom management techniques. Classroom management techniques are a compilation of methods designed to manage the classroom environment and thereby enhance the learning of *all* students. Although the methods used in classrooms vary across teachers and grade levels, several commonalities have been identified by Smith, Polloway, Patton, and Dowdy (1995):

- Posted classroom rules that are stated simply and positively
- Consistent application of classroom rules by the teacher
- Established consequences for rules that are broken
- Offering class incentives for rule-abiding behavior
- Informing parents of classroom rules and consequences
- Following a regular classroom schedule

Classroom Climate.   It is in the best interest of all students, including students with ADHD, to create a positive, warm, and inviting classroom climate. According to work by Pfiffner and Barkley (1990), a positive relationship between a teacher and a student with ADHD may improve not only students' immediate academic and social functioning but their long-term functioning as well. Students with ADHD, however, receive more intense negative attention from teachers and peers (e.g., reprimands, negative feedback) (Frederick & Olmi, 1994). Given that students with ADHD tend to have more behavioral and academic problems than other students, a negative cycle could easily begin (see Figure 4.1).

Behavior Management Strategies.   To avoid falling into the trap of a negative cycle, teachers can provide students with positive teacher attention when the student is engaging in appropriate behavior. Tilson and Bender (1997) suggest that teachers can begin the class period on a positive note by "meeting the student with ADHD at the door to the classroom with a smile and a welcoming comment" (p. 195). Other methods include

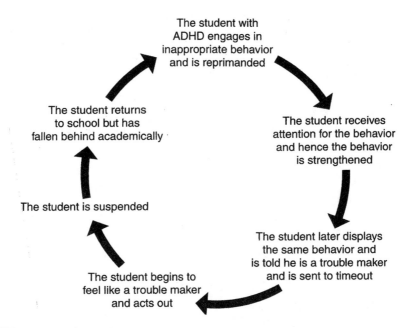

FIGURE 4.1. Negative cycle associated with inappropriate behavior.

- Identifying the student's strengths and drawing attention to these strengths (e.g., pair him or her with a student who may be struggling)
- Establishing behavior support programs that focus on positive behaviors and positive reinforcement
- Allowing the student to help out in the classroom by running errands, distributing handouts, and so on

Seating.   One factor that can easily be manipulated in helping to manage student behavior is placement of seats in the classroom. The highest rates of off-task behavior in children without ADHD have been found with traditional row seating, followed by cluster seating. Large circle seating has been associated with the least amount of social interaction (Rosenfeld, Lambert, & Black, 1985). Mulligan (2001) surveyed general education teachers in northern New England, and found that preferential seating was viewed as one of the most frequently used and effective strategies for managing behavior of children with ADHD. Research has also found that children with ADHD are also more likely to be off task during the afternoon (Dane, Schachar, & Tannock, 2000), thus it is particularly important that seating arrangements be considered during the afternoon hours. Because students with ADHD are frequently off task, placing a student's desk near the teacher so that he or she can be closely monitored is frequently recommended. Theoretically, the closer a student with ADHD is seated to the teacher, the less likely he or she will be distracted by other students and off task. It is also frequently recommended that students with ADHD be seated away from windows, doors, and high-traffic areas to reduce distractions. Schilling, Washington, Billingsley, and Deitz (2003) recently studied the effects of therapy balls versus chairs on in-seat behavior and writing productivity in children with ADHD and found that the therapy balls improved both in-seat behavior and writing productivity. Lastly, it is probably wise to seat students with ADHD next to good role models, that is, students who usually are on task and engage in appropriate classroom behavior.

Functional Behavior Analysis.   Research suggests that off task or disruptive behavior is the most frequent complaint of teachers with students with ADHD. As mentioned in chapter 3, studies have found that the primary reasons students are off task are

1. To escape or avoid tasks
2. For peer attention
3. For teacher attention
4. To have access to tangible objects
5. For self-stimulation

Functional behavior analysis (FBA) is invaluable in gaining an understanding of a student's specific behavior problems and factors that may be maintaining these behaviors. Before any intervention is designed and applied, it is critical that teachers define the student's problem in measurable terms, identify the frequency and duration of the problem, identify antecedents and consequences, and, lastly, define the desired behavior. The Functional Behavior Analysis Worksheet found in Appendix I may be useful in this process; following the suggestions that appear in Figure 4.2 may also be helpful. After functional behavior analysis has been completed, an intervention can be developed as well as a plan for evaluating the effectiveness of the intervention. For example, functional behavior analysis may reveal that a student's problem behavior is being off task after the teacher has instructed the students to complete a math assignment. In this scenario, the student may dislike math and, to avoid doing the assignment, he or she looks around the room and plays with objects on the desk. Functional behavior analysis would reveal that the student is playing with objects and looking around the room to escape or avoid the math task. A possible intervention is that the student could play with objects on the desk or run an errand for the teacher *after* he or she completed a specified amount of work on the math assignment. Thus, in this situation, off-task behavior is decreased and replaced with a desired behavior, completion of the math assignment. Alternatively, functional behavior analysis may reveal that the student is off task (looking around the room and playing with objects on the desk) because he or she is gaining attention from other classmates. The intervention may consist of reinforcing the classmates for ignoring the off-task behavior. The critical element is that, for each student, the teacher determines the function of the undesirable behavior before trying an intervention program. Recently, Hoff, Ervin, and Friman (2005) described in detail the use of FBA in designing an intervention program to decrease disruptive behavior in boys with ADHD. This approach could easily be adopted for students with ADHD enrolled in regular educational programs. For additional information and examples of the use of functional behavior analysis with students with ADHD, see Broussard and Northup (1995, 1997) or DuPaul and Ervin (1996).

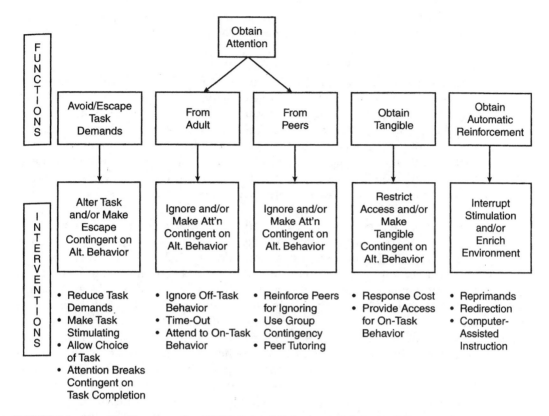

FIGURE 4.2. Possible Functions for ADHD-Related Behavior and Associated Interventions.

Source: From "Functional Assessment of Behaviors Related to Attention-Deficit/Hyperactivity Disorder: Linking Assessment to Intervention Design," by G. J. DuPaul and R. A. Ervin, 1996, *Behavior Therapy*, 27, p. 614. Copyright 1996 by the Association for Advancement of Behavior Therapy. Reprinted by permission of the publisher.

Proactive Strategies.   As DuPaul and Weyandt (2006b) recently described, teachers can use proactive strategies to decrease the likelihood of problem behavior occurring with children with ADHD. Specifically, by using FBA, teachers can identify antecedents that might trigger problematic behavior and change the conditions so that a child with ADHD displays a more desirable behavior. For example, teachers can provide students with a menu of assignments that the student must complete within a certain time period and the student is permitted to choose the assignment he or she wishes to complete. Alternatively, if a student with ADHD is habitually off task and disruptive during seat work (e.g., silent reading) teachers may opt to have the student complete the reading assignment on the computer. Giving students with ADHD the opportunity to choose the academic task with which they would like to work may improve academic productivity (Dunlap et al., 1994). For example, if several English tasks are assigned (e.g., reading or a written language assignment), allowing the student to decide which task he or she would like to work on has been found to increase task involvement. Being able to choose academic assignments has been found to decrease undesirable behaviors in students with ADHD (Powell & Nelson, 1997). Proactive strategies differ from reactive strategies that are interventions that take place *after* the problematic behavior occurs (e.g., punishment) (Ervin, DuPaul, Kern, & Friman, 1998).

Token Economies and Reinforcement Principles.   A token economy is a type of contingency-based program that involves the delivery of a consequence following a specific behavior. There are three basic types of consequences: positive reinforcement, negative reinforcement, and punishment. Simply stated, behaviors that are followed by reinforcement will likely increase whereas behaviors that are not reinforced or punished will likely decrease. It is important to note that positive reinforcement involves the *delivery* of a consequence while negative reinforcement involves the *removal* of (or escape from) an aversive situation or stimulus. Both types of reinforcement serve to increase behavior. Punishment, however, involves the delivery of a consequence that *decreases* a behavior. For example, teacher attention and verbal praise are the most commonly used forms of positive reinforcement in the classroom and have been found to effectively change behavior in many students (White, 1975). Verbal reprimands are the most common form of punishment used in the classroom; others include time-out, being sent to the principal's office, and loss of privileges. Teachers and principals often inadvertently negatively reinforce students' behavior by removing them from the classroom or enforcing out-of-school suspension. Imagine, for example, that a student acts out because he or she does not want to be in a physical education class. The teacher sends the student to the hallway for 15 minutes. The student has thus escaped a situation he or she did not want to be in, which increases the likelihood that he or she will act out again in the future. Now imagine that the hallway is an exciting and fun place to be; passersby say hello, friends walk by, and other teachers stop to chat with the student. In this situation, the student's acting out behavior has also been positively reinforced. The reason in-school suspension programs are often more effective than out-of-school suspension programs is that students do not enjoy in-school suspension. Usually students must work the entire time and are not permitted to talk or engage in enjoyable activities. Out-of-school suspension, however, can be great fun, especially if students are permitted to watch television, listen to music, shop, and engage in other pleasurable activities. In other words, in-school suspension is usually truly punishing whereas out-of-school suspension can be rewarding.

Research suggests that teacher attention and praise do not significantly alter the behavior of children with ADHD (e.g., Abramowitz, O'Leary, & Rosen, 1987; North et al., 1995). Interventions that incorporate token economies, however, have been found to be highly successful in decreasing disruptive behavior and increasing on-task behavior in students with ADHD. Tokens are tangible objects such as poker chips, points, or checkmarks that are provided immediately after a specific desired behavior has occurred (DuPaul & Weyandt, 2006a, 2006b). These tokens can be cashed in later for an activity or other privilege of the student's choice. The delivery rate, number of tokens, and specific privileges vary depending on the behavior and the contract agreed upon by the teacher and student. DuPaul, Stoner, Tilly, and Putnam (1991) recommend that eight steps be followed when a token reinforcement system is developed (see Table 4.5).

TABLE 4.5   Steps Involved in Designing a School-Based Token Reinforcement System

1. Identify the classroom situations that are problematic for the student and are targeted for intervention. Rating scales and direct observations can help to determine these situations.
2. Select specific behaviors to be targeted and include the specific actions (e.g., appropriate interactions with peers during recess) or behavioral products (e.g., number of math problems to be completed in a specific period of time).
3. Select secondary reinforcers (e.g., checkmarks, poker chips, colored pieces of paper).
4. Develop a list of rewarding activities or privileges for which the tokens can be exchanged. Be sure to develop this list jointly with the student!
5. Break down the targeted behaviors into component parts. For example, "successful completion of assignment" can be defined as completing a certain number of items within a specified time period, attaining a certain level of accuracy, and reviewing the work before requesting the teacher's feedback. The number of tokens that will be awarded for completing each component and target behavior should be decided upon with the student, and should be based on task difficulty.
6. Tokens should be exchanged for activities or privileges at least on a daily basis. In general, the longer the delay between receiving tokens and exchanging them for activities or privileges, the less effective the program will be.
7. The efficacy of the intervention should be evaluated on a regular basis by using multiple assessment procedures. A daily chart can be kept of percentage of work completion, percentage of time on task, frequency of completion of target behaviors, and so on. It is important to decide how the program will be evaluated and to collect data on the student's target behaviors prior to implementing the intervention. In this way, a comparison can be made concerning the target behaviors with regard to how the student was performing before and after the intervention. This procedure will also help to determine whether the intervention should be modified and whether new target behaviors should be added or old behaviors deleted.
8. In order to increase the likelihood that the student's behavioral changes will generalize to other settings and situations, the procedures described in 1–7 should be applied to additional problematic situations. Lastly, the use of tokens, privileges, and activities must be faded in a gradual fashion. For example, instead of awarding tokens for each component of a target behavior, a token could be awarded for completion of several components. Eventually, the tokens may be phased out entirely and replaced with a less time consuming program such as contingency contracting (i.e., the activities or privileges are awarded after the target behavior has been completed, based on a mutually agreeable contract between the teacher and the student without the use of tokens).

Source: From "Interventions for Attention Problems," by G. J. DuPaul, G. Stoner, W. D. Tilly, and D. Putnam, in *Interventions for Achievement and Behavior Problems*, by G. Stoner, M. R. Shinn, and H. M. Walker (Eds.), 1991, Silver Spring, MD: National Association of School Psychologists. Adapted with permission.

Token Economies and Response Cost.   Token economies that are based exclusively on positive reinforcement are less effective at changing behavior in students with ADHD than programs that involve both positive reinforcement and mild punishment, that is, *response cost* (Pfiffner & O'Leary, 1987).

For example, Rapport and Gordon (1987) developed *The Attention Training System (ATS)*. The ATS is an electronic module with a point counter and red light, and it is placed on the student's desk. The teacher can control the number of points that the student earns and whether the light is on or off from anywhere in the room. The child is instructed that he or she will automatically receive points for every minute he or she is on task. The student is also told that the red light will appear and one point will be deducted from the student's total points when he or she is off task. The ATS has been found to be highly effective at decreasing off-task behavior and in one study was equally as effective as medication (Rapport, Murphy, & Bailey, 1982).

Teacher–Student Contracts.   A teacher and a student can collaboratively create a written and signed contractual agreement that specifies the behaviors that a student must display in order to receive certain privileges or activities (i.e., contingency contracts). Depending on the student's age, severity of symptoms, and length of delay between the goal behavior and the privilege, contingency contracting may be less effective at managing behavior than some of the other methods covered thus far. Several important points must be considered when developing contingency contracts

- The age of the student
- The complexity of the contract (simpler is better)
- Goal behaviors must be observable and attainable
- The length of time between the behavior and delivery of the privilege must be reasonable, preferably on a daily basis
- The privileges or activities must be desirable for the student

Time-Out.   Time-out is a form of punishment designed to decrease the occurrence of a particular behavior. For example, if a student is out of seat during a reading group, the student could be told that his/her talking is unacceptable and as a consequence he/she must be removed from the reading group for a specified period of time. Various time-out procedures exist and are, in general, effective with many students who act out. Time-out should only be used in conjunction with an ongoing positive reinforcement program and as a last resort. In order to increase the likelihood that time-out will be effective, several principles should be followed. Time-out should be implemented

- By trained staff
- When the child is being removed from a reinforcing environment
- Consistently but not excessively
- For a brief period of time (e.g., 1–5 minutes)
- After functional behavior analysis has been conducted on the behavior
- Only when it has been found to decrease, not increase, the behavior

Peer Interventions.   Peer interventions, such as opportunities to spend time with peers, have most often been used to increase appropriate behavior (e.g., acquisition of skills) in children and adolescents. Recently, however, teachers and researchers have begun to explore the use of peer interventions in decreasing disruptive classroom behavior. Research has demonstrated that students, including children with ADHD, are more likely to continue to be disruptive in the classroom when they receive attention from their peers. Given this information, Broussard and Northup (1997) investigated whether peer attention for appropriate behavior (e.g., sitting quietly, remaining on task) and loss of attention for disruptive behavior (e.g., talking, out of seat, playing with objects) would influence the behavior of students with and without ADHD (ages 7 to 9). In this study (Broussard & Northup, 1997), peer attention was provided by allowing the students to earn time with a peer and doing something fun together (e.g., playing a game, art project) after the student had earned a certain number of coupons (tokens). The teacher placed the coupons on the student's desk when the student was following classroom rules and was nondisruptive (i.e., on task). When the student was disruptive, he lost coupons (response cost). Results revealed substantial increases in on-task behavior and reduction of disruptive behavior for all students during the peer intervention. In other words, this study supports the potential effectiveness of peer attention in reducing disruptive classroom behavior in children with and without ADHD. This type of intervention is relatively simple to design and implement and could easily be adapted to middle and high school students.

Classroom-Wide Reinforcement Programs.   A criticism of token economy programs is that they provide students with ADHD special attention or rewards at the exclusion of the other students. To help address this concern, McNeil (1995) developed a classroom-wide reinforcement program called *The ADHD Classroom Kit: An Inclusive Approach to Behavior Management* (Kit). The kit was designed to improve the behavior of all students and incorporates techniques based on scientific studies. The program is based on consequences of behavior including positive reinforcement and mild punishment. For example, when students display appropriate behavior, they are rewarded with labeled praises, happy faces, or games; and if they display inappropriate behavior, they may receive a sad-face warning, sad faces, or loss of game-playing privileges. In addition to these consequences, the kit incorporates peer-mediated interventions such as cooperative-learning exercises and group-based rewards. Preliminary research with the kit suggests that it can be highly effective at developing, maintaining, and managing classroom-wide behavior, including the behavior of students with ADHD (e.g., Anhalt, McNeil, & Bahl, 1998). Rosenbaum, O'Leary, and Jacob (1975) explored whether the behavior of students with ADHD would improve if the entire class benefited from changes in their behavior. Specifically, the entire class was informed that a particular student was having difficulty concentrating and completing his work. The student as well as the class was told that every hour the student's behavior would be checked and, if he were on task, both he and the class would receive a reward. The results indicated that this method was superior to an individualized reinforcement program. Thus, in some cases, class-wide reinforcement programs may significantly improve the behavior of students with ADHD.

Self-Monitoring/Self-Management.   Self-monitoring or self-management is an intervention strategy that requires a student to monitor and record occurrences of his or her own behavior. The purpose of this technique is to help students to become more aware of their own behavior and to eventually become more responsible for managing their own behavior. Although the findings have been mixed, some studies have found that self-management strategies can be effective at decreasing disruptive behavior and increasing on-task behavior in students with ADHD (e.g., Abikoff et al., 1988; Kotkin, 1998; Shapiro, DuPaul, & Bradley-Klug, 1998). Moreover, Mulligan (2001) found that teachers preferred this strategy over peer tutoring or time-out when working with students with ADHD. Typically, the student and teacher agree on a goal behavior for the student (e.g., percentage of time on task) and the conditions of the self-monitoring program (i.e., how frequently the student will monitor his/her behavior). During activities or assignments, the student is prompted by the teacher to check his/her behavior by an auditory (e.g., tone, beep, word), visual (hand signal, colored paper), or physical cue (e.g., shoulder squeeze). The student then records on a form located on or in his/her desk, whether he/she was engaging in a specified behavior (e.g., on task) (see Table 4.6 for an example). It is important that teachers understand that students with ADHD have tremendous difficulty paying attention and often *do not know how* to pay attention. Self-monitoring techniques can help the student with ADHD (as well as all students) learn how to attend, become more self-aware, and remain focused for longer periods of time.

TABLE 4.6   Self-Monitoring Chart

Name: _____   **Assignment:** _____

When my teacher signaled me, I was working on my assignment.

Place a checkmark under Yes or No:

Signaled	Yes	No
1. _____		
2. _____		
3. _____		
4. _____		
5. _____		
6. _____		
7. _____		
8. _____		
9. _____		
10. _____		

Note: From Weyandt (2001).

Self-monitoring strategies tend to be more effective if they are used in conjunction with positive self-reinforcement (i.e., a desired privilege or activity) and mediation (DuPaul & Stoner, 2003). Depending on the type of program employed, students may evaluate and reinforce their own performance with tokens that can later be exchanged for a desired privilege or activity. For example, a student and a teacher determine that a reasonable goal is for the student to be on task 85% of the time during a math assignment. At random periods during the assignment, the teacher signals to the student to monitor his or her behavior. The student would then record a check mark on a form located on his or her desk for being on task. At the end of the math assignment, the percentage of time on task would be calculated; if the student reached the goal, he or she would then reward himself/herself with a predetermined privilege or desired activity. Research has found that self-monitoring in conjunction with self-reinforcement can increase on-task behavior and academic accuracy in students with and without ADHD (Hinshaw, Henker, & Whalen, 1984). It is also useful to require students to plot their performance on a graph so that their current performance can be directly compared to past performance. Fuchs and Fuchs (1987) found that when students plotted and displayed their data, their achievement improved significantly relative to students who did not graph their data. Keeping a visual record such as a graph enables students to assess and evaluate their own behavior and establish goals for future behavior. For more information about self-monitoring, see Lloyd, Landrum, and Hallahan (1991) and research with students with ADHD see DuPaul and Stoner (2003) and Barkley (2004).

Problem-Solving Techniques.   Various cognitive–behavioral programs have been developed to help improve the impulsivity, self-control, and problem-solving deficits characteristic of many individuals with ADHD. Most of these programs involve teaching students to think about their behavior before acting and include basic problem-solving techniques (e.g., how to systematically and successfully complete a task). Although the number of steps may vary, most problem-solving programs include (a) identification and definition of the problem, (b) generation of alternative solutions, (c) choosing a solution, (d) trying the solution and evaluating its effectiveness, and (e) choosing another alternative if necessary. Kendall (1992), for example, has developed a 20-session *Stop and Think* program for students with ADHD; the program involves a therapist teaching students to use a specific problem-solving process to help improve their academic skills and interpersonal relationships (for a critique of this program, see Perla, 1996). Similar to the self-monitoring literature, research findings concerning problem-solving programs for children with ADHD have been inconsistent, with some studies reporting success with these programs while other studies have not found problem-solving programs effective in the treatment of ADHD (e.g., Barkley, Edwards, Laneri, Fletcher, & Metevia, 2001; Frame, 2004; Houck, King, Tomlinson, Vrabel, & Wecks, 2002). Studies by Kendall and Braswell (1982) and Urbain and Kendall (1980), as well as others, have found support for these programs; however, the majority of studies have not found them to be effective at improving academic performance of students with ADHD (Abikoff, 1991). Other studies (e.g., Hinshaw, Henker, & Whalen, 1984) indicate that a combination of medication and cognitive behavioral train-

TABLE 4.7   Suggestions for Decreasing Behavioral Problems in Students With ADHD

- Establish and post classroom rules and expectations
- Adhere to a classroom routine
- Create a safe, warm, and positive classroom environment
- Arrange seating to minimize distractions
- Create assignments that allow for physical movement
- Capitalize on the student's strengths
- Provide extra supervision during unstructured tasks
- Use token economy programs
- Involve peers in behavior management programs
- Establish a class-wide peer tutoring program
- Use self-monitoring programs in combination with positive reinforcement
- Create teacher-student contracts

Note: From Weyandt (2001).

ing is optimally effective at improving the social behavior of students with ADHD. In addition, a few studies suggest that problem-solving techniques may be more effective with adolescents than younger children with ADHD, particularly when dealing with the secondary emotional problems such as low self-esteem or anger-management difficulties that may accompany ADHD (Fehlings, Roberts, Humphries, & Dawe, 1990). Beginning in 1992 the National Institute of Mental Health (NIMH) conducted a multisite study on the effectiveness of various interventions in treating ADHD in childhood. Results indicated that the benefits of medication management in combination with behavioral management were superior to behavior management used in isolation (Jensen, Hinshaw, Swanson, Greenhill, et al., 2001). Follow up studies after 24 months revealed the benefits of medication management were superior to a combined approach or a behavioral approach used in isolation (MTA Cooperative Group, 2004). A summary of interventions to decrease behavior problems appears in Table 4.7.

Social–Emotional Issues

As discussed in chapter 1, socially, many children with ADHD display problems with aggressiveness, defiance, stubbornness, and verbal hostility toward others. Emotionally, it is not uncommon for children with ADHD to have mood swings, temper tantrums, low frustration tolerance, and anger management difficulties. In addition, teachers tend to rate students with ADHD as more severely maladjusted than students without the disorder. As adolescents, individuals with ADHD are often emotionally immature, less popular, and more socially isolated. Studies also indicate that adolescents with ADHD are more likely to engage in risk-taking behavior and are at greater risk for using and abusing substances. During adulthood, individuals with ADHD continue to have interpersonal relationship difficulties and social skill deficits and are at greater risk for antisocial behavior and work-related problems Although these social and emotional problems are not components of ADHD, they frequently emerge after years of struggling with academic, social, and behavioral difficulties.

It is important to understand that treatment of the social–emotional problems that might accompany ADHD addresses the secondary problems and not the disorder per se. In other words, an individual with ADHD and low self-esteem problems may benefit from cognitive-restructuring therapy; however, his or her attention and impulsivity problems are likely to remain. The following summary provides an overview of interventions that may be used to help address the social and emotional problems of some individuals with ADHD.

Social Skills Training. Although some individuals with ADHD may be popular and have good interpersonal skills, many have significant social skill performance deficits that can contribute to peer rejection and feelings of rejection and isolation. The majority of children with ADHD have problems in interacting with their peers; and peers describe children with ADHD as aggressive, disruptive, intrusive, domineering, and noisy. Interestingly, earlier research reported that children with ADHD were less knowledgeable about appropriate behavior and social skills; however, recent research suggests that they are able to describe appropriate social responses but they do not demonstrate this knowledge when involved in a social situation (i.e., their deficits are in performance rather than knowledge). Thus, various social skill training programs have been developed to try to help individuals with ADHD acquire and apply appropriate social skills, and several can be purchased commercially (e.g., see Begun, 1995).

Commercial and Research-Based Programs. Many of these programs teach children at the preschool and elementary level the importance of sharing, taking turns, waiting patiently, listening, and attending to the needs of others. At the middle and high school level, programs often emphasize cooperation, effective communication skills, how to develop and maintain friendships, and conflict resolution. Techniques vary among programs, but traditional instruction, modeling, practice, coaching, and feedback are often used at all grade levels. Other programs are more research based, such as Guevremont's (1990) comprehensive program that includes four skill areas: (a) social entry, (b) conversational skills, (c) conflict resolution, and (d) anger control. Training occurs in small groups on a weekly basis, and each session involves teaching, learning, and practicing of specific skills. Homework is also assigned to encourage individuals to practice the skills at home, school, and when spending time with peers. A major goal of this program is for individuals with ADHD to acquire skills that they use after they complete the program (i.e., generalization). Tutty, Gephart, and Wurzbacher (2003) recently evaluated the effectiveness of an 8-week social skills and behavioral program for children ages 5 to 12 with ADHD and reported that the program was effective at improving social skill functioning and was highly acceptable to teachers. Preliminary social skill improvement studies with preschool and elementary age children with ADHD have also produced promising results (Chang et al., 2004; Gol & Jarus, 2005; Webster-Stratton, Reid, & Hammond, 2001). Recently, Antshel and Remer (2003) evaluated the efficacy of an 8-week social skills training program in 30 girls and 90 boys with ADHD and found improvements in children's cooperation, assertion, and empathy skills. Sheridan, Dee, Morgan, McCormick, and Walker (1996) from the University of Utah developed a multimethod intervention program for social skill deficits in children with ADHD. The program included (a) the use of stimulant medication; (b) teaching and practice of weekly skills (social entry, maintaining interaction, and solving problems); and (c) parent training. Preliminary studies support the effectiveness of this multimethod program.

Given the importance of interpersonal relationships throughout childhood, adolescence, and adulthood, the importance of social skill training for individuals with ADHD seems obvious. More research is needed, however, to determine which programs are most effective at different age levels and which are most effective at maintaining appropriate social skills in a variety of settings.

Anger Management Training. Teachers and peers describe many individuals with ADHD as aggressive, and research indicates that children and adolescents with ADHD report having more anger than their peers (Kitchens, Rosen, & Braaten, 1999). Recently, Brooks and Boaz (2005) interviewed 66 parents of adolescents with ADHD and 44% described their children as aggressive and 70% as defiant. Auerbach, Atzaba-Poria, Berger, and Landau (2004) suggested that infants as young as 7 months of age who are at risk for ADHD show greater levels of anger compared to those who are at low risk for ADHD. Children and adolescents who are aggressive tend to be disliked and rejected by others, which places these individuals at risk for negative outcomes later in life (Parker & Asher, 1987). Waschbusch et al. (2002) reported that boys with ADHD and co-existing oppositional defiant disorder or conduct disorder were especially reactive to provocation from their peers, had higher heart rate acceleration, anger, and behavioral aggression than boys without ADHD. Even research with college students with high ADHD symptoms has reported that these young adults experience more anger while driving, and are more aggressive and risk prone while driving. According to Guevremont (1990), learning to control one's anger is necessary to break the pattern of aggressive, disruptive, and annoying behavior frequently demonstrated by individuals with ADHD. One method of teaching individuals with ADHD to learn more effective ways of coping with and expressing anger is to include it as part of a large social skills training program. Guevremont, for example, included anger control sessions as the fourth component of his comprehensive social skills training program. Similarly, Kendall's (1992) *Stop and Think* program addresses conflict and anger management skills within the framework of problem solving. Barkley, Guevremont, Anastopoulos, and Fletcher (1992) compared three family therapy programs for treating family conflicts in adolescents with ADHD and found all three approaches reduced family conflicts and anger during these conflicts. Other programs are more specific and teach individuals to

- Identify common external events that trigger anger
- Identify internal cues associated with anger
- Consider alternatives to use when angry
- Use self-statements to control anger

Self-Esteem.   Given the information concerning the likelihood of academic failure and poor peer interactions, students with ADHD are at risk for having low self-esteem (Kelley et al., 1989). As Barber, Grubbs, and Cottrell (2005) recently noted, the cumulative effect of years of low self-esteem may have major life consequences and efforts should be made to foster self-esteem in students with ADHD. Pisecco, Wristers, Swank, et al. (2001) found that children's early history of behavioral problems and low academic self-concept were associated with the development of more serious social problems in adolescence. Teachers can help to improve the self-esteem of these students by providing positive experiences in the classroom. For example, teachers can

- Assign tasks that can be successfully completed
- Focus on and draw attention to the strengths of the student
- Help the student to set and attain goals and objectives
- Place the student in small groups with supportive peers
- Reinforce appropriate use of social skills in all students

In addition, teachers should capitalize on the strengths of students with ADHD. For example, if a student with ADHD is particularly clever in math or art, he or she might be paired with a student who is less skilled in those areas. An older student with ADHD could also be encouraged to work with younger children in a helping or nurturing manner. In other words, teachers should help build success experiences for all students with ADHD, particularly those with low self-esteem.

Education About ADHD.   One method to empower individuals with ADHD is to help them become educated about the disorder. Numerous books are available about ADHD for all age levels, including information developed for children (story books), adolescents, adults, and parents or spouses of individuals with the disorder. In addition to books, videos, and Web sites, local and national ADHD organizations are available that provide invaluable information about the nature and treatment of ADHD. Support groups for parents or for individuals with ADHD are also available in many schools and local communities (see the books and other ADHD resources listed in Appendix G).

In-School Counseling, Support Groups and Group Counseling.   According to a review article by Pelham, Wheeler, and Chronis (1998), research studies have *not* supported the effectiveness of individual and play therapy for children with ADHD. In other words, just talking about attention and impulsivity problems does not appear to reduce these symptoms in individuals with ADHD. This is not surprising, however, given that the attention, impulsivity, and hyperactivity symptoms of ADHD are believed to have a physiological basis. However, depending on the nature of the counseling as well as the student's problems, counseling may be helpful in addressing some of the emotional issues that may accompany ADHD. For example, if a student with ADHD is performing poorly academically as a result of severe test anxiety, he or she may benefit from relaxation and desensitization training administered one on one by the school counselor or school psychologist. Similarly, if an adolescent with ADHD is suffering from depression and it is adversely affecting his or her school performance, the student may benefit from cognitive restructuring training with the school counselor. Robinson, Sclar, Skaer, and Galin (2004) studied the types of treatments children with ADHD (ages 5–18) received during 1995–1999 in the United States and reported that the most common type of treatment was medication used alone (42%) followed by medication used with counseling/therapy (32%). Only 10% of the children received counseling services alone. In-school and community-based support groups for students with ADHD can also be helpful in providing students with a safe place to air their concerns, questions, or ideas about the disorder. Group counseling can also be useful for teaching students with ADHD conflict management skills, time management strategies, or study skills. Numerous games and activities are commercially available for use in individual and group settings (see Appendix G for more information).

Home-Based Interventions

Education About ADHD

For parents who have lived with a child or adolescent with ADHD since infancy, finally receiving a diagnosis of ADHD can be a relief. On the other hand, learning that one's child has a disability can be frightening and overwhelming. To help parents better cope with their son or daughter's disability, a wealth of information about ADHD is available in the form of books, videos, Web sites, and local and national ADHD organizations. Support groups for parents are also available in many communities (see the books and other ADHD resources listed in Appendix G).

Home–School Collaboration

Consistent communication between home and school is frequently recommended as a method to increase the likelihood of a successful educational experience for students with ADHD (Foy & Earls, 2005). Home–school contingency programs, which require parents to provide positive reinforcement in the home based on school reports, have been found to improve the behavior and academic performance of students with ADHD. Barkley (1994), for example, recommends the use of a daily school-behavior report card to help address behavior management problems at school (Table 4.8). To use the card, Barkley recommends:

1. The teacher presents the student with a clean card each morning.
2. The teacher lists on the left-hand side the student's target behaviors or academic performance skills that will be the focus of the program.
3. At the end of the class period, the teacher gives the student a rating that reflects how well the student did for each behavior during the class period.

TABLE 4.8   Daily School Behavior Report Card

Child's Name_____   **Date**_____

Teachers: Please rate this child's behavior today in the areas listed below. Use a separate column for each subject or class period. Use the following ratings: 1 = excellent, 2 = good, 3 = fair, 4 = poor, 5 = very poor. Then initial the box at the bottom of your column. Add any comments about the child's behavior today on the back of this card.

	Class Periods/Subjects						
Behaviors to be Rated							
Class Participation							
Performance of Class Work							
Follows Classroom Rules							
Gets Along Well With Other Children							
Quality of Homework, If Any Given							
Teacher's Initials							

Place comments on back of card.

---Cut Along Here After Photocopying---------------------------------

Daily School Behavior Report Card

Child's Name_____   **Date**_____

Teachers: Please rate this child's behavior today in the areas listed below. Use a separate column for each subject or class period. Use the following ratings: 1 = excellent, 2 = good, 3 = fair, 4 = poor, 5 = very poor. Then initial the box at the bottom of your column. Add any comments about the child's behavior today on the back of this card.

	Class Periods/Subjects						
Behaviors to be Rated							
Teacher's Initials							

Place comments on back of card.

Source: From "Using a Daily School Behavior Report Card," by R. A. Barkley, 1996, *The ADHD Report, 4,* p. 15. Adapted with permission.

4. The cards are sent home on a daily basis initially but can be reduced to several times a week and eventually faded out completely.
5. Consequences are to be delivered at home (e.g., praise and attention, tangible rewards).

To increase the likelihood that daily report card programs are successful, only a limited number of target behaviors should be included (not more than five), behaviors that the student is already doing well should be included in the program, and the program should be individually tailored for each student. Additionally, if the student has more than one teacher, all teachers should complete and initial the card, or each teacher should develop their own card. To help students complete homework assignments, reminder notices can be written on the back of each card.

Structured Homework Time

To help address the organizational needs of students with ADHD, a structured time period should be set aside after school for children and adolescents to complete their homework. This time period should remain the same to help the child establish an after-school routine. Reinforcement programs can be used to help children and adolescents stay motivated and complete their assignments in a timely manner. It is crucial, however, that the privileges (television watching, Internet use, computer-video games, reading novels or magazines, talking on the telephone) be given *after* the child or adolescent has completed his/her homework. Too often, parents fall into the trap of telling their children they can "talk on the phone for 10 minutes but then they have to do their homework." In this example, the incentive or pleasurable activity has already occurred; thus, the motivation for completing the homework has been lost. It is also important that parents limit the amount of time that their child is expected to work on homework so that he or she is not doing schoolwork the entire evening.

Tutoring

For students with ADHD and low academic performance, tutoring may be helpful for improving their skills. It is important that the amount of time and the quality of the tutoring are reasonable and enjoyable so the child or adolescent does not associate schoolwork with a negative experience. Tutoring can be costly, however, so this option may not be available to many parents.

Parenting Skills Training

Research with families with children who have ADHD indicates that these parents report high levels of stress and are more commanding and negative in their parenting style than parents of children without ADHD (Barkley, Anastopoulos, Guevremont, & Fletcher, 1992; Campbell, 1990; Cunningham & Boyle, 2002). Additional studies have found that children with ADHD are more likely to be victims of family violence, physical abuse, and require more frequent emergency room attention than children without ADHD (Becker & McCloskey,

2002; Harrison & Sofronoff, 2002; Heffron, Martin, Welsh, & Perry, 1987). Parents of children with ADHD tend to report more marital problems, higher rates of psychiatric illness, and lower self-esteem than parents of children without ADHD (Cunningham & Boyle, 2002; Mash & Johnston, 1983). Sayal, Taylor, and Beecham (2003) found that parents who perceived their children's ADHD as a serious problem were more likely to use mental health services, and experience diminished work ability. DuPaul, McGoey, Eckert, and Van Brakle (2001) found that parents of children with ADHD aged 3 to 5 experienced greater stress, and were more likely to display negative behavior toward their children than parents of children without ADHD. Just as teachers must learn techniques to manage classroom behavior, parents can often benefit from learning how to manage their child's behavior in the home environment. Parents can also benefit from understanding the importance of good parenting skills that apply to all children including the use of rules and responsibilities, consequences, consistency, love and affection, praise, and interest and involvement in the child's life.

Parenting Skills Training Programs. Numerous parent training programs are available for parents of ADHD children and adolescents, and many programs offer effective strategies for behavior management, problem solving, improving communication skills, modeling appropriate behavior, enhancing the self-esteem of the ADHD child, and conflict resolution. For example, Anastopoulos, Smith, and Wien (1998) describe in detail a 10-step, 10- to 12-session parent training program developed by Russell Barkley (1997b). The goals of this program are to train and provide supervision of parents in the use of behavior management techniques, to facilitate parental adjustment of having a child with ADHD, to increase parental compliance with the program, and to provide parents with coping skills that will lead to happier, less stressful lives for themselves and their children. Frankel, Myatt, Cantwell, and Feinberg (1997) from the UCLA School of Medicine developed an 11-session parent training program designed to improve the social skills of children with ADHD. Pisterman and colleagues (1992) studied 57 families with preschool-age children with ADHD across 12 parent training sessions. Parents were provided with training in reinforcement and punishment techniques, guided readings, homework, and instructions for managing problematic behavior. In general, research has supported the effectiveness of these programs, as well as others, at improving parenting skills as well as parent–child relationships. Interestingly, Sonuga-Barke and colleagues (2001, 2002) found that preschool children whose mothers reported high levels of ADHD symptoms showed significantly less improvement after participating in an 8-week parent training program.

Cunningham (1998) developed a large-group intervention program for families called *the community parent education program (COPE)*. The objective of the COPE program is to provide easily accessible family intervention services from a community-based model. The COPE program integrates principles from a variety of sources including family systems theory, social–cognitive psychology, large and small group theory, and social learning theories. The curriculum of the program is highly involved and includes methods to improve family relationships, self-regulation, problem solving, and so on. Preliminary studies support the long-term effectiveness of this program at enhancing family relationships, decreasing behavior management problems, and increasing problem-solving skills. Barkley (1997b) published a 10-session parent training program, *Defiant Children*, that is also available in Spanish. *Defiant Children* is a highly structured program that includes training materials for therapists, assessment materials, and numerous homework exercises and handouts for parents. Recently, Hechtman, Abikoff, Klein, Greenfield, et al. (2001; Hechtman, Abikoff, Klein, Weiss, et al., 2001) studied the effectiveness of a multimethod intervention for ADHD including parent training. Results indicated that parent training was associated with improvement in mothers' negative parenting and knowledge of parenting principles in general. More research is needed concerning the effectiveness of parent-training programs and family therapy interventions for ADHD, however, as these programs differ substantially with regard to length of intervention and content of the program (Bjornstad & Montgomery, 2005; Newby, Fischer, & Roman, 1991).

Token Economies and Parent–Child Contracts

The token economy and contingency contracts discussed in the school interventions section can also be applied in the home. For example, parents can follow the same guidelines that appear in Table 4.5 for establishing a token economy and simply include behaviors that are problematic in the home environment (e.g., not following through on chores). The parent and child could decide collaboratively when tokens should be administered and the privileges for which they could be exchanged. A home-based reinforcement list could also be created (Table 4.3). Similarly, a contingency contract can be established whereby privileges are earned after completion of target behaviors and tokens could be omitted.

Promoting Self-Esteem

As mentioned previously, individuals with ADHD are at risk for developing problems with self-esteem. Parents as well as other family members can play a critical role in enhancing the self-esteem of children and adolescents with ADHD. Drs. Gerard Banez and Stacy Overstreet (1998) have identified four types of negative thinking that are characteristic of individuals with low self-esteem, including

- Judging oneself overly harshly
- Overgeneralizing negative feedback
- Dwelling on failures in areas that are highly important
- Blaming oneself for mistakes and not accepting personal successes

According to Banez and Overstreet (1998), parents can play a vital role in helping children and adolescents with ADHD identify and understand their negative thought patterns and to replace these with helpful thinking. For example, parents can encourage their children to

1. Evaluate their own thoughts by asking provoking questions such as "How do you feel when you think that?" or "Why do you think that?" (p. 8).
2. Replace their negative thoughts with more positive ones (e.g., "I always mess up" to "Sometimes I do a really good job").
3. Realize they are responsible for their successes.
4. Encourage children to not feel ashamed when they make mistakes but rather ask what can be learned from the experience.

Banez and Overstreet (1998) also recommend that parents

- Model (i.e., think aloud) positive, constructive thoughts.
- Downplay a child's failures and instead reassure the child that trying is what is important.
- Encourage their children to use problem-solving strategies.
- Openly express their own feelings in appropriate ways and encourage their children to do so as well.
- Recognize and reinforce their child's positive behavior and pay less attention to the negative behavior.
- Collaborate with their children and schedule extra time for activities that foster good communication and listening skills.

In an article published by the National Association of School Psychologists (Weill, 1995) it is recommended that parents build self-confidence in their children with ADHD by encouraging them to participate in noncompetitive sports (e.g., gymnastics, swimming); teaching them friendship and game-playing skills; and building on their strengths. In general, helping children to find an area in which they can experience success and drawing attention to this strength are likely to enhance their self-esteem. This area need not be an academic skill but could involve physical skills (e.g., rollerblading, skateboarding, dance, athletics); helping skills (e.g., volunteering at a local community agency); or technical skills (e.g., art, carpentry, computers). The National Association of School Psychologists offers a variety of publications concerning ways in which parent can help to foster a healthy self-esteem in the children and adolescents (see Appendix G for Web site information).

Counseling Interventions

Depending on the unique needs of the individual, adolescents and adults with ADHD may benefit from a variety of counseling services, particularly those that are skill focused rather than talk-therapy focused. More research is needed, however, to explore the short- and long-term effectiveness of these interventions in treating individuals with ADHD. Given that many adolescents and adults with ADHD have difficulty with interpersonal skills, self-control, and organizational skills, the following interventions may be beneficial. For more information about interventions for adults with ADHD, see Goldstein and Teeter-Ellison's, *Clinicians Guide to Adult ADHD: Assessment and Intervention*, 2002.

- Career counseling
- Time management
- Anger/conflict management
- Study and academic skills training
- Problem-solving training
- Communication skills training
- Organizational skills training
- Substance abuse counseling
- Couples/marriage counseling
- Financial management counseling

Summary

Numerous environmentally based interventions are available for ADHD, ranging from instructional interventions and behavior management and support programs for the classroom to individual counseling and skills training to address co-existing emotional problems and skill deficits. Behavioral interventions for the classroom and parent-training programs have received the most empirical support for improving the behavioral symptoms associated with ADHD. In addition to the environmentally based approaches, medication and alternative treatments are available. These later approaches are discussed in chapter 5.

5 ADHD—How Is It Treated? Medication and Alternative Approaches

The purpose of this chapter is to provide an overview of medication and alternative approaches that are available for the treatment of ADHD. A wealth of information is available concerning the use of medication for ADHD, and the reader is strongly encouraged to seek additional information (see references provided throughout the chapter). Based on recent media attention and the number of books available on alternative interventions, there appears to be a widespread interest in alternative treatments for ADHD. Relative to what is known about medication treatment, however, significantly less empirical information is available concerning the appropriate use and effectiveness of alternative treatments for the disorder. Recently, the scientific community has begun to study the potential usefulness of a variety of nontraditional interventions such as biofeedback, diet, massage, and sensory integration training, with some findings more encouraging than others. Clearly, many questions remain unanswered, and well-designed, scientific studies are needed to determine whether these approaches may be beneficial for children, adolescents, and adults with ADHD.

Medication

A large body of research exists concerning the treatment of ADHD with medication, particularly stimulant medication. Depending on an individual's medical history, co-existing disorders, and specific ADHD symptoms, additional non-stimulant medications are also available such as atomoxetine (Strattera), antidepressants, and antihypertensive medications. This chapter emphasizes the use and effects of stimulant medication, given that stimulants are the most commonly prescribed and extensively studied medications for individuals with ADHD (DuPaul, Barkley, & Conner, 1998). Additional medications are also covered briefly; the reader is encouraged to refer to the references cited for additional information concerning these medications. As noted by Weyandt (2004) and others, medications are not a panacea for ADHD nor are they harmless. The most effective treatment for ADHD is an individually tailored, multimethod approach that often involves the use of medication in combination with behavioral interventions.

Stimulant Medication

The use of stimulant medication is one of the most widely studied and effective treatment methods available for ADHD. A plethora of studies attest to the short-term benefits of medication in improving the academic, social, and behavioral functioning of children, adolescents, and adults with ADHD. Despite the scientifically documented benefits and minimal side effects associated with stimulant medications, the use of stimulants with children and adolescents with ADHD remains controversial (NIH, 2000). As reviewed in chapter 1, proponents argue that stimulants are unnecessary, potentially harmful, and a way of medicating children into submission. Contributing to the controversy are numerous antimedication books, the media's coverage of rare but traumatic cases involving stimulant medication, and several nationally recognized groups that have protested the use of stimulants with children and adolescents at national and international conferences. In addition, stimulant prescriptions have increased substantially within the last decade with some researchers estimating a five-fold increase or higher (Greenhill, 2001). Habel, Schaefer, Levine, Bhat, and Elliott (2005) reported a 4% increase between 1996 and 2000 in California among children aged 2 to 18 years. Although these numbers initially seem alarming, studies also indicate that only 50% of children with ADHD receive appropriate care and treatment (Hoagwood et al., 2000; Hoagwood, Jensen, Feil, Vitiello, & Bhatara, 2000). The CDC recently reported that only 56% of children with ADHD were treated with medication. Stevens, Harman, and Kelleher (2005) recently reported disparities in treatment of ADHD and found that (a) children without insurance had lower levels of care, (b) White American children where more likely to be diagnosed with ADHD than African-American and Hispanic-American children, (c) African-Americans were less likely to take stimulant medication compared to white American children. Unfortunately, a great deal of inaccurate information has been reported concerning the use and effects of stimulant medication in children and adolescents with ADHD, which has added fuel to the ADHD controversy. For in-depth information concerning the use of stimulants, namely Ritalin, in children, adolescents, and adults, see *Ritalin: Theory and Practice*, second edition, edited by Drs. Greenhill and Osman (1999) or *Stimulant Drugs and ADHD: Basic and Clinical Neuroscience*, edited by Drs. Solanto, Arnsten, and Castellanos (2001).

Pharmacology of Stimulant Medications.   Stimulants increase the arousal level of the central nervous system (CNS), and for many years it was commonly believed that they had a paradoxical effect when used with individuals with ADHD (i.e., they are already "hyper"). However, research suggests that the CNS of individuals with ADHD is underaroused, not hyperaroused, and numerous articles have been published about the stimulation-seeking behavior of individuals with ADHD (e.g., Abikoff et al., 1996; Anderson et al., 2000; Antrop, Roeyers, Van Oost, & Buysse, 2000). Stimulants, therefore, increase the arousal level of individuals with ADHD just as they do in individuals without the disorder. Stimulants are thought to increase arousal by targeting neurotransmitter systems such as dopamine and norepinephrine and increasing their efficiency or availability for cellular communication in the brain. These neurotransmitters are dispersed throughout the brain but are concentrated in regions involved in arousal, attention, concentration, motor planning and motor control, and self-regulation—the very behaviors impaired in individuals with ADHD. As mentioned in chapter 2, recent brain imaging studies have found increased activity in these brain regions believed to be dysfunctional in ADHD, following administration of stimulants (methylphenidate, Ritalin) (Rosa-Neto et al., 2005; Volkow, Fowler, Wang, Ding, & Gatey, 2002). These studies suggest that stimulants interfere with the normal re-uptake process of dopamine and therefore more of this neurotransmitter is available for cellular communication. Although the precise mechanisms by which stimulants improve the symptoms associated with ADHD are not fully understood, these studies suggest that stimulants help to normalize brain functioning in individuals with ADHD (Volkow, Wang, Fowler, & Ding, 2005). For more information concerning the pharmacology of stimulants, see Schachar and Ickowicz (1999) or *Stimulant Drugs and ADHD: Basic and Clinical Neuroscience*, edited by Drs. Solanto, Arnsten, and Castellanos (2001).

Types of Stimulant Medications. The most frequently used stimulants are listed in Table 5.1. Methylphenidate (Ritalin, Concerta, Metadate) is the most commonly prescribed stimulant, and according to Zito et al. (2003), 80% of children treated with stimulants are treated with methylphenidate. For most stimulants, two forms are available, short acting (given twice or more daily) and sustained release (given once daily). Methylphenidate is effective in the treatment of ADHD in children, adolescents, and adults (Beiderman & Spencer, 2002; Findling, Short, & Manos, 2001). The appropriate dosage should be *individually determined* and generally ranges from 5 mg to more than 20 mg. According to DuPaul and Stoner (2003), sustained-release medications are preferred over short acting medications as they can be given before a child goes to school and therefore confidentiality can be maintained. It is important to note that perhaps as many as 30% of children with ADHD may not respond well to Ritalin (Spencer et al., 1996). Researchers have attempted to identify factors that can predict an individual's response to stimulant medication. Although inconclusive, a number of factors have been associated with a positive response to stimulant medication including high levels of inattentiveness, hyperactivity and restlessness, low levels of anxiety, and good parental management (DuPaul, Barkley, & Connor, 1998; Thomson & Varley, 1998). Winsberg and Comings (1999) found that the presence of a certain transporter gene (DAT1) was predictive of whether a sample of children with ADHD responded well to methylphenidate. Other researchers have suggested that performance on neuropsychological tasks and physiological tasks can predict with 80% to 90% accuracy who will respond well to medication (e.g., Hermens, Cooper, Kohn, Clarke, & Gordon, 2005; Sangal & Sangal, 2004).

When individuals respond poorly to Ritalin, other stimulants such as Adderall, non-stimulants (Strattera), or other forms of medication—such as antidepressants—may be useful. Auiler, Liu, Lynch, and Gelotte (2002) noted,

TABLE 5.1 Stimulant Medications

Generic Name	Trade Name
Methylphenidate	Ritalin, Concerta, Metadate, Methylin
Dextroamphetamine	Dexedrine
Dexmethylphenidate	Focalin
Amphetamine Salts	Adderall

however, that food consumption might alter the effects of Adderall more than methylphenidate (i.e., concentrations of methylphenidate were unaffected by a high fat breakfast). Adderall is available in 5, 10, 20, and 30-mg tablets; and research supports its safety and effectiveness in treating ADHD in children and adolescents (Manos, Short, & Findling, 1999; McGough, Pataki, & Suddath, 2005). Research also suggests that Adderall may be used successfully with children and adolescents who had no response or an adverse response to Ritalin, and in some cases Adderall may be superior to methylphenidate (Pliszka, Browne, Olvera, & Wynne, 2000). Faraone and Biederman (2002) reported that Adderall can also improve aggressive, disruptive behavior in children and adolescents with ADHD. Questions have been raised about the safety of Adderall, however, following the sudden death in 12 boys (ages 7–16) who had been taking the medication. As a result of the deaths, the Canadian drug regulatory agency suspended the sale of Adderall in the Canadian market in February 2005. The United States FDA investigated the cases, did not remove Adderall from the market, and issued a statement that patients and parents of patients taking Adderall should discuss any concerns with the prescribing physician (www.fda.gov).

Other less commonly used stimulants include Dexedrine and Cylert. Dexedrine, like Ritalin, is available in short-acting or sustained-release forms. Efron, Jarman, and Barker (1997) compared the effects of dexedrine and methylphenidate on teacher and parent ratings of children with ADHD and concluded that both medications resulted in improvement but methylphenidate was superior to dexedrine on most measures. Although Cylert was used in the past to treat ADHD, today it is rarely used because it takes several weeks before the full effect is reached, is more difficult and time-consuming to determine an optimal dose, and, more importantly, has been found to cause liver damage (Berkovitch, Pope, & Phillips, 1995; Marotta & Roberts, 1998).

Benefits of Stimulant Medication.   A large body of literature supports the short-term effectiveness of stimulants in improving the attention and behavioral symptoms of ADHD in children, adolescents, and more recently adults (see Biederman & Spencer, 2002; Handen, Feldman, Lurier, & Hazar-Murray, 1999; Kooij et al., 2004; Spencer et al., 1996, for a review). The American Academy of Pediatrics recently reviewed and analyzed the literature concerning the effectiveness of medications in treating ADHD and concluded that the evidence strongly supported the use of stimulants in treating the core symptoms (Brown et al., 2005). Studies have also reported improvements in academic accuracy and productivity, as well as performance on curriculum-based measures (Rapport, DuPaul, Stoner, & Jones, 1986; Stoner, Carey, Ikeda, & Shinn, 1994). DuPaul, Anastopoulos, Kwasnik, Barkley, and McMurray (1996) also found improvements in children's behavioral self-concept when they were taking Ritalin compared to when they were taking a placebo. Numerous studies have found enhanced social interactions between children with ADHD and their parents, teachers, and peers when taking stimulants. A 1990 study by Dr. William Pelham from the Western Psychiatric Institute in Pittsburgh, Pennsylvania, found that even the baseball performance of boys with ADHD was significantly improved when they were taking Ritalin versus a placebo (Pelham, McBurnett,

Murphy, Clinton, & Thiele, 1990). Butte, Treuth, Voigt, Llorente, and Heird (1999) found that stimulant medications decreased the physical activity level and amount of energy expended by boys and girls with ADHD (ages 6–12) while they rode a stationary bike, did schoolwork, and watched a movie. Pliszka et al. (2000) found that stimulants reduced inattentive and oppositional behaviors and resulted in overall improvement as measured by parent ratings on the Conners Global Index (CGI). Recently, Arnold and colleagues (2003) compared the effectiveness of medication and behavioral treatment over a 14-month period with Caucasian, African-American, and Latino children 7 to 9 years of age and concluded that treatment response did not differ by ethnicity, and therefore treatment for ADHD should be the same for children regardless of their socioeconomic status or ethnicity.

Long-Term Effects of Stimulants. Despite the documented short-term effectiveness of stimulants, a number of long-term studies had failed to find significant differences between individuals with ADHD who had and had not been medicated (Mannuzza et al., 1993; Weiss & Hechtman, 1993). Gillberg and colleagues (1997), however, conducted a 15-month study with children ages 6 to 11 and the results indicated that stimulants were superior to placebos in improving attention and behavior over the 15-month period. More recently, Wilens and colleagues (2005) studied more than 200 children treated with methylphenidate over 24 months and found sustained improvements based on parental reports. Moreover, this study found minimal negative effects on growth, blood pressure, tics, or laboratory measures. Hechtman, Abikoff, Klein, Weiss, et al. (2004) also found significant improvement in academic performance of children treated with methylphenidate and this improvement has maintained over 2 years. Compared to earlier studies, more recent long-term studies have been better designed and more attentive to diagnostic criteria, attrition, and noncompliance issues (i.e., not taking the medication or failing to take it properly). Thus, recent findings support that stimulant medication has short-term as well as longer term effects on improving attention and behavioral symptoms in children with ADHD (Jensen, 2002).

Concerns About Stimulant Medication. Although stimulants have been used for decades, concerns remain about their use in treating children and adolescents with ADHD. As mentioned previously, some special interest groups and mental health professionals vehemently oppose the use of medication in treating child and adult psychological or behavioral disorders. Some common concerns and issues related to the use of stimulant medication include

- When to medicate
- Rate of medication treatment
- Monitoring of medication
- Medication side effects
- Abuse potential
- Misconceptions
- Long-term risks

When to Medicate.   Teachers and parents are often confused as to when medication is needed. According to DuPaul and Barkley (1990), the following factors (as well as others) should be considered:

1. The child's age
2. The severity of the child's symptoms and disruptive behavior
3. Prior use of other treatments
4. The financial resources of the family
5. Presence of anxiety or tic disorder symptoms
6. Parental attitude toward use of medication
7. Adequacy of adult and medical supervision
8. The child's attitude toward medication

Parents and children should not be coerced into taking medication. In addition, they must be able to afford the medication. Other interventions (e.g., behavior management, education) should be tried before a trial of medication, and ongoing supervision must be available. In general, the more severe the symptoms, the greater the likelihood that a child, adolescent, or adult will benefit from medication. Not everyone shows improvement with stimulant medication, however, and individuals with coexisting anxiety or other disorders may benefit from other types of medication. In the case of adolescents, Dr. Howard Schubiner (1998), a physician, suggests that medication is generally indicated when

1. There is a positive diagnosis of ADHD.
2. There is documented moderate to severe impairment in school and/or home functioning.
3. The adolescent has agreed to take the medication and the parents concur with the adolescent's decision.
4. The adolescent has not abused alcohol, marijuana, or other illicit substances.
5. There are no present medical contraindications such as hypertension, cardiovascular problems, or chronic diseases that are aggravated by psychoactive medication.

Rate of Medication Treatment.   In 1996 it had been estimated that 1.5 million children in North America received medication for ADHD (Safer, Zito, & Fine, 1996). In 2003, this figure rose to 2.5 million (CDC, 2005). The Centers for Disease Control reported that 4.4 million children ages 4 to 17 had been diagnosed with ADHD in the United States and 56% took medication for the disorder (CDC, 2005). Others have reported that approximately two thirds of children with ADHD receive medication at some point during childhood or adolescence (Hoagwood et al., 2000). Studies also indicate that boys are prescribed medication more frequently than girls with a ratio of about 3:1, and African-American youth are prescribed medication half as often as Caucasian youth (e.g., Zito, Safer, dos Reis, Magder, & Riddle, 1997). The rate of medications prescribed for preschoolers has increased substantially (Zito et al., 2000). In 1994, Safer and

Krager reported that the rate of medication treatment for elementary school students with ADHD rose from 1.07% in 1971 to 5.96% in 1987. For middle school students, the rate increased from 0.59% in 1975 to 2.98% in 1993, and from 0.22% in 1983 to 0.70% in 1993 for high school students. LeFever, Butterfoss, and Vislocky (1999) investigated (a) the prevalence rate of ADHD and (b) the percentage of students in Grades 2 through 5 who were receiving medication for ADHD in two southeastern Virginia school districts. According to their findings, the prevalence rate was 2 to 3 times higher than the expected rate of 3%, and, in addition, 17% of Caucasian boys, 9% of African-American boys, 7% of Caucasian girls, and 3% of African-American girls were receiving medication for ADHD.

Based on these studies, it would appear that stimulants are overused for school-age children. Not all studies support this notion, however. In 1998, the American Medical Association's Council on Scientific Affairs (Goldman et al., 1998) conducted a large-scale study and concluded that (a) the prevalence of ADHD in children and adolescents has remained relatively stable since 1975, (b) it is not being overdiagnosed, and (c) medication for the disorder is not being overprescribed. Similarly, Jensen et al. (1999) investigated the prevalence and type of treatment for students age 9 to 17 years in four U.S. communities (Atlanta, Georgia; New Haven, Connecticut; Westchester, New York; and San Juan, Puerto Rico). Overall, 5.1% of the children and adolescents met *DSM-IV* criteria. Significant differences existed across communities, however, with Puerto Rico having the lowest prevalence rate (1.6%) and Georgia having the highest (9.4%). Contrary to LeFever's study, only 12.5% of the total group had been treated with stimulant medication during the past year. In terms of other interventions, 3% of the children and adolescents had received treatment from a psychiatrist and 12% from a psychologist, implying that the majority of children with ADHD are not receiving needed services. Lastly, Angold, Erkanli, Egger, and Costello (2000) reported that the use of stimulants had increased substantially among children in the Great Smoky Mountains (North Carolina) and that these medications were frequently prescribed inappropriately. Reid, Hakendorf, and Prosser (2002) reported that the patterns of stimulant use in Australian children are similar to those in the United States, while rates are somewhat lower in Israel (Fogelman, Vinker, Guy, & Kahan, 2003).

Studies have been conflicting in terms of who is prescribing stimulant prescriptions. For example, Hoagwood, Jensen, Feil, Vitiello, and Bhatara (2000) reported that family practitioners were more likely to prescribe medication for ADHD than psychiatrists or pediatricians and were less likely to recommend mental health services for individuals with ADHD. More recently, Habel and colleagues (2005) reported that 55% of stimulant prescriptions were written by physicians in pediatrics and 45% were written by physicians in psychiatry. Interestingly, Stockl and colleagues (2003) surveyed 1,000 physicians who had a history of prescribing stimulant medication to children or adolescents and found 58% indicated they would prefer prescribing a noncontrolled medication that does not have abuse potential rather than stimulants. However, 92% agreed that stimulants are effective in treating ADHD and that ADHD causes serious problems for patients with the disorder. Parents also appear to have concerns about the use of stimulant medication for the treatment of ADHD. For example, Dosreis et al. (2003) found that 55% of parents were hesitant to use medication with their children and 38% believed that too many children receive medication for ADHD. Similarly, Bussing and Gary (2001) conducted focus groups with parents of children with ADHD and evaluated parental perceptions of various treatment approaches for ADHD. Bussing and Gary reported that most parents in their study described medication as a difficult treatment approach to consider and accept for their children.

What these studies suggest is that parents and physicians have concerns about the use of stimulant medication to treat ADHD and on a *nationwide* scale medication does not appear to be overprescribed. The studies also suggest, however, that many individuals with ADHD are not receiving necessary services, and in some communities the rate of ADHD and the use of medication to treat the disorder seems alarmingly high. Clearly, more research is needed to better understand the variability of diagnosis and treatment of ADHD across the United States.

Monitoring Medication.   When medication is used with children and adolescents, it should be closely monitored to assess effectiveness, proper dosage, and potential side effects. Unfortunately, assessment of medication effectiveness is frequently determined by subjective reports by parents and very little, if any, objective information (Barkley, 1998; Hoagwood et al., 2000). Ideally, monitoring of medication would be accomplished by collaboration between a physician and a school representative. For example, the physician could prescribe on a weekly or biweekly basis, varying doses of medication including a placebo. The child's teacher, parent, or school representative would not be privy to the amount of medication. The school representative (e.g., school psychologist) would be in charge of distributing and gathering teacher and parent rating scales (e.g., Academic Performance Rating Scale and behavioral scales such as the ADHD Rating Scale, see Appendixes B and C) and interpreting the results for the physician. For example, see Table 5.2. Direct observations of the child or adolescent could also be used to help gather information about the effectiveness of the medication with regard to the child's behavioral, academic, and social functioning. In this way, the physician could determine the appropriate dosage for the child or adolescent based on academic, social, and behavioral feedback from the teacher, parents, and school psychologist. DuPaul and Barkley (1993) provide an excellent discussion of various behavioral methods that can be used to help establish and monitor medication treatment. Recently, Gureasko-Moore, DuPaul, and Power (2005) found that nearly 55% of school psychologists in their study were involved in medication monitoring. Ardoin and Martens (2000) found that a small group of children with ADHD were able to accurately report whether or not they were taking medication or placebo, behavioral changes, and adverse effects of the medication. Smith and colleagues (2000) reported that adolescents with ADHD were also able to provide valid information about their behavior while taking methylphenidate. As Hyman et al. (1998), noted, however, practical issues often come into play such as teacher compliance in filling out measures, obtaining physician cooperation, and supplying adequate placebos when trying to titrate and monitor medication effectiveness and side effects with children with ADHD.

With regard to ongoing supervision, Schubiner (1998) recommends that patients follow up with their physician 1 month after the initial prescription was

TABLE 5.2   Steps to School-Based Medication Evaluation

1. Parent obtains prescription (e.g., Ritalin, 5 mg) from pediatrician.
2. Staff member not involved directly with evaluation (e.g., school nurse) and physician determine order of administration of several doses (e.g., 5, 10, 15, 20 mg) including a nonmedication trial.
3. Parent (or school nurse) administers dose according to predetermined schedule on a daily basis.
4. Assessment measures collected on a weekly (daily) basis:
   a. Teacher ratings
   b. Parent ratings
   c. Side effects ratings
   d. Observations of classroom behavior by independent observer during individual written seatwork
5. Assessment measures must be taken to reflect the child's behavior during the active phase of the medication (i.e., 2–4 hours postingestion).
6. Determine if there are significant changes in behavior (especially academic) at any dose.
7. Determine the lowest dose that brings about the greatest change with the fewest side effects.
8. Report results to child's pediatrician.

Source: From *ADHD in the Schools: Assessment and Intervention Strategies* (p. 160), by G. J. DuPaul and G. Stoner, 2003, New York: Guilford Press. Reprinted with permission.

given, maintain telephone contact during the first month, and schedule office visits whenever side effects occur. Schubiner also recommends that patients return for office visits every 3 to 4 months while they are taking medication. These visits will help to determine the optimal dose of medication and to monitor potential side effects. Another important factor to monitor in children taking medication is compliance (whether they continue to take the medication as prescribed). Recently, Bussing and colleagues (2005) reported that more than one third of children who were prescribed stimulant medications for ADHD were no longer taking it during the second and third follow-up stages of the 2-year study. In terms of supervision of medication in schools, Musser and colleagues (1998) reported that during school hours, 44% of children and 37% of schools in central Wisconsin reported that stimulants were stored in unlocked locations. In this study, 10% of schools allowed students to carry their own stimulant medication to and from school.

Medication Side Effects.   Numerous studies are available addressing the side effects associated with stimulant medication treatment. See Greenhill, Halperin, and Abikoff (1999) and the *Physician's Desk Reference* (2006) for a detailed review of this information. The type, number, and severity of side effects vary among individuals and tend to be dose-dependent (Rapport, Randall, & Moffitt, 2002), According to Rapport and Moffitt (2002) changes in weight, blood pressure, and heart rate can accompany treatment with stimulants but these changes are usually transient, dose-dependent, and easily altered with changing the dose of the medication. Additional potential side effects include

- Weight loss
- Sleep disturbances
- Headaches
- Stomachaches
- Mood changes

According to work by Barkley, McMurray, Edelbrock, and Robbins (1990), who investigated the use of methylphenidate in children, decreased appetite, insomnia, and irritability are the most common side effects (approximately 50% of the children displayed these side effects), followed by stomachaches and headaches (33% of the children). Most of these symptoms, however, will dissipate within 1 to 2 weeks. More severe but rare side effects may include seizures, psychosis, increased blood pressure, or motor tics (*Physician's Desk Reference*, 2006). Law and Schachar (1999), however, investigated whether stimulant medication (methylphenidate) caused tics in 91 children with ADHD. Based on their findings, methylphenidate was no more likely than placebo to cause tics or to worsen preexisting tics. In fact, the study found that the majority of children with preexisting tics experienced improvement in their tic symptoms when taking medication. More recent research by Wilens et al. (2005) and Palumbo, Spencer, Lynch, Co-Chien, and Faraone (2004) have reported that methylphenidate does not induce or exacerbate tics, and the Tourette's Syndrome Study Group (2002) came to a similar conclusion. Other studies have found an association between tic disorders and stimulant medication usage, so perhaps more research is needed to fully understand this relationship (Varley, Vincent, Varley, & Calderon, 2001).

Several studies have indicated that preschool-age children may be more susceptible to methylphenidate side effects than older children (Connor, 2002; Handen, Feldman, Lurier, & Huzar-Murray, 1999). Short, Manos, Findling, and Schubel (2004), however, found that side effects were infrequent in preschool children when the optimal dose level was attained. Side effects should be of serious concern to physicians as well as individuals taking medication. For example, parents, teachers, and perhaps individuals taking stimulant medication should be asked about the presence and severity of symptoms such as appetite changes, sleep problems, irritability, headaches, and so on. Procedures such as checking blood pressure, height, weight, and heart rate will also assist in monitoring potential side effects. Barkley (1998) has developed a side effects rating scale (Stimulant Drug Side Effects Rating Scale, p. 531) that can be used to help evaluate the presence and degree of side effects in individuals taking stimulant medications for ADHD.

Misconceptions. Several misconceptions continue to exist about side effects including the idea that stimulant medication causes growth suppression. Based on numerous studies, the American Academy of Pediatrics (1987) concluded that use of stimulant medication does not cause any weight or height suppression in children and adolescents. Recently, Zachor and colleagues (in press) assessed the effects of long-term (3 year) stimulant medication treatment on the height and weight of children with ADHD and also concluded that stimulants did not significantly interfere with these measures.

Another misconception is that stimulant medication such as Ritalin is addictive when taken as prescribed. According to Greenhill, Halperin, and Abikoff (1999), there is little evidence of individuals developing tolerance to methylphenidate, and furthermore, individuals who stop taking stimulants do not experience withdrawal symptoms. Many children, adolescents, and adults continue to respond to the same dose of stimulant medication, and, depending on the type of stimulant, it is usually in and out of the system within a few hours. Stimulants do have the potential for *abuse*, however, and Williams and colleagues (2004) recently reported that 6% of 450 adolescents referred for substance abuse treatment were diagnosed as methylphenidate or dextroamphetamine abusers. Gordon, Tulak, and Troncale (2004) found that 33% of adolescents with ADHD who were treated for substance abuse had reported abusing stimulants commonly used to treat ADHD. Fatality cases have also been reported due to the intranasal abuse of methylphenidate (Massello & Carpenter, 1999). In central Wisconsin, Musser et al. (1998) reported that 16% of children taking stimulants had been approached to sell, trade, or give away their medication. Prescription stimulants are also misused among middle and high school students based on research by McCabe, Teter, and Boyd (2004) and McCabe, Knight, Teter, and Wechsler (2005). Specifically, these researchers surveyed students in Grades 6 through 11 in a Midwestern public school system, and 4.5% reported the illicit use of stimulant medication. In addition, 23% reported being approached to sell, trade, or give away their prescription medication. The illicit use of stimulants was lowest among African-American students, and highest among those who did not plan to attend college. A number of studies have reported illicit use of stimulants among college students. For example, Low and Gendaszek (2002) surveyed undergraduate students at a small college in Maine, and found that 35% of the students sampled reported illicit use of stimulants. Common reasons for using stimulants illegally included (a) to improve intellectual performance (23%), (b) to be more efficient on academic assignments (22%), and (c) for recreational purposes, that is, in combinations with alcohol (19%) (known as "pharming," Kadison, 2005). Male college students reported more illicit use of stimulants than female college students. Teter, McCabe, Boyd, and Guthrie (2003) found only 3% of students from the University of Michigan reported illicit use of stimulants and males and females did not differ in their use. In a 2005 study conducted in the Midwest, 17% of male college students and 11% of female college students reported illicit use of stimulant medication. Similar to the Low and Gendaszek study, this study found that students tended to use stimulants to improve academic performance and for recreational purposes (Hall, Irwin, Bowman, Frankenberger, & Jewett, 2005). Lastly, McCabe and colleagues (2005) surveyed more than 10,000 college students from 119 colleges across the United States and found that 6.9% of students reported illicit use of stimulants. An interesting finding in this study was that illicit use of stimulants varied tremendously across universities with the highest use among students who attended universities in the Northeast region of the United States. Clearly, the misuse of stimulant medication is a potentially serious public health issue and more research is needed to better understand the problem and to develop methods to decrease misuse of stimulants. Although methylphenidate can be and is misused by adolescents and young adults, it is thought to be relatively nonaddictive (Volkow et al., 2001). Kollins (2003) reported that the pharmacokinetic properties of methylphenidate are substantially different from other types of stimulants that are often abused (e.g., cocaine) therefore lessening its abuse and addiction potential.

Another misconception is that one dosage level is appropriate for all individuals with ADHD depending on their age and body weight. It is important to note that the ideal amount of medication varies among individuals, even among individuals of the same age, gender, and weight. For example, Rapport, Quinn, DuPaul, Quinn, and Kelly (1989) demonstrated that children of the same age and weight responded quite differently to medication dosages in terms of their behavior and academic functioning. For some children, the optimal dose was 10 mg of methylphenidate, whereas for others the optimal dose was 20 mg. For more information about predicting clinical responses and appropriate dosages of medication, see Rapport and Denney (1999).

Finally, some have questioned whether learning that takes place while students are taking medication is retained when the students are not taking the medication (this concept is known as *state-dependent learning*). Based on several studies involving children who have taken medication and were then presented with a learning task (e.g., memory game), state-dependent learning does not appear to occur (e.g., Becker-Mattes, Mattes, Abikoff, & Brandt, 1985; Stephens, Pelham, & Skinner, 1984). In other words, if an individual learns new information while he or she is medicated, this information is likely to be retained even when he or she is not medicated.

Long-Term Risks.   Parents and teachers have questioned whether use of medication in childhood increases the likelihood of drug use and abuse in adolescence and young adulthood. Several long-term studies have investigated this issue and have found that for most individuals the use of medication on a regular basis is not associated with an increased risk of drug involvement and, in many cases, is actually associated with a *decreased* risk (Chilcoat & Breslau, 1999; Weiss & Hechtman, 1993). In a 13-year study which followed children with ADHD through adolescence and young adulthood, Barkley, Fischer, Smallish, and Fletcher (2003) recently interviewed them about their length of stimulant medication treatment and drug use. Results revealed that stimulant-treated children had no greater risk for experimenting with drugs during adolescence or frequency of drug use in adulthood. Thus, these studies debunk the myth that treatment with stimulants during childhood leads to a greater risk of experimentation, use or abuse of drugs in adolescence or adulthood. It is also important to note that a plethora of studies indicate that medication can dramatically improve an individual's academic, social, and behavioral functioning. Given the large body of research that associates poor academic performance and behavioral problems with increased risk of substance use and abuse, withholding medication could conceivably increase the likelihood of drug usage in adolescence and adulthood. Nevertheless, stimulants are controlled substances that can be lethal when abused. It is therefore, good clinical, ethical, and professional practice for parents, teachers, and medical personnel to closely monitor the storage and use of medication.

A recent study proposed that treatment with stimulants might cause specific chromosomal abnormalities in individuals with ADHD, abnormalities that were associated with increased risk of cancer (El-Zein et al., in press). In response to the study, the national association, CH.A.D.D. (Children and adults with ADHD) issued a press release criticizing the study for its small sample size (12 children), need for replication, and noted that the children were not studied before stimulant treatment and therefore the findings are only relational, not causal. At this point, the findings by El-Zein et al. are only preliminary and more studies are needed to further investigate the potential relationship between stimulants and chromosomal alterations. However, in February 2006, an FDA advisory panel voted 8 to 7 that stimulant medications should carry "black box" warnings about an increased risk of cardiovascular problems and sudden death. This recommendation was based on 25 deaths that occurred (19 were children) while adults and children were taking stimulants for ADHD. Organizations such as CH.A.D.D. have responded by saying the panel's decision was "premature" (www.ChADD.org). Clearly more studies are needed to better understand the potential deleterious health effects of stimulants and factors that may moderate these effects.

Nonstimulant Medication

In November 2002, the FDA approved the use of Strattera (atomoxetine) for the treatment of ADHD. Strattera is a nonstimulant, nonantidepressant medication that targets different neurotransmitters in the brain than stimulants. Specifically, Strattera prevents the re-uptake of norepinephrine (while stimulants target dopamine) at the cellular level causing more of this neurotransmitter to be available at the level where brain cells communicate. Since its approval, a relatively large number of studies have investigated and supported the effectiveness of Strattera at improving ADHD symptoms in children and adolescents, including both males and females (e.g., Biederman, Heiligenstein, et al., 2002; Kaplan et al., 2004; Kelsey et al., 2004; Perwien et al., 2004; Simpson & Plosker, 2004; Spencer, Heiligenstein, et al., 2002; Weiss et al., 2005). Preliminary studies have also found that Strattera is equally as effective as methylphenidate at treating ADHD (Kratochvil et al., 2002). Recently, however, concerns have been raised about the possibility that Strattera increases suicidal thoughts in children and adolescents, and in September 2005, the FDA ordered that the makers of Strattera, Eli Lilly, carry a prominent "black box" warning on its label. This is the FDA's most serious alert and was based on Eli Lilly's research with 1,357 children who were taking Strattera compared to children who were not taking the medication. Results revealed that 5 of the 1,357 children reported suicidal thoughts while no children in the control group had reported these thoughts. It is important to note that one child attempted suicide and survived, and no other children attempted suicide in this study.

Antidepressant Medication

Although antidepressants are used less frequently than stimulants to treat ADHD, tricyclic antidepressant medication may be useful for individuals with ADHD who do not respond to stimulants. Williams and colleagues (2004) found that 23% of 450 adolescents referred for substance abuse treatment reported nonmedical use of methylphenidate and dexedrine and therefore suggested that antidepressants or other nonstimulant medications be used with substance abusing individuals with ADHD. Antidepressants can also be effective with individuals who have co-existing affective disorders such as depression (Table 5.3). Stimulants result in increasing the arousal level of the CNS by affecting the amount or efficiency of neurotransmitters, primarily dopamine, that is available for cellular communication in the brain. Antidepressants, however, primarily affect the neurotransmitters serotonin and norepinephrine. For more information concerning the pharmacology of antidepressants, see Schachar and Ickowicz (1999).

The most commonly used tricyclic antidepressants for individuals with ADHD include imipramine (Tofranil), desipramine (Norpramin), and nortriptyline (Pamelor). These medications are usually reserved for adults with ADHD due to their ability to increase blood pressure and rapid heart rate in some children and adolescents (Popper, 2000). Tricyclic antidepressants are slower acting than stimulants and may take 4 to 6 weeks to show effects. Side effects may include drowsiness, dry mouth, nausea, constipation, tremors, increased or decreased blood pressure, or, in rare cases, seizures or death (*Physician's Desk Reference*, 2005). Another type of antidepressant, selective serotonin reuptake inhibitors (SSRIs) can be used in conjunction with stimulants to treat co-existing anxiety disorders or depression and include sertraline (Zoloft), fluoxetine (Prozac), paroxetine (Paxil), and fluvoxamine (Luvox). SSRIs have been found to have fewer side effects and therefore better tolerated in children and adolescents. A third type of antidepressant is bupropion (Wellbutrin), which is believed to affect multiple neurotransmitter systems, and has been found to be effective at treating ADHD in adults; preliminary studies have supported its effectiveness with adolescents (Daviss et al., 2001; Wilens et al., 2003). Side effects of SSRIs may include, among others, headache, agitation, tremor, nausea, dizziness, increased blood pressure, sexual dysfunction, or gastrointestinal problems (*Physician's Desk Reference*, 2006). It is important to note that re-

TABLE 5.3   Antidepressant Medications

Generic Name	Trade Name
Trycyclics	
Imipramine	Tofranil
Desipramine	Norpramin
Nortriptyline	Pamelor
SSRIs	
Sertraline	Zoloft
Fluoxetine	Prozac
Paroxetine	Paxil
Fluvoxamine	Luvox
Other	
Bupropion	Wellbutrin

search indicates that stimulants are superior to antidepressants at improving ADHD symptoms, and far more research is available concerning the use and safety of stimulants than antidepressants in treating ADHD. In addition, the FDA has *not* approved the use of antidepressants for the specific treatment of ADHD. For a review of the use of antidepressants in treating children, adolescents, and adults, see Emslie, Walkup, Pliszka, and Ernst (1999), Geller, Reising, Leonard, Riddle, and Walsh (1999), Popper (2000).

Alpha2 Noradrenergic Agonists

Unlike stimulants and antidepressants that appear to affect the amount of neurotransmitters that are available for cellular transmission, alpha2 noradrenergic agonists interfere with the release of certain neurotransmitters (e.g., norepinephrine). The most frequently used alpha2 noradrenegric agonist for ADHD is Clonidine and was originally used as a treatment for Tourette's syndrome. Clonidine has been used successfully with children with ADHD who have co-existing sleep disorders, conduct disorder, and/or tic disorders (e.g., Wilens et al., 1994). Although Clonidine is effective at reducing behavior symptoms associated with ADHD (e.g., impulsivity, aggression), it has been found to impair cognitive functions such as attention and memory (Coull, Middleton, Robbins, & Sahakian, 1995). Other side effects associated with Clonidine include fatigue, sedation, irritability, and skin irritation. Recently Hazell and Stuart (2003) explored the effectiveness of Clonidine used in conjunction with a stimulant for the treatment of children ages 6 to 14 with ADHD and co-existing oppositional defiant disorder or conduct disorder. Results revealed that conduct symptoms were reduced as well as ADHD symptoms, however, a number of transient side effects were reported such as decreased blood pressure, dizziness, and sedation. For additional information concerning Clonidine, see an excellent review article by Connor, Fletcher, and Swanson (1999). For more information concerning other alpha2 noradrenergic agonists and infrequently prescribed and less efficacious medications (e.g., benzodiazepines, lithium), see George and Mortimer (1998) as well as Popper (2000).

Combined Treatments

Bhatara, Feil, Hoagwood, Vitiello, and Zima (2004) examined national trends in the use of multiple types of medication used in conjunction with stimulants to treat children and adolescents. Results revealed a five-fold increase in the use of two or more psychotropic medication prescribed to children under the age of 18 between the years 1993–1998. Typically, a combination of medications is used in the treatment of ADHD when individuals with the disorder have co-existing issues such as depression, anxiety, and Tourette's syndrome. Although this approach may make common sense, research is lacking concerning the safety and efficacy of combining stimulants with other types of medications in the treatment of ADHD (Waxmonsky, 2005).

What has been studied more thoroughly, however, is the combination of stimulant medication with behavioral approaches. As mentioned in chapter 4, a substantial number of studies have found that the most effective method for treating ADHD is a multimethod approach, particularly a *combination* of medication and behavior modification (e.g., Jensen et al., 2005; Kolko, Bukstein, & Barron, 1999; Pelham, Gnagy, et al., 2000), although other studies suggest that medication used in isolation is superior to a multimethod approach (Hechtman, Abikoff, Klein, Greenfield, et al., 2004; Hechtman, Abikoff, Klein, Weiss, et al., 2004). As Rapport, Chung, Shore, and Isaacs (2001) noted, treatments that are designed to target the underlying physiology and core features of ADHD are more likely to result in improvement of symptoms than interventions that target peripheral behaviors (e.g., following rules, enhancing academic skills). Medication is primarily effective at improving attention and on-task behavior, while behavior modification can effectively reduce the aggressive, acting out, and inappropriate social behavior frequently characteristic of individuals with ADHD. In addition, other forms of treatment such as social skills training, parent training, career counseling, conflict management, and so on may be necessary depending on the specific needs of an individual as well as the setting (e.g., home, school, workplace). The bottom line is that treatment should be individually tailored to the needs of the child while taking into account factors such as availability of interventions, cost, practical considerations, compliance, and family values, to name a few.

Alternative Approaches

As mentioned in chapter 1, use of alternative approaches to treat ADHD is not uncommon, and some studies have reported that 12% to 54% of parents use approaches such as biofeedback, faith healing, homeopathy, or dietary modifications or supplements to treat their children with ADHD (Bussing, Zima, Gary, & Garvan, 2002; Brue & Oakland, 2002; Chan, Rappaport, & Kemper, 2003). Sinha and Efron (2005) reported that 67% of 105 families in Melbourne, Australia reported using complementary and alternative medicine in the treatment of ADHD. Although many alternative treatments are available for ADHD they are less well studied than the traditional treatments presented previously in this chapter and in chapter 4. The following sections summarize the most popular alternative treatments. Also see Arnold (1999) for a review of the research findings concerning additional alternative and complementary methods in the treatment of ADHD.

Biofeedback

A variety of biofeedback (neurofeedback) techniques exist, but those that have been used most frequently with individuals with ADHD involve measuring brain waves or muscular tension. Biofeedback consists of attaching electrodes to an individual's scalp (or other body parts), and the electrodes are connected to a machine. The machine measures various body functions such as changes in brain waves or muscular tension. Individuals are encouraged to increase or decrease brain activity and are provided with feedback about these changes on a computer or television screen. With children, video games may be used and the child gains points by increasing or decreasing certain brain waves (e.g., Play Attention, www.playattention.com). The underlying theory of biofeedback treatment for ADHD is that the brain waves of individuals with the disorder differ from those without ADHD and that individuals with the disorder can alter their brain waves after numerous sessions of biofeedback training. A few studies have found differences in brain wave patterns (EEG) of children and adolescents with ADHD, although many others have not (e.g., Mann, Lubar, Zimmerman, Miller, & Muenchen, 1990; Baving, Laucht, & Schmidt, 1999). Regardless of these findings, there is no evidence to support the idea that aberrant brain waves are *responsible* for ADHD.

Biofeedback as a treatment for ADHD has recently received attention from the media, and many clinicians attest to its effectiveness. With regard to scientific studies, several investigations have found that biofeedback decreases ADHD symptoms (e.g., Lubar, 1991; Potashkin & Beckles, 1990) although others have not (Culbert, Kajander, & Reaney, 1996). Although biofeedback is unlikely to be harmful and may eventually prove to be beneficial in the treatment of ADHD, the scientific evidence does not currently support the use of this intervention over more traditional and substantiated interventions. In a recent review of the EEG biofeedback literature, Loo and Barkley (2005) noted that many of the biofeedback studies have serious methodological weakness and concluded, "although the existing studies of EEG biofeedback claim promising results in the treatment of ADHD, the promise of EEG biofeedback as a legitimate treatment cannot be fulfilled without studies that are scientifically rigorous" (p. 73).

Caffeine

Given that coffee contains caffeine and caffeine is a central nervous system stimulant, coffee has also been recommended as an alternative treatment for ADHD. Several research studies have explored whether children with ADHD would benefit from caffeine, but most of these studies have serious methodological problems. Nevertheless, a few studies have found that caffeine, when compared to placebo or no treatment, resulted in improved teacher and parent ratings of children's behavior (Garfinkel, Webster, & Sloman, 1981; Leon, 2000). It should also be noted that some studies found that children with ADHD who were treated with caffeine experienced significant side effects such as irritability, agitation, bowel problems, and sleep disturbances (e.g., Firestone, Davey, Goodman, & Peters, 1978). Caffeine is also known to worsen anxiety symptoms, heart arrhythmias, and in toxic doses can induce psychotic symptoms (Broderick & Benjamin, 2004). Given these findings, caffeine is not recommended as an alternative treatment for ADHD. The reader is referred to Leon (2000) for a review of the effects of caffeine on the cognitive and behavioral performance of children with attention-deficit/hyperactivity disorder.

Diet Modification

Two main dietary approaches used in the treatment of ADHD included dietary restriction/elimination and supplementation. The first to popularize dietary changes for treatment of ADHD was Benjamin Feingold (1975) in the early 1970s, as discussed in chapter 1. More recent advocates of the dietary approach recommend exclusion of foods that are high in sugar and refined carbohydrates and all "suspect foods" that a child "loves and craves" (e.g., Block, 1996, p. 92). Many others recommend that foods containing artificial dyes and additives be eliminated from the diet.

In general, scientific studies indicate that elimination of sugar does *not* result in an improvement in ADHD symptoms (Goldman, Lerman, Contois, & Udall, 1986; Wolraich, Wilson, & White, 1995). Shaywitz and colleagues (1994) investigated whether a widely used artificial sweetener, *aspartame*, affected the behavior or cognitive skills (e.g., attention, planning, memory) in children with ADHD. Similar to the sugar studies, no differences were found in behavior or cognitive skills when children were taking aspartame versus a placebo. Shaywitz and colleagues also measured the children's blood and urine levels and concluded that aspartame does not appear to affect brain chemistry and nervous system functioning.

Multiple elimination diets have also been recommended in the treatment of ADHD (e.g., the oligoantigenic dye). In addition to eliminating dyes, additives, and sugar, multiple elimination diets recommend the removal of dairy products, wheat, corn, yeast, soy, citrus, egg, chocolate, and nuts from a child's dietary regimen. Several studies have reported improvement in children's behavior while adhering to these diets (e.g., Egger, Carter, Graham, Gumley, & Soothill, 1985; Schmidt et al., 1997) but as Rojas and Chan (2005) recently noted, many of these studies also suffer from serious methodological problems. Moreover, elimination diets that exclude main sources of nutrients and energy such as dairy products and carbohydrates may actually be harmful if the individual does not consume a well-balanced and adequate diet—which is difficult to accomplish when multiple staple foods are eliminated from the diet. In addition, Krummel, Seligson, and Guthrie (1996) argue that dietary restrictions could negatively affect family dynamics and relationships.

In terms of supplementation, a variety of substances have been recommended such as fatty acids, glyconutrients, phytonutrients, mega vitamins, and mega minerals such as magnesium. For example, one popular dietary supplement, Phyto-BearsÆ, has been recommended for children with ADHD as has Pedi-Active A.D.D.Æ by Nature's Plus. A few studies have supported the use of glyconutritional supplements for decreasing the severity of ADHD symptoms according to parent ratings; however, more research is needed as these studies have not been well designed (i.e., no placebo or control group) (Dykman & Dykman, 1998; Dykman & McKinley, 1997). In a recent review of the fatty acid literature, Rojas and Chan (2005) concluded studies have not demonstrated "any clear benefit of essential fatty acid supplementation on symptoms of ADHD" and noted that in some cases ADHD symptoms worsened with supplementation (pp. 126–127). Recently, Harding, Judah, and Gant (2003) compared the visual and auditory performance of 10 children with ADHD treated with Ritalin and 10 children with ADHD treated with a combination of dietary supplements (e.g., vitamins, minerals, phytonutrients, fatty acids) over a 4-week period and found that both groups improved significantly on the behavioral tasks. The authors concluded that dietary supplements were equally effective as Ritalin at improving ADHD symptoms. This study, like many others, however, only included 20 children and laboratory measures were used rather than more meaningful real-life measures such as teacher report, behavior observation, academic performance, and so on. In other words, it is unknown whether the supplementation would have improved classroom academic performance as well as classroom behavior.

Magnesium is another supplement that has received attention in the treatment of ADHD. For example, Starobrat-Hermelin and Kozielec (1997) reported that 50 children with ADHD in their study had magnesium deficiencies and after 6 months of magnesium supplementation their levels returned to normal. Specific information concerning academic and behavioral functioning was not provided, however, thus the relevance of these findings are unclear. More recently, Mousain-Bosc, Roche, Rapin, and Bali (2004) reported that "hyperexcitable" children showed a decrease in aggressive behavior after 1 to 6 months of magnesium supplementation. Arnold et al. (2005), however, found magnesium levels to be normal in children with ADHD but reported they had low levels of zinc and these levels were related to parent and teacher ratings with respect to inattention. In summary, the role, if any, mineral such as magnesium and zinc (as well as other minerals) may play in ADHD in uncertain. Based on the few studies that have been conducted and the problems that characterize these studies, the literature does not support the use of supplementation in the reliable treatment of ADHD.

In general, despite the testimonials and strong beliefs of many that support the use of nutritional supplements for treatment of ADHD, the scientific studies are not encouraging. In a recent review of treatment alternatives for ADHD, Arnold (1999) concluded that "megavitamin multiple combinations have enough evidence to warn physicians and the public away from their indiscriminate use" and "essential fatty acid supplementation, glyconutritional supplementation, RDA vitamins, and single vitamin megadosages do not enjoy the database necessary for making clinical practice recommendations" (p. 41).

Massage and Yoga

Clinicians such as Mary Ann Block (1996) recommend the use of osteopathic manipulative therapy as a treatment for ADHD. According to Dr. Block, this therapy involves the physician's use of his or her hands to help improve the body's nervous, vascular, and immune systems. Although Dr. Block describes anecdotal reports of improvement in ADHD patients, she does not refer to any scientific studies. Field, Quintino, Hernandez-Reif, and Koslovsky (1998), however, conducted a study with 28 adolescents with ADHD to explore the potential effects of massage and relaxation therapies. Based on self-reports as well as teacher ratings, the adolescents with ADHD who received massage therapy fidgeted less, were more on task, and were "happier" than adolescents who received relaxation training. More recently, Khilnani, Field, Hernandez-Reif, and Schanberg (2003) studied 30 students with ADHD (ages 7–18) who were randomly assigned to receive or not receive massage therapy. Results revealed that students who participated in massage therapy for 20 minutes, twice per week for 1 month showed significant improvements in classroom behavior compared to those without ADHD who did not receive massage therapy. With regard to yoga, very few studies have been conducted to explore the potential effects of yoga in the treatment of ADHD. Jensen and Kenny (2004) compared the parent and teacher ratings of boys with ADHD who participated in a 20-

session yoga group and found on both the parent and teacher rating scales that yoga may be of value as a complementary treatment for ADHD, particularly during times of the day when medication effects wear off. Although these preliminary studies are encouraging, additional research is needed to determine whether other studies would find similar results and whether the beneficial effects of massage therapy and yoga are short- or long-term and whether they are associated with substantial changes in academic, behavioral, and/or social functioning.

Sensory Integration Training

Sensory integration training involves the use of exercise to help develop and facilitate connections among nerve cells in individuals with ADHD. The theory is based on the idea that individuals with ADHD have faulty arousal systems and certain exercises can enhance attention and increase arousal of the central nervous system. Banaschewski, Besmens, Zieger, and Rothenberger (2001) at the University of Gottingen, Germany, noted that children with ADHD have a decreased ability to regulate motor behavior and have difficulties with a variety of motor skills. Consequently these researchers created a 20-session sensorimotor program and implemented it with six children with ADHD. Results revealed that only three children completed the study and they evidenced "slight" improvement in sensorimotor coordination. Improvement was also observed on parent rating scales. This study is obviously flawed in terms of scientific rigor and is characteristic of many of the sensorimotor-ADHD-integration studies. Drs. Barbara Ingersoll and Sam Goldstein (1993), authors of *Attention Deficit Disorder and Learning Disabilities: Realities, Myths, and Controversial Treatments*, summed up the literature well when they concluded there is no scientific evidence to support the use of sensory integration training as a treatment for ADHD. Furthermore, many of these programs can be costly, and effective treatments may be withheld or delayed while a child, adolescent, or adult is participating in sensory integration training.

Additional Alternative Interventions

Additional alternative interventions are recommended for ADHD including homeopathy (Frei et al., in press), exercise (Tantillo, Kesick, Hynd, & Dishman, 2002), weighted vests (VandenBerg, 2001), music therapy (Jackson, 2003), and green, outdoor settings (Kuo & Taylor, 2004) to name a few. Although some of these alternative interventions may prove to be beneficial in the treatment of ADHD at this point they should be considered exploratory interventions that require rigorous, scientific investigation before they are viewed as legitimate treatments.

Summary

Interventions for ADHD vary widely and include educational strategies and accommodations, behavior support programs, medication, individual counseling, family interventions, and skills training. Additional interventions have been recommended but not scientifically supported for the treatment of ADHD, such as sensory integration training, caffeine, and the Feingold Diet. Other alternative interventions, including biofeedback, massage, and exercise require additional scientific scrutiny. Given the good intentions of parents, teachers, and other professionals, claims of new and effective treatments for ADHD can be enticing, particularly those that make intuitive sense. The clinician and the consumer must be skeptical and cautious, however, and would benefit from relying on well-studied and substantiated interventions. This is not to say that new treatments for ADHD will not emerge, but rather to warn and remind the reader to look for convincing and scientific evidence before committing time and resources to unproven and in many cases, costly, interventions.

Background Questionnaires

Example of a Background Questionnaire Used in a Child Guidance Clinic or School

Childhood History Form

Child's Name: _____

Birthdate: _____ Age _____ Sex _____

Home Address: _____
$\qquad$ Street $\qquad$ City

_____ Home Phone _____
$\qquad$ State $\qquad$ Zip $\qquad$ Area Code

Child's School _____
$\qquad$ Name $\qquad$ Address

Grade _____ Special Placement (if any) _____

Child is presently living with:

_____ Natural Mother _____ Natural Father _____ Stepmother _____ Stepfather

_____ Adoptive Mother _____ Adoptive Father _____ Foster Mother _____ Foster Father

_____ Other Specify _____

Non-residential adults involved with this child on a regular basis:

_____

_____

Source of referral: Name _____

Address _____ Phone _____

Briefly state main problem of this child: _____

_____

_____

_____

PARENTS

Mother _____

Occupation _____ Business Phone _____

(continued)

Source: From Managing Attention Deficit Hyperactivity Disorder in Children: A Guide for Practitioners (2nd ed.) (pp. 667–674), by S. Goldstein & M. Goldstein, 1998, New York: John Wiley & Sons, Inc. Copyright © 1995, *Childhood History Form*, 2nd Edition, Salt Lake City, UT: Neurology, Learning and Behavior Center. Reprinted by permission of John Wiley & Sons, Inc.

Age _____ Age at time of pregnancy with patient _____

School: Highest grade completed _____

            Learning problems _____

            Attention problems _____

            Behavior problems _____

Medical Problems _____

Have any of your blood relatives experienced problems similar to those your child is experiencing? If so, describe: _____

_____

_____

Father _____

Occupation _____ Business Phone _____

School: Highest grade completed _____

            Learning problems _____

            Attention problems _____

            Behavior problems _____

Medical Problems _____

Have any of your blood relatives experienced problems similar to those your child is experiencing? If so, describe: _____

_____

_____

SIBLINGS

1. _____
2. _____
3. _____
4. _____
5. _____
6. _____

PREGNANCY—Complications

Excessive vomiting _____ hospitalization required _____

Excessive staining/blood loss _____ threatened miscarriage _____

Infection(s) (specify) _____

Toxemia _____ Operation(s) (specify) _____

Other illness(es) (specify) _____

Smoking during pregnancy _____ # cigarettes per day _____

Alcoholic consumption during pregnancy _____

    Describe if beyond an occasional drink _____

Medications taken during pregnancy _____

X-ray studies during pregnancy _____
Duration of pregnancy (weeks) _____

DELIVERY

Type of Labor: Spontaneous _____ Induced _____ Duration (hrs.) _____
Type of Delivery: Normal _____ Breech _____ Caesarean _____
Complications: Cord around neck _____ Hemorrhage _____
    Infant injured during delivery _____ Other _____
    Birth Weight _____

POST DELIVERY PERIOD

Jaundice _____ Cyanosis (turned blue) _____ Incubator Care _____
Infection (specify) _____
Number of days infant was in the hospital after delivery _____

INFANCY PERIOD

Were any of the following present—to a significant degree—during the first few years of life? If so, describe:

    Did not enjoy cuddling _____
    Was not calmed by being held or stroked _____
    Difficult to comfort _____
    Colic _____ Excessive restlessness _____
    Excessive irritability _____
    Diminished sleep _____
    Frequent head banging _____
    Difficulty nursing _____
    Constantly into everything _____

TEMPERAMENT

Please rate the following behaviors as your child appeared during infancy and toddler-hood:

    Activity Level: How active has your child been from an early age? _____
_____

    Distractibility: How well did your child pay attention? _____
_____

    Adaptability: How well did your child deal with transition and change? _____
_____

(continued)

Approach/Withdrawal: How well did your child respond to new things (i.e., places, people, food)? _____

_____

Intensity: Whether happy or unhappy, how aware are others of your child's feelings?

_____

_____

Mood: What was your child's basic mood? _____

_____

Regularity: How predictable was your child in patterns of sleep, appetite, etc.? _____

_____

MEDICAL HISTORY

If your child's medical history includes any of the following, please note the age when the incident or illness occurred and any other pertinent information:

Childhood diseases (describe ages and any complications) _____

_____

Operations _____

Hospitalization for illness _____

_____

Head injuries _____

Convulsions _____ with fever _____ without fever _____

Coma _____

Persistent high fevers _____

Eye problems _____

Tics (i.e., eye blinking, sniffing, any repetitive, non-purposeful movements) _____

_____

Ear problems _____

Allergies or asthma _____

Poisoning _____

Sleep _____

   Does your child settle down to sleep? _____

   Sleep through the night without disruption? _____

   Experience nightmares, night terrors, sleep walking, sleep talking? _____

_____

   Is your child a very restless sleeper? _____

   Does your child snore? _____

Appetite _____

_____

PRESENT MEDICAL STATUS

Height _____ Weight _____

Present Illnesses for which the child is being treated _____

Medications child is taking on ongoing basis? _____

DEVELOPMENTAL MILESTONES

If you can recall, record the age at which your child reached the following developmental milestones. If cannot recall exactly, check item at right:

	Age	Early	Normal	Late
Smiled	_____	_____	_____	_____
Sat without support	_____	_____	_____	_____
Crawled	_____	_____	_____	_____
Stood without support	_____	_____	_____	_____
Walked without assistance	_____	_____	_____	_____
Spoke first words	_____	_____	_____	_____
Said phrases	_____	_____	_____	_____
Said sentences	_____	_____	_____	_____
Bladder trained, day	_____	_____	_____	_____
Bowel trained, night	_____	_____	_____	_____
Rode tricycle	_____	_____	_____	_____
Rode bicycle (without training wheels)	_____	_____	_____	_____
Buttoned clothing	_____	_____	_____	_____
Tied shoelaces	_____	_____	_____	_____
Named colors	_____	_____	_____	_____
Named coins	_____	_____	_____	_____
Said alphabet in order	_____	_____	_____	_____
Began to read	_____	_____	_____	_____

COORDINATION

Rate your child as Good, Average, or Poor on the following skills:

Walking _____

Running _____

Throwing _____

Catching _____

Shoelace tying _____

Buttoning _____

Writing _____

(continued)

Athletic abilities _____
Excessive number of accidents
  compared to other children _____

COMPREHENSION AND UNDERSTANDING

Do you consider your child to understand directions and situations as well as other children his or her age? _____
_____
If not, why not? _____
_____
How would you rate your child's overall level of intelligence compared to other children?
Below Average _____ Above Average _____ Average _____

SCHOOL HISTORY

Were you concerned about your child's ability to succeed in kindergarten? If so, please explain: _____
_____
Rate your child's school experiences related to academic learning:
  Nursery School _____
  Kindergarten _____
  Current Grade _____
To the best of your knowledge, at what grade level is your child functioning:
  Reading _____ Spelling _____ Arithmetic _____
Has your child ever had to repeat a grade? If so, when? _____
Present class placement: Regular Class _____ Special class (if so, specify)
_____
Kinds of special counseling or remedial work your child is currently receiving _____
_____
Describe briefly any academic school problems _____
_____
_____
Rate your child's school experiences related to behavior as Good, Average or Poor:
  Nursery school _____
  Kindergarten _____
  Current grade _____
Does your child's teacher describe any of the following as significant classroom problems?
  Doesn't sit still in his or her seat _____
  Frequently gets up and walks around the classroom_____
  Shouts out. Doesn't wait to be called on _____
  Won't wait his or her turn _____

Doesn't cooperate well in group activities _____

Typically does better in a one-to-one relationship _____

Doesn't respect the rights of others _____

Doesn't pay attention during storytelling or show and tell _____

Describe briefly any **other** classroom behavioral problems _____

_____

_____

As best you can recall, please use the following space to provide a general description of your child's school progress in each grade. Use the back of this form if extra space is needed:

_____

_____

_____

_____

_____

_____

PEER RELATIONSHIPS

Does your child seek friendships with peers? _____

Is your child sought by peers for friendship? _____

Does your child play with children primarily his or her own age? _____

Younger? _____ Older? _____

Describe briefly any problems your child may have with peers: _____

_____

_____

_____

HOME BEHAVIOR

All children exhibit, to some degree, the behaviors listed below. Check those that you believe your child exhibits to an excessive or exaggerated degree when compared to other children his or her own age.

Fidgets with hands, feet or squirms in seat _____

Has difficulty remaining seated when required to do so _____

Easily distracted by extraneous stimulation _____

Has difficulty awaiting his turn in games or group situations _____

Blurts out answers to questions before they have been completed _____

Has problems following through with instructions (usually not due to opposition or failure to comprehend) _____

Has difficulty paying attention during tasks or play activities _____

(continued)

Shifts from one uncompleted activity to another _____

Has difficulty playing quietly _____

Often talks excessively _____

Interrupts or intrudes on others (often not purposeful or planned but impulsive) _____

Does not appear to listen to what is being said _____

Loses things necessary for tasks or activities at home _____

Boundless energy and poor judgment _____

Impulsivity (poor self-control) _____

History of temper tantrums _____

Temper outbursts _____

Frustrates easily _____

Sloppy table manners _____

Sudden outbursts of physical abuse of other children _____

Acts like he or she is driven by a motor _____

Wears out shoes more frequently than siblings _____

Excessive number of accidents _____

Doesn't seem to learn from experience _____

Poor memory _____

A "different child" _____

How well does your child work for a short term reward? _____

How well does your child work for a long term reward? _____

Does your child create more problems, either purposeful or non-purposeful, within the home setting than his or her siblings? _____

_____

Does your child have difficulty benefitting from his experiences? _____

_____

Types of discipline you use with your child _____

_____

_____

Is there a particular form of discipline that has proven effective? _____

_____

Have you participated in a parenting class or obtained other forms of information concerning discipline and behavior management? _____

_____

INTERESTS AND ACCOMPLISHMENTS

What are your child's main hobbies and interests? _____

_____

What are your child's areas of greatest accomplishment? _____

_____

What does your child enjoy doing most? _____

_____

What does your child dislike doing most? _____

_____

What do you like about your child? _____

_____

LIST NAMES AND ADDRESSES OF ANY
OTHER PROFESSIONALS CONSULTED:
(Including family doctor)

1. _____
2. _____
3. _____
4. _____

ADDITIONAL REMARKS:

Please write any additional remarks you may wish to make regarding your child.

_____

_____

_____

_____

_____

APPENDIX B

ADHD Rating Scale-IV: School Version

Child's name _____ Sex: M F   Age_____   Grade _____

Completed by: _____

Circle the number that *best describes* this student's school behavior over the past 6 months (or since the beginning of the school year).

	Never or rarely	Sometimes	Often	Very often
1. Fails to give close attention to details or makes careless mistakes in schoolwork.	0	1	2	3
2. Fidgets with hands or feet or squirms in seat.	0	1	2	3
3. Has difficulty sustaining attention in tasks or play activities.	0	1	2	3
4. Leaves seat in classroom or in other situations in which remaining seated is expected.	0	1	2	3
5. Does not seem to listen when spoken to directly.	0	1	2	3
6. Runs about or climbs excessively in situations in which it is inappropriate.	0	1	2	3
7. Does not follow through on instructions and fails to finish work.	0	1	2	3
8. Has difficulty playing or engaging in leisure activities quietly.	0	1	2	3
9. Has difficulty organizing tasks and activities.	0	1	2	3
10. Is "on the go" or acts as if "driven by a motor."	0	1	2	3
11. Avoids tasks (e.g., schoolwork, homework) that require sustained mental effort.	0	1	2	3
12. Talks excessively.	0	1	2	3
13. Loses things necessary for tasks or activities.	0	1	2	3

136

	Never or rarely	Sometimes	Often	Very often
14. Blurts out answers before questions have been completed.	0	1	2	3
15. Is easily distracted.	0	1	2	3
16. Has difficulty awaiting turn.	0	1	2	3
17. Is forgetful in daily activities.	0	1	2	3
18. Interrupts or intrudes on others.	0	1	2	3

Academic Performance Rating Scale

Student _____ Date _____

Age_____   Grade _____ Teacher _____

For each of the below items, please estimate the above student's performance over the *past week*. For each item, please circle *one* choice only.

1. Estimate the percentage of written math work *completed* (regardless of accuracy) relative to classmates.	0–49%	50–69%	70–79%	80–89%	90–100%
	1	2	3	4	5
2. Estimate the percentage of written language arts work *completed* (regardless of accuracy) relative to classmates.	0–49%	50–69%	70–79%	80–89%	90–100%
	1	2	3	4	5
3. Estimate the *accuracy* of completed written math work (i.e., percent correct of work done).	0–64%	65–69%	70–79%	80–89%	90–100%
	1	2	3	4	5
4. Estimate the *accuracy* of completed written language arts work (i.e., percent correct of work done).	0–64%	65–69%	70–79%	80–89%	90–100%
	1	2	3	4	5
5. How consistent has the quality of this child's academic work been over the past week?	Consistently poor	More poor than successful	Variable	More successful than poor	Consistently successful
	1	2	3	4	5

Source: From "Teacher Ratings of Academic Skills: The Development of the Academic Performance Rating Scale," by G. J. DuPaul, M. D. Rapport, and L. M. Perriello, 1991, *School Psychology Review, 20*, pp. 299–300. Copyright © 1991 by the National Association of School Psychologists. Reprinted by permission of the publisher.

6. How frequently does the student accurately follow teacher instructions and/or class discussion during *large-group* (e.g., whole class) instruction?	Never	Rarely	Sometimes	Often	Very often
	1	2	3	4	5

7. How frequently does the student accurately follow teacher instructions and/or class discussion during *small-group* (e.g., reading group) instruction?	Never	Rarely	Sometimes	Often	Very often
	1	2	3	4	5

8. How quickly does this child learn new material (i.e., pick up novel concepts)?	Very slowly	Slowly	Average	Quickly	Very quickly
	1	2	3	4	5

9. What is the quality or neatness of this child's handwriting?	Poor	Fair	Average	Above average	Excellent
	1	2	3	4	5

10. What is the quality of this child's reading skills?	Poor	Fair	Average	Above average	Excellent
	1	2	3	4	5

11. What is the quality of this child's speaking skills?	Poor	Fair	Average	Above average	Excellent
	1	2	3	4	5

12. How often does the child complete written work in a careless, hasty fashion?	Never	Rarely	Sometimes	Often	Very often
	1	2	3	4	5

13. How frequently does the child take more time to complete work than his/her classmates?	Never	Rarely	Sometimes	Often	Very often
	1	2	3	4	5

14. How often is the child able to pay attention without you prompting him/her?	Never	Rarely	Sometimes	Often	Very often
	1	2	3	4	5

(continued)

	Never	Rarely	Sometimes	Often	Very often
15. How frequently does this child require your assistance to accurately complete his/her academic work?	Never 1	Rarely 2	Sometimes 3	Often 4	Very often 5
16. How often does the child begin written work prior to understanding the directions?	Never 1	Rarely 2	Sometimes 3	Often 4	Very often 5
17. How frequently does this child have difficulty recalling material from a previous day's lessons?	Never 1	Rarely 2	Sometimes 3	Often 4	Very often 5
18. How often does the child appear to be staring excessively or "spaced out"?	Never 1	Rarely 2	Sometimes 3	Often 4	Very often 5
19. How often does the child appear withdrawn or tend to lack an emotional response in a social situation?	Never 1	Rarely 2	Sometimes 3	Often 4	Very often 5

APPENDIX D

Evaluation of School Behaviors

Operational Definitions of Behaviors in the TOAD System

1. Talking Out: Spoken words, either friendly, neutral, or negative in content, directed at either the teacher without first obtaining permission to speak or unsolicited at classmates during inappropriate times or during work periods.

2. Out of Seat: The child is not supporting his weight with the chair. Up on knees does not count as out of seat behavior.

3. Attention Problem: The child is not attending either to independent work or to a group activity. The child is therefore engaged in an activity other than that which has been directed and is clearly different from what the other children are doing at the time. This includes the child not following teacher directions.

4. Disruption: The child's actions result in consequences that appear to be interrupting other children's work. These behaviors might include noises or physical contact. They may be intentional or unintentional.

Source: TOAD System. From *Managing Attention Disorders in Children: A Guide for Practitioners* (2nd ed.) (pp. 288–289), by S. Goldstein & M. Goldstein, 1998. New York: John Wiley & Sons, Inc. Copyright © 1990, John Wiley & Sons, Inc. Reprinted by permission of John Wiley & Sons, Inc.

Observations

Target Student _____ M/F ____ Grade _____ Date _____

School _____ Teacher _____

Observer _____

Class Activity _____

Position ❏ Teacher directed   ❏ Teacher directed   ❏ Independent
            whole class   small group   work session

Directions: Ten-second interval. Observe each student *once:* then record data. This is a partial interval recording. If possible, collect full 15 minutes under teacher directed or independent condition. If not, put a slash when classroom condition changes. *Classmates observed must be the same sex as the target student.*

	1					2					3				
Target															
Student*															

*Classmates of same sex

	4					5					6				
Target															
Student*															

*Classmates of same sex

	7					8					9				
Target															
Student*															

*Classmates of same sex

	10					11					12				
Target															
Student*															

*Classmates of same sex

	13					14					15				
Target															
Student*															

*Classmates of same sex

Note: To observe class, begin with the first same-sex student in row 1. Record each subsequent same-sex student in following intervals. Data reflect an average of classroom behavior. *Skip unobservable students.*

ON-TASK CODES: Eye contact with teacher or task and performing the requested task.

OFF-TASK CODES:

T = *Talking Out/Noise:* Inappropriate verbalization or making sounds with object, mouth, or body.

O = *Out of Seat:* Student fully or partially out of assigned seat without teacher permission.

I = *Inactive:* Student not engaged with assigned task and passively waiting, sitting, etc.

N = *Noncompliance:* Breaking a classroom rule or not following teacher directions within 15 seconds.

P = *Playing with Object:* Manipulating objects without teacher permission.

+ = *Positive Teacher Interaction:* One-on-one positive comment, smiling, touching, or gesture.

− = *Negative Teacher Interaction:* One-on-one reprimand, implementing negative consequence, or negative gesture.

APPENDIX E

Adult Rating Scale

Name/ID Number: _____ Birth Date: _____ Current Date: _____

Age: _____ Gender: _(M) / (F)_ Status: _Single / Divorced / Married_

Below is a list of behaviors or problems that some people have. To the right of each item indicate, in your opinion, how much of a problem each one is for you. *Please be sure to provide an answer to each question.*

	Not at all	Just a little	Pretty much	Very much
1. Physical restlessness, excessive fidgeting				
2. Difficulty concentrating				
3. Easily distracted				
4. Impatient				
5. "Hot" or explosive temper				
6. Unpredictable behavior				
7. Shift often from one uncompleted task to another				
8. Difficulty completing tasks				
9. Impulsive				
10. Talk excessively				
11. Often interrupt others				
12. Often lose things				
13. Forget to do things				
14. Engage in physically daring activities, reckless				
15. Always on the go, difficulty sitting still				
16. Does not appear to listen to others when spoken to				
17. Difficulty sustaining attention				
18. Difficulty doing things alone				
19. Frequently get into trouble with the law				
20. Difficulty delaying gratification				
21. Lack of organization skills				
22. Inconsistent school/work performance				
23. Inability to establish and maintain a routine				
24. Performing below level of competence in school/work				
25. Overexcitability				

APPENDIX F

Key Questions for Assessing Comorbidity/Differential Diagnosis

Name of Adolescent _____ Date _____

Name of Respondent _____

Please respond to each of the following questions by circling YES or NO.

OPPOSITIONAL DEFIANT DISORDER

1. Which of the following negativistic, hostile, and defiant behaviors is your adolescent currently exhibiting, and has he or she been exhibiting them for at least 6 months? (Circle YES if the behavior occurs now and has occurred for at least 6 months.)

    a. Often loses temper   YES   NO

    b. Often argues with adults   YES   NO

    c. Often actively defies or refuses to comply with adults' requests or rules
                                                                         YES   NO

    d. Often deliberately annoys people   YES   NO

    e. Often blames others for his or her mistakes or misbehavior
                                                                         YES   NO

    f. Is often touchy or easily annoyed by others YES   NO

    g. Is often angry and resentful   YES   NO

    h. Is often spiteful or vindictive   YES   NO

CONDUCT DISORDER

2. Which of the following behaviors is your adolescent currently exhibiting, and has your adolescent been exhibiting for the past 6—12 months? (Circle YES if behavior is currently exhibited and has occurred over the past 6—12 months.)

Aggression to people and animals

    a. Often bullies, threatens, or intimidates others
                                                                         YES   NO

    b. Often initiates physical fights   YES   NO

c. Has used a weapon that can cause serious physical harm to others (e.g., a bat, brick, broken bottle, knife, gun)   YES   NO

d. Has been physically cruel to people   YES   NO

e. Has been physically cruel to animals   YES   NO

f. Has stolen while confronting a victim (e.g., mugging, purse snatching, extortion, armed robbery)   YES   NO

g. Has forced someone into sexual activity   YES   NO

Destruction of property

h. Has deliberately engaged in fire-setting with the intention of causing serious damage
                                            YES   NO

i. Has deliberately destroyed others' property (other than by fire-setting)
                                            YES   NO

Deceitfulness or theft

j. Has broken into someone else's house, building, or car
                                            YES   NO

k. Often lies to obtain goods or favors or to avoid obligations (i.e., "cons" others)
                                            YES   NO

MOOD DISORDERS

3. In the past month, has your adolescent felt or acted depressed, most of the day, every day, for any period of time?   YES   NO

4. If YES, did the depressed mood last at least 2 weeks?
                                            YES   NO

5. Did the depressed mood interfere with daily functioning in school, at home, with peers, or in recreation?   YES   NO

6. Have there been any other periods of depressed mood earlier in your adolescent's life, lasting most of the day, every day, for at least 2 weeks?
                                            YES   NO

7. Has your adolescent been depressed, most of the time, for the past year?
                                            YES   NO

8. Has your adolescent become depressed, for several days, in response to any acutely upsetting event (e.g., breakup with boyfriend/girlfriend, failing a test, argument with you)?
                                            YES   NO

9. Has there been any period, within the past month, when your adolescent felt or acted abnormally irritable (e.g., screaming, shouting, yelling, etc., with extreme intensity)?   YES   NO

10. Did this period of irritability last for more than a few hours, even for days or weeks?
                                            YES   NO

(continued)

11. Has there ever been any other period, earlier in your adolescent's life, when he or she was abnormally irritable for long periods of time?

    YES   NO

12. Has there been any period, within the past month, when your adolescent felt or acted very elated, manic, or in a high mood (not connected with drugs)?

    YES   NO

13. Did this period of elation or mania last more than a few hours, even for days or weeks?

    YES   NO

14. Has there ever been any other period, earlier in your adolescent's life, when he or she was abnormally elated, manic, or in a high mood (not connected with drugs) for long periods?   YES   NO

ANXIETY DISORDERS

15. Has your adolescent ever had a panic attack, in which he or she suddenly felt very frightened, anxious, or extremely uncomfortable?

    YES   NO

16. Has your adolescent ever been afraid of going out of the house alone, being in a crowd, standing in line, traveling on buses, trains, or riding in cars?

    YES   NO

17. Has your adolescent ever been afraid of doing things in front of other people, like speaking, eating, or writing, or of interacting with other people?

    YES   NO

18. Has your adolescent ever been afraid of going to school (e.g., truly afraid, not trying to avoid school)?   YES   NO

19. Has your adolescent ever been very afraid of things like flying, heights, seeing blood, thunder, lightening, closed places, animals, or insects?

    YES   NO

20. Has your adolescent ever been bothered by thoughts that didn't make any sense and kept coming back even when he or she tried not to have them?

    YES   NO

21. Has your adolescent ever had things that he or she had to do over and over again and couldn't resist (e.g., compulsive acts such as washing hands, checking something, touching things in a certain order, walking a certain way)?

    YES   NO

22. Has your adolescent ever been in a very dangerous/traumatic situation, or witnessed firsthand a very dangerous/traumatic situation? (violence, physical/sexual abuse, accident, near-death situation, etc.)   YES   NO

23. If YES to 22, has your adolescent ever had these things come back over and over again in nightmares, flashbacks, or obsessive thoughts?

    YES   NO

24. In the past 6 months, has your adolescent been generally worried, anxious, and nervous for at least half of the time (not in response to just one event)?
                                        YES   NO

TIC/MOVEMENT DISORDERS

25. Has your adolescent ever had any tics (involuntary, rapid, recurrent movements such as eye blinking, twitches, or head turning, etc.)?
                                        YES   NO

26. Does your adolescent ever say words or make other sounds, besides burping or hiccups, that are not intended, that keep repeating, and that he or she can't stop?
                                        YES   NO

27. Has your adolescent ever had any unusual habits, movements, etc.?
                                        YES   NO

EATING/SLEEP DISORDERS

28. Has your adolescent ever had a period of being underweight? For girls, during this time, did she stop menstruating or have irregular periods?
                                        YES   NO

29. Has your adolescent ever been afraid of getting fat or believed that he or she is fat when in reality he or she is not?   YES   NO

30. Has your adolescent ever engaged in out-of-control eating (e.g., eating a lot in a short time and feeling out of control about it)?   YES   NO

31. Has your adolescent ever gotten rid of unwanted food and calories through vomiting, using laxatives, excessive
exercise, or fasting?   YES   NO

32. Does your adolescent have any difficulty with sleep (getting to sleep, staying asleep, waking up)?   YES   NO

PSYCHOTIC SYMPTOMS

33. Has your adolescent ever reported seeing, hearing, smelling, or feeling things that were not based in reality?   YES   NO

34. Has your adolescent ever reported having any of the following possibly delusional beliefs:

    a. People were taking special notice of him or her
                                        YES   NO

    b. Receiving special messages from TV, radio, newspaper, etc.
                                        YES   NO

    c. Feeling important and having special powers that others don't have
                                        YES   NO

    d. Something strange happening to his or her body despite doctor finding nothing
                                        YES   NO

    c. Feeling he or she committed a crime and should be punished
                                        YES   NO

(continued)

f. Something external to the teenager is controlling his or her thoughts and actions against his or her will (beyond normal complaints that parents are too controlling)

YES   NO

g. Thoughts that are not his or her own are being put into his or her head

YES   NO

h. Thoughts are being broadcast so others can hear them

YES   NO

DRUGS/ALCOHOL

35. Does your adolescent have any problems with alcohol or drugs?

YES   NO

APPENDIX G

Resources for ADHD Information

For Individuals With ADHD

For Adolescents

CH.A.D.D. (1996). *ADD and adolescence: Strategies for success from CH.A.D.D.* Columbia, MO: Hawthorne Educational Services, Inc. 800-542-1673. Fax (800-442-9509).

Greenbaum, J., & Markel, G. (2001). *Helping adolescents with ADHD and learning disabilities: Ready to use tips, techniques, and checklists for school success.* Paramus, NJ: The Center for Applied Research in Education.

Nadeau, K. G. (1998). *Help4ADD@High School.* Bethesda, MD: Advantage Books.

Parker, R. N. (1992). *Making the grade: An adolescent's struggle with ADD.* Hawthorne Educational Services, Inc. (800-542-1673) Fax (800-442-9509).

Robin, L. (1998). *ADHD in adolescents.* New York: Guilford Press.

Taymans, J. M., West, L. L., Sullivan, M., & Scheiber, B. (2000). *Unlocking potential: College and other choice for people with LD and AD/HD.* Woodbine House.

Quinn, P. (1995). *Adolescents and ADD: Gaining the advantage.* Washington, DC: Magination Press.

Quinn, P., & Stern, J. (2001). *Putting on the breaks, revised edition.* Magination Press. Available at Child's Work, Child's Play (800-962-1141) or Hawthorne Educational Services, Inc. (800-542-1673) Fax (800-442-9509).

Wender, P. (2001). *ADHD: Attention deficit hyperactivity disorder in children, adolescents, and adults.* New York: Oxford University Press.

Zeigler Dendy, C. A., & Zeiler, A. (2003). *A bird's-eye view of life with ADD and ADHD: Advice from young survivors.* Cedar Bluff, AL: Cherish the Children. <www.crisdency.com>

For Adults With ADHD

Barkley, R. (2006). *ADHD: A handbook for diagnosis and treatment.* New York: Guilford Press.

Bell, M. T. (2002). *You, your relationship, and your ADD.* Oakland, CA: New Harbinger Publishing Company.

Brown, D. (2000). *Learning a living: A guide to planning your career and finding a job for people with learning disabilities, attention deficit disorder, and dyslexia.* Bethesda, MD: Woodbine House, Inc.

Hallowell, E. M., & Ratey, J. (1994). *Driven to distraction.* NY: Pantheon.

Katz, L. J., Goldstein, G., & Beers, S. R. (2001). *Learning disabilities in older adolescents and adults.* New York: Kluwer Academic/Plenum Press.

Kelly, K., & Ramundo, P. (1995). *You mean I'm not lazy, stupid, or crazy? A self-help book for adults with attention deficit disorder.* Hawthorne Educational Services, Inc. (800-542-1673) Fax (800-442-9509).

Kolberg, J., & Nadeau, K. (2002). *ADD-friendly ways to organize your life*. New York: Brunner-Routledge.

Monastra, V. J. (2004). *Parenting children with ADHD: 10 lessons that medicine cannot teach*. American Psychological Association.

Murphy, K., & Levert, S. (1995). *Out of the fog: Coping strategies for adult attention deficit disorder*. New York: Hyperion.

Nadeau, K. (1996). *Adventures in fast forward: Life, love, and work for the ADD adult*. Florence, KY: Brunner/Mazel.

Nadeau, K., & Quinn, P. (Eds.). (2002). *Understanding women with AD/HD*. Silver Spring, MD: Advantage Books.

Novotni, M. (2000). *What does everybody know that I don't?*. Plantation, FL: Specialty Press, Inc.

Solden, S. (2002). *Journeys through ADDulthood*. NY: Walker Publishing Co.

Weiss, L. (1992). *Attention deficit disorder in adults*. Hawthorne Educational Services, Inc. (800-542-1673) Fax (800-442-9509).

Weiss, L. (1994). *The attention deficit disorder in adults workbook*. Hawthorne Educational Services, Inc. (800-542-1673) Fax (800-442-9509).

For Children

Caffrey, J. A. (1997). *First star I see* (for girls with ADHD). Hawthorne Educational Services, Inc. (800-542-1673) Fax (800-442-9509).

Carpenter, P., & Ford, M. (1999). *Sparky's excellent misadventures: My A.D.D. journal*. Magination Press.

Galvin, M. (2001). *Otto learns about his medicine: A story about medication for children with ADHD*. Magination Press.

Gantos, J. (2000). *Joey Pigza loses control*. Farrar, Straus and Giroux.

Gehret, J. (1996). *Eagle eyes: A child's guide to paying attention* (2nd ed.). Hawthorne Educational Services, Inc. (800-542-1673) Fax (800-442-9509).

Gordon, M. (1991). *Jumpin' Johnny get back to work! A child's guide to ADHD/hyperactivity*. Hawthorne Educational Services, Inc. (800-542-1673) Fax (800-442-9509).

Kraus, J., & Martin, W. (2004). *Copy stories: A kid's book about living with ADHD*. Washington, DC: Magination Press.

Moss, D. (1989). *Shelly the hyperactive turtle*. Available at Child's Work, Child's Play (800-962-1141).

Nadeau, K. G., Dixon, E. B., & Beyl, C. (2004). *Learning to slow down and pay attention: A book for kids about ADHD (3rd edition)*. Magination Press.

Switzer, N. (2005). *Stop the traffic and let me out: A book about ADHD*. BookSurge Publishing.

Taylor, J. F. (2006). *The survival guide for kids with ADD or ADHD*. Free Spirit Publishing.

For College Students

Bramer, J. (1996). *Succeeding in college with attention deficit disorders*. Hawthorne Educational Services, Inc. (800-542-1673) Fax (800-442-9509).

Kravets, M., & Wax, I. (2002). *The K & W guide to colleges for the learning disabled*. New York: HarperCollins.

Mooney, J., & Cole, D. (2000). *Learning outside the lines: Two ivy league students with learning disabilities and AD/HD give you the tools for academic success and educational revolution*. New York: Simon and Schuster.

Murphy, K., & Levert, S. (1995). *Out of the fog: Coping strategies for adult attention deficit disorder*. New York: Hyperion.

Nadeau, K. (1994). *College survival guide for students with ADD or LD*. New York: Brunner/Mazel.

Quinn, P. O. (2001). *ADD and the college student, revised*. Hawthorne Educational Services, Inc. (800-542-1673) Fax (800-442-9509).

Roberts, S. M., & Jansen, G. (1997). *Living with ADD: A workbook for adults with attention deficit disorder*. Hawthorne Educational Services, Inc. (800-542-1673) Fax (800-442-9509).

For Family Members

For Brothers and Sisters
Gehret, J. (1992). *I'm somebody too*. Verbal Images Press.
Gordon, M. (1992). *My brother's a world-class pain: A sibling's guide to ADHD/hyperactivity*. Hawthorne Educational Services, Inc. (800-542-1673) Fax (800-442-9509).

For Parents
Alexander-Roberts, C. (1994). *The ADHD parenting handbook: Practical advice for parents from parents*. Hawthorne Educational Services, Inc. (800-542-1673) Fax (800-442-9509).
Alexander-Roberts, C. (2001). *ADHD and teens*. Dallas, TX: Taylor Trade Publishing.
Ashley, S. (2005). *ADD and ADHD answer book*. Sourcebooks.
Barkley, R. A. (2000). *Taking charge of ADHD (Revised Edition)*. NY: Guilford Publications, Inc. (800-365-7006).
Block, M. A. (1996). *No more Ritalin: Treating ADHD without drugs*. Kensington Publishing Corporation.
Block, M. A. (2001). *No more ADHD*. Block System.
Copeland, E. D., & Love, V. (1991). *Attention please! A comprehensive guide for successfully parenting children with attention disorders and hyperactivity*. Hawthorne Educational Services, Inc. (800-542-1673) Fax (800-442-9509).
Goldstein, S., & Goldstein, M. (1989). *Why won't my child pay attention?* Hawthorne Educational Services, Inc. (800-542-1673) Fax (800-442-9509).
Honos-Webb, L. (2005). *The gift of ADHD: How to transform your child's problems into strengths*. Santa Clara, CA: New Harbinger Publications.
Jensen, P. S. (2004). *Making the system work for your child with ADHD*. The Guilford Press.
Lavin, P., & Lavin, K. (2005). *A comprehensive guide for parenting the ADHD child*. PublishAmerica.
Martin, K. (2005). *Celebrate! ADHD*. Washington, DC: Cantwell-Hamilton Press.
Nadeau, K. G. (2000). *Understanding girls with AD/HD*. Silver Spring, MD: Advantage Books.
Reiff, M. I., Tippins, S., & LeTourneau, A. A. (2004). *ADHD: A complete and authoritative guide*. American Academy of Pediatrics.
Robin, A. (1998). *ADHD in adolescents: Diagnosis and treatment*. New York: Guilford Press (800-365-7006).
Shapiro, L. E. (1996). *Sometimes I know I drive my mom crazy but I know she is crazy about me*. Hawthorne Educational Services, Inc. (800-542-1673) Fax (800-442-9509).
Shaywitz, S., & Shawitz, B. (1992). *Attention deficit disorder come of age—Toward the 21st century*. Austin TX: Pro-Ed. (512) 451-3246.
Stevens, L. J. (2000). *Twelve effective ways to help your ADD/ADHD child: Drug-free alternatives for attention deficit disorders*. Avery.
Weiss, L. (1996). *Give your ADD teen a chance: A guide for parents of teenagers with attention deficit disorder*. Colorado Springs, CO: Pinon Press.
Wilens, T. E. (2004). *Straight talk about psychiatric medications for kids, revised edition*. The Guilford Press.
Zeigler Dendy, C. A. (1995). *Teenagers with ADD: A parents' guide (The Special-Needs Collection)*. Bethesda, MD: Woodbine House.

Intervention Information (Child, Adolescent, and Adult)

Barkley, R. A. (1997). *Defiant children: A clinician's manual for assessment and parent training*. New York: Guilford Press (800-365-7006).

Barkley, R. A. (2006). *Attention deficit hyperactivity disorder: A handbook for diagnosis and treatment (3rd ed.)*. New York: Guilford Press (800-365-7006).

Feingold Association, PO Box 6550, Alexandria, VA 22306 (703-768-FAUS).

Flick, G. L. (2002). *ADD/ADHD behavior-change resource kit: Ready-to-use strategies & activities for helping children with attention deficit disorder*. Jossey-Bass.

Greenbaum, J., & Markel, J. (2001). *Helping adolescents with ADHD & learning disabilities: Ready-to-use tips, techniques, and checklists for school success*. Paramus, NJ: Jossey-Bass.

Goldstein, S., & Goldstein, M. (1999). *Managing ADHD in children: A guide for practitioners*. New York: John Wiley & Sons (212-850-6011) Fax (212-850-6008).

O'Dell, N. E., & Cook, P. (2004). *Stopping ADHD*. NY: Penguin Group.

Rief, S. F. (2002). *The ADD/ADHD checklist*. San Francisco, CA: Jossey-Bass.

Rief, S. F. (2003). *The ADHD book of lists: A practical guide for helping children and teens with attention deficit disorders*. San Francisco, CA: Jossey-Bass.

Rief, S. F. (2005). *How to reach and teach children with ADD/ADHD: Practical techniques, strategies, and interventions*. San Francisco, CA: Jossey-Bass.

Robin, A. L. (2002). Lifestyle issues. In S. Goldstein & A. Teeter Ellison (Eds.), *Clinician's guide to adult ADHD: Assessment and intervention* (pp. 280–291). New York: Academic Press.

Safren, S. A., Sprich, S., Perlman, C. A., & Otto, M. W. (2005). *Mastering your adult ADHD: A cognitive-behavioral treatment program*. Oxford University Press.

Teeter, P. (1998). *Interventions for ADHD: Treatment in a developmental context*. New York: Guilford Press (800-365-7006).

For Counselors and School Psychologists
ADD Warehouse
300 NW 70th Avenue
Suite 102
Plantation, Florida
www.addwarehouse.com
Fax 954-792-8545
(800) 233-9273

Child's Work Child's Play (800) 962-1141
Games available:
Jumpn' Jake Settles Down (3–12 years)
Look Before You Leap! (3–12 years)
Stop, Relax, and Think (6–12 years)
The Solutions Kit for ADHD (6–12 years)

For Teachers
ADD Warehouse
300 NW 70th Avenue
Suite 102 Plantation, Florida
www.addwarehouse.com
Fax 954-792-8545
(800) 233-9273

Child's Work, Child's Play (educational materials) (800) 962-1141.

Copeland, E. D., & Love, V. L. (1995). *Attention without tension: A teacher's handbook on attention disorders (ADHD and ADD)*. Plantation, FL: Specialty Press.

Davis, L., & Sirotowitz, S. (1996). *Study strategies made easy: A practical plan for school success*. Plantation, FL: Specialty Press.

DuPaul, G., & Stoner, G. (2003). *ADHD in the schools (2nd edition)*. New York: Guilford Press (800-365-7006).

Minskoff, E., & Allsopp, D. (2002). *Academic success strategies for adolescents with learning disabilities and ADHD*. Brookes Publishing Company.

Parker, H. C. (1992). *Attention deficit accommodation plan for teaching (ADAPT)*. Hawthorne Educational Services, Inc. (800-542-1673) Fax (800-442-9509).

Parker, H. C., & Gordon, M. (1992). *Teaching the child with attention deficit disorders: A slide program for in-service teacher training*. Columbia, MO: Hawthorne Educational Services, Inc. (800-542-1673) Fax (800-442-9509).

Parker, H. C. (2005). *The ADHD handbook for schools: Effective strategies for identifying and teaching students with attention-deficit/hyperactivity disorder*. Specialty Press/A.D.D. Warehouse.

Pfinner, L. (1996). *All about ADHD: The complete practical guide for classroom teachers*. NY: Scholastic.

Quinn, P., & McCormick, A. (1998). *Re-thinking AD/HD: A guide to foster success in students with AD/HD at the college level*. Silver Spring, MD: Advantage Books.

Quinn, P., Ratey, N., & Maitland, T. (2000). *Coaching college students with AD/HD: Issues and answers*. Silver Spring: MD: Advantage Books, LLC.

Zeigler Dendy, C. A. (2000). *Teaching teens with ADD and ADHD: A quick reference guide for teachers and parents*. Bethesda, MD: Woodbine House.

General Information

Legal Information About ADHD

Latham, P. S., & Latham, P. H. (1996). *Documentation and the law*. Hawthorne Educational Services, Inc. (800-542-1673) Fax (800-442-9509).

Latham, P. S., & Latham, P. H. (2002). What clinician's need to know about legal issues relative to ADHD. In S. Goldstein, & Ellison, A. T. (Eds.), *Clinician's Guide to Adult ADHD: Assessment and Intervention* (pp. 205–219). Boston: Academic Press.

Martín, J. L. (1998). *Overview of Basic IDEA Issues: ARD Committees, Parents, LRE, IEPs, and Avoiding Due Process Hearings*. Austin, TX: Richards Lindsay & Martin, L.L.P. <http://www.504idea.org/IDEA_ Basics.pdf>

Richards, D. M. (2002). *An overview of §504*. Austin, TX: Richards Lindsay & Martin, L. L. P. <http://www.504idea.org/504_ Overview_ Fall_a 2003.pdf>

Streett, S., & Smith, T. E. C. (1996). *Section 504 and public schools: A practical guide*. PO Box 251186, Little Rock, AR 72225 (501-569-3016).

U.S. Department of Education. (1999). *Free appropriate public education for students with disabilities: Requirements under section 504 of the Rehabilitation Act of 1973*. <http://www.ed.gov/about/offices/list/ocr/docs/edlite-FAPE504.html>

Overview of Research Findings Concerning ADHD

Barkley, R. A., & Gordon, M. (2002). Research on comorbidity, adaptive functioning, and cognitive impairments in adults with AD/HD: Implications for a clinical practice. In S. Goldstein & A. Teeter Ellison (Eds.), *Clinician's guide to adult ADHD: Assessment and intervention* (pp. 43–69). New York: Academic Press.

Barkley, R. A. (2005). *ADHD and the nature of self-control*. NY: The Guilford Press.

Barkley, R. A. (2006). *Attention deficit hyperactivity disorder: A handbook for diagnosis and treatment (3rd ed.).* New York: Guilford Press (800-365-7006).

Brown, T. (Ed.). (2000). *Attention deficit disorders and comorbidities in children, adolescents, and adults.* Washington, DC: American Psychiatric Press.

Goldstein, S., & Goldstein, M. (1998). *Managing ADHD in children: A guide for practitioners.* New York: John Wiley & Sons (212-850-6011) Fax (212-850-6008).

Zentall, S. S. (2005). *ADHD and education: Foundations, characteristics, methods, and collaboration.* Prentice Hall.

Professional Assessment Materials

ADHD: A Clinical Workbook (Barkley, R., & Murphy, K.) NY: Guilford Press (800-365-7006).

ADHD Rating Scale IV (DuPaul, G., Power, T., Anastopoulos, A., & Reid, R.) NY: Guilford Press (800-365-7006).

Behavior Assessment Scale for Children (BASC). (Kamphaus, R., & Reynolds, C.) American Guidance Systems. Ages: 4–18. (800-328-2560).

Child Behavior Checklist, Teacher Report Form, and Youth Self Report (Achenbach, T). Center for Children, Youth, and Families. University of Vermont, 1 South Prospect Street, Burlington, VT 05401.

Conners Rating Scales—Revised, and Conners Adult ADHD Rating Scales (Conners, K.) Multi-Health Systems, Inc. Ages 3–17 and Adults (800-456-3003).

Videotapes

ADDA. (2001). *ADD: Transition to college—Passport for success.* Silver Spring, MD: ADDvance Seminars. www.add.org

Barkley, R. A. (1992). *ADHD—What do we know?* (36 minutes). Hawthorne Educational Services, Inc. (800-542-1673) Fax (800-442-9509).

Barkley, R. A. (1993). *ADHD in the classroom: Strategies for teachers.* (40 minutes). Hawthorne Educational Services, Inc. (800-542-1673) Fax (800-442-9509).

Barkley, R. A. (1997). *Understanding the defiant child.* NY: Guilford Press.

Barkley, R. A. (1997). *ADHD in Adults.* Guilford Press.

George Washington University. (1996). *ADD: The race inside my head.* 614-488-1174.

Goldstein, S. (1991). *It's just attention disorder: A video guide for kids.* (30 minutes). Hawthorne Educational Services, Inc. (800-542-1673) Fax (800-442-9509).

Phelan, T. W. (1990). *All about ADD: Parts 1 and 2.* (108 and 85 minutes). Hawthorne Educational Services, Inc. (800-542-1673) Fax (800-442-9509).

Rief, S. (2004). *ADHD & LD: Powerful teaching strategies and accommodations.* Educational Resource Specialists.

Rief, S. F. (2005). *ADHD book of lists & ADHD & LD video set.* John Wiley & Sons. Hawthorne Educational Services, Inc. (800-542-1673) Fax (800-442-9509).

Quinn, P. (1993). *ADD and the college student and approaching college for students with ADD.* Washington, DC: Pediatric Development Center. 202-966-1561.

Web sites

www.ama-assn.org

www.chadd.org

www.healthyplace.com

www.504idea.org/

www.nimh.nih.gov/publicat/adhd.cfm

www.apa.org

www.add.org

www.webmd.com

www.ed.gov

www.cdc.gov/ncbddd/adhd/

National Associations and Support Groups

Adult ADD Association
1225 East Sunset Drive
Suite 640
Bellingham, WA 98226

American Psychiatric Association
1400 K Street, North West
Washington, DC 20005
(202-682-6000)

American Psychological Association (APA)
750 First Street, North East
Washington, DC 20002
(202-336-5500)

Attention Deficit Disorder Association (ADDA)
19262 Jamboree Road
Irving, CA 92715
(800-487-2282)

Children and Adults with Attention Deficit Disorders (CH.A.D.D.)
8181 Professional Place, Suite 201
Landover, MD 20785
(301-306-7070)

Learning Disabilities Association (LDA)
4156 Library Road
Pittsburgh, PA 15234
(412-341-1515)

On-Line ADD Support Room
America Online: Search for "ADD"
CompuServe: Search for "Go ADD"
Newsletters & Magazines
Netscape: Search for ADD or ADHD

ADDult News
Johnson, M. J.
2620 Ivy Place
Toledo, OH 43613

The ADHD Report
Barkley, R. A., and Associates
Guilford Publications, Inc.
72 Spring Street
New York, NY 10012
(800-365-7006)

Brakes: The Interactive Newsletter for Kids with ADHD
Quinn, B., & Stern, J.
Magination Press
19 Union Square West
New York, NY 10003
(800-825-3089)

Chadder and Chadder Box (CH.A.D.D.)
8181 Professional Place, Suite 201
Landover, MD 20785
(301-306-7070)

Suggested Outline for an In-Service Training on ADHD

I. **What Is ADHD?** (Handouts)
   - Current diagnostic criteria
   - Prevalence rates
   - Gender ratio

II. **What Causes ADHD?** (Video Clips)
   - No single cause
   - Prenatal theories
   - Neurochemical theories
   - Neuroanatomical theories
   - Other
   - Myths

III. **Problems in the Classroom?** (Examples)
   - Academic underachievement
   - Learning problems
   - Organizational
   - Behavioral
   - Other

IV. **How Is It Treated?** (Handouts, Video Clips, Examples)
   - Academic interventions
   - Behavioral interventions
   - Skills training (social skills, problem solving, organization)
   - Counseling
   - Home-school collaboration
   - Support groups
   - Medication
   - Other
   - Myths

V. **Legal Issues** (Handouts, Examples)
   - ADA, IDEA, and 504

Note: From Weyandt (2001).

APPENDIX I

Functional Behavior Analysis Worksheet

To help identify the factors that might be triggering and sustaining problem behaviors observe the student's behavior and record the following information. Be sure to provide specific descriptions.

Date: _____ Time: _____ Teacher: _____ Student: _____

Precipitating Conditions	Behavior (Describe)	Consequences (What follows?)	Function (Hypothesized)
Academic instruction	_____	Loss of privilege	Attention
Small group activity	_____	Peer attention	Avoidance
Solitary seat work	_____	Teacher attention	Intimidation
Unstructured activity	_____	Time-out	Stimulation
Other _____	_____	Verbal reprimand	Tangibles
Other _____	_____	Other _____	Other _____
Additional Information _____			

After defining the problem behavior, answer each of the following:

1. How frequently does the problem occur?

2. How long does the problem behavior last?

3. In what situations does the problem behavior occur?

4.. In what situations does the problem behavior not occur?

5. What is the desired behavior?

Note: From Weyandt (2001).

APPENDIX J

Social Skills Assessment

(Parent Form)

Name _____ Date _____

Individual Completing This Form _____

( ) Mother   ( ) Father   ( ) Foster Parent

Description: Please check any statements which you feel describe your child or adolescent. Please make note if there are differences in your child's behavior with siblings or peers.

Not True	Sometimes True	Frequently True	My Child:
_____	_____	_____	appears socially isolated. For example, he or she spends a large proportion of time engaged in solitary activities, and may be judged independent and capable of taking care of himself/herself.
_____	_____	_____	interacts less with friends, appearing shy and timid. My child can be described as somewhat overanxious with others.
_____	_____	_____	spends less time involved in activities with other children due to a lack of social skills and/or appropriate social judgment.
_____	_____	_____	appears to have fewer friends than other children due to negative, bossy, or annoying behaviors that "turn off" others.
_____	_____	_____	spends less time with friends than most due to awkward or bizarre behaviors.
_____	_____	_____	distrubs others: teases, provokes, fights, interrupts others.
_____	_____	_____	openly strikes back with angry behavior to the teasing of others.

Source: From S. Goldstein. (1988). *Social Skills Assessment Questionnaire.* Printed with permission of the author.

Not True	Sometimes True	Frequently True	My Child:
____	____	____	can be argumentative and must have the last word in verbal exchanges.
____	____	____	displays physical aggression toward objects or persons.
____	____	____	will manipulate or threaten peers.
____	____	____	speaks to others in an impatient or cranky tone of voice: says uncomplimentary or unpleasant things to others. For example may engage in name calling or ridicule.
____	____	____	will respond when other children initiate conversation.
____	____	____	will engage in long conversations.
____	____	____	will share laughter with friends.
____	____	____	will spontaneously contribute to a family discussion.
____	____	____	can take a leadership role at home.
____	____	____	will work with family members on projects.
____	____	____	can verbally initiate with family members.

Additional Comments: _____

_____

_____

_____

REFERENCES

Abidin, R. R. (1983). *Parenting stress index*. Charlottesville, VA: Pediatric Psychology Press.

Abikoff, H. (1991). Cognitive training in ADHD children: Less to it than meets the eye. *Journal of Learning Disabilities, 24*, 205–209.

Abikoff, H., Courtney, M. E., Szeibel, P. J., & Koplewicz, H. S. (1996). The effects of auditory stimulation on the arithmetic performance of children with ADHD and nondisabled children. *Journal of Learning Disabilities, 29*, 238–246.

Abikoff, H., Ganeles, D., Reiter, G., Blum, C., Foley, C., & Klein, R. G. (1988). Cognitive training in academically deficient ADHD boys receiving stimulant medication. *Journal of Abnormal Child Psychology, 16*, 411–432.

Abramowitz, A., O'Leary, S., & Futtersak, M. (1988). The relative impact of long and short reprimands on children's off-task behavior in the classroom. *Behavior Therapy, 19*, 243–247.

Abramowitz, A., O'Leary, S., & Rosen, L. (1987). Reducing off-task behavior in the classroom: A comparison of encouragement and reprimands. *Journal of Abnormal Child Psychology, 15*, 153–163.

Achenbach, T. M. (2001). *Manuals for the Child Behavior Checklist, Teachers Report Form, and the Youth Self-Report and 2001 Profiles*. Burlington, VT: University of Vermont.

Acker, M. M., & O'Leary, S. G. (1987). Effects of reprimands and praise on appropriate behavior in the classroom. *Journal of Abnormal Child Psychology, 15*, 549–557.

Alberts, E., & van der Meere, J. (1992). Observations of hyperactive behavior during vigilance. *Journal of Clinical Psychology and Psychiatry, 33*, 1355–1364.

Alberts-Corush, J., Firestone, P., & Goodman, J. T. (1986). Attention and impulsivity characteristics of the biological and adoptive parents of hyperactive and normal control children. *American Journal of Orthopsychiatry, 56*, 413–423.

Alessandri, S. M. (1992). Attention play on social behavior in ADHD preschoolers. *Journal of Abnormal Child Psychology, 20*, 289–302.

American Academy of Pediatrics. (1987). Committee on drugs report: Medication for children with attention deficit disorder. *Pediatrics, 80*, 5.

American Academy of Pediatrics. (2000). Clinical practice guideline: Diagnosis and evaluation of the child with attention-deficit/hyperactivity disorder. *Pediatrics, 105*, 1158–1170.

American Psychiatric Association. (1968). *Diagnostic and statistical manual of mental disorders* (2nd ed.). Washington, DC: Author.

American Psychiatric Association. (1980). *Diagnostic and statistical manual of mental disorders* (3rd ed.). Washington, DC: Author.

American Psychiatric Association. (1987). *Diagnostic and statistical manual of mental disorders* (3rd ed. rev.). Washington, DC: Author.

American Psychiatric Association. (1994). *Diagnostic and statistical manual of mental disorders* (4th ed.). Washington, DC: Author.

American Psychiatric Association. (2000). *Diagnostic and statistical manual of mental disorders* (4th ed., text revision). Washington, DC: Author.

Americans with Disabilities Act of 1990, 42 U.S.C. §§ 12101 et seq.

Amin, K., Douglas, V. I., Mendelson, M. J., & Dufresen, J. (1993). Separable/integral classification by hyperactive and normal children. *Development and Psychopathology, 5*, 415–431.

Anastopoulos, A. D. (1993). Assessing ADHD with the child behavior checklist. *The ADHD Report, 1*, 3–4.

Anastopoulos, A. D., Smith, J. M., & Wien, E. E. (2006). Counseling and training parents. In R. A. Barkley (Ed.), *Attention-deficit/hyperactivity disorder: A handbook for diagnosis and treatment* (2nd ed., pp. 453–479). New York: Guilford Press.

Anastopoulos, A. D., Spisto, M. A., & Maher, M. C. (1994). The WISC-III freedom from distractibility factor: Its utility in identifying children with attention-deficit/hyperactivity disorder. *Psychological Assessment, 6*, 368–371.

Anderson, G. M., Dover, M. A., Yang, B. P., Holahan, J. M., Shaywitz, S. E., Marchione, K. E., et al. (2000). Adrenomedullary function during cognitive testing in attention-deficit/hyperactivity disorder. *Journal of the American Academy of Child and Adolescent Psychiatry, 39*, 635–643.

Andrés, M. A., Catalá, M. A., & Gómez-Beneyto, M. (1999). Prevalence, comorbidity, risk factors and service utilization of disruptive behavior disorders in a community sample of children in Valencia (Spain). *Social Psychiatry and Psychiatric Epidemiology, 34*, 175–179.

Angello, L. M., Volpe, R. J., DiPerna, J. C., Gureasko-Moore, S. P., Gureasko-Moore, D. P., Nebrig, M. R., et al. (2003). Assessment of attention-deficit/hyperactivity disorder: An evaluation of six published rating scales. *School Psychology Review, 32*, 241–262.

Angold, A., Erkanli, A., Egger, H. L., & Costello, J. E. (2000). Stimulant treatment for children: A community perspective. *Journal of the American Academy of Child and Adolescent Psychiatry, 39*, 975–987.

Anhalt, K., McNeil, C. B., & Bahl, A. B. (1998). The ADHD classroom kit: A whole-classroom approach for managing disruptive behavior. *Psychology in the Schools, 35*, 67–79.

Antrop, I., Buysse, A., Roeyers, H., & Van Oost, P. (2005). Activity in children with ADHD during waiting situations in the classroom: A pilot study. *British Journal of Educational Psychology, 75*(Pt. 1), 51–69.

Antrop, I., Roeyers, H., Van Oost, P., & Buysse, A. (2000). Stimulation seeking and hyperactivity in children with ADHD. Attention deficit hyperactivity disorder. *Journal of Child Psychology and Psychiatry, 41*, 225–231.

Antshel, K. M., & Remer, R. (2003). Social skills training in children with attention deficit hyperactivity disorder: A randomized-controlled clinical trial. *Journal of Clinical Child and Adolescent Psychology, 32*, 153–165.

Ardoin, S. P., & Martens, B. K. (2000). Testing the ability of children with attention deficit hyperactivity disorder to accurately report the effects of medication on their behavior. *Journal of Applied Behavior Analysis, 33*, 593–610.

Armstrong, T. (1995). *The myth of the ADD child.* New York: Dutton Press.

Arnold, L. E. (1999). Treatment alternatives for attention-deficit/hyperactivity disorder (ADHD). *Journal of Attention Disorders, 3*, 30–48.

Arnold, L. E., Bozzolo, H., Hollway, J., Cook, A., Disilvestro, R. A., Bozzolo, D. R., et al. (2005). Serum zinc correlates with parent- and teacher-rated inattention in children with attention-deficit/hyperactivity disorder. *Journal of Child and Adolescent Psychopharmacology, 15*, 628–636.

Arnold, L. E., Elliot, M., Sachs, L., Bird, H., Kraemer, H. C., Wells, K. C., et al. (2003). Effects of ethnicity on treatment attendance, stimulant response/dose, and 14-month outcome in ADHD. *Journal of Consulting and Clinical Psychology, 71*, 713–727.

Ashenafi, Y., Kebede, D., Desta, M., & Alem, A. (2000). Socio-demographic correlates of mental and behavioural disorders of children in Southern Ethiopia. *East African Medical Journal, 77*, 565–569.

Asherson, P., & IMAGE Consortium. (2004). Attention-deficit hyperactivity disorder in the post-genomic era. *European Child and Adolescent Psychiatry, 13*(Suppl. 1), I50–I70.

Asherson, P., Kuntsi, J., & Taylor, E. (2005). Unravelling the complexity of attention-deficit hyperactivity disorder: A behavioural genomic approach. *British Journal of Psychiatry, 187*, 103–105.

Auerbach, J. G., Atzaba-Poria, N., Berger, A., & Landau, R. (2004). Emerging developmental pathways to ADHD: Possible path markers in early infancy. *Neural Plasticity, 11*, 29–43.

Auiler, J. F., Liu, K., Lynch, J. M., & Gelotte, C. K. (2002). Effect of food on early drug exposure from extended-release stimulants: Results from the Concerta, Adderall XR Food Evaluation (CAFÉ) Study. *Current Medical Research and Opinion, 18*, 311–316.

Banaschewski, T., Besmens, F., Zieger, H., & Rothenberger, A. (2001). Evaluation of sensorimotor training in children with ADHD. *Perceptual and Motor Skills, 92*, 137–149.

Banez, G. A., & Overstreet, S. (1998). Parental strategies for promoting self-esteem in children and adolescents with ADHD. *The ADHD Report, 6*, 8–9.

Barbaresi, W., Katusic, S., Colligan, R., Weaver, A., Pankratz, V. Mrazek, D., et al. (2004). How common is attention-deficit/hyperactivity disorder? Towards resolution of the controversy: Results from a population-based study. *Acta Paediatrica, 93*, 55–59.

Barbaresi, W. J., & Olsen, R. D. (1998). An ADHD educational intervention for elementary schoolteachers: A pilot study. *Journal of Developmental and Behavioral Pediatrics, 19*, 94–100.

Barber, S., Grubbs, L., & Cottrell, B. (2005). Self-perception in children with attention deficit/hyperactivity disorder. *Journal of Pediatric Nursing, 20*, 235–245.

Barkley, R. A. (1990). *Attention-deficit/hyperactivity disorder: A handbook for diagnosis and treatment.* New York: Guilford Press.

Barkley, R. A. (1994). Choosing a teacher for a child with ADHD. *The ADHD Report, 2*, 1–3.

Barkley, R. A. (1996). Using a daily school-behavior report card. *The ADHD Report, 4*, 1–2, 13–16.

Barkley, R. A. (1997a). Behavioral inhibition, sustained attention, and executive functions: Constructing a unifying theory of ADHD. *Psychological Bulletin, 12*, 65–94.

Barkley, R. A. (1997b). *Defiant children: A clinician's manual for assessment and parent training* (2nd ed.). New York: Guilford Press.

Barkley, R. A. (2002). Major life activity and health outcomes associated with attention-deficit/hyperactivity disorder. *Journal of Clinical Psychiatry, 63*(Suppl. 12), 10–15.

Barkley, R. A. (2004). Adolescents with attention deficit/hyperactivity disorder: An overview of empirically based treatments. *Journal of Psychiatric Practice, 10*, 39–56.

Barkley, R. A. (2006). *Attention-deficit/hyperactivity disorder: A handbook for diagnosis and treatment* (3rd ed.). New York: Guilford Press.

Barkley, R. A., Anastopoulos, A. D., Guevremont, D. G., & Fletcher, K. E. (1991). Adolescents with ADHD: Patterns of behavioral adjustment, academic functioning, and treatment utilization. *Journal of the American Academy of Child and Adolescent Psychiatry, 30*, 752–761.

Barkley, R. A., Anastopolous, A. D., Guevremont, D. C., & Fletcher, K. E. (1992). Adolescents with attention-deficit/hyperactivity disorder: Mother-adolescent interactions, family beliefs and conflicts, and maternal psychopathology. *Journal of Abnormal Child Psychology, 20*, 263–288.

Barkley, R. A., Cunningham, C., & Karlsson, J. (1983). The speech of hyperactive children and their mothers: Comparisons with normal children and stimulant drug effects. *Journal of Learning Disabilities, 16*, 105, 110.

Barkley, R. A., DuPaul, G. J., & McMurray, M. B. (1990). A comprehensive evaluation of attention deficit disorder with and without hyperactivity. *Journal of Consulting and Clinical Psychology, 58*, 775–789.

Barkley, R. A., Edwards, G., Laneri, M., Fletcher, K., & Metevia, L. (2001). The efficacy of problem-solving communication training alone, behavior management training alone, and their combination for parent-adolescent conflict in teenagers with ADHD and ODD. *Journal of Consulting and Clinical Psychology, 69*, 926–941.

Barkley, R. A., Fischer, M., Edelbrock, C. S., & Smallish, L. (1990). The adolescent outcome of hyperactive children diagnosed by research criteria: An 8-year prospective followup study. *Journal of the American Academy of Child and Adolescent Psychiatry, 29*, 546–557.

Barkley, R. A., Fisher, M., Smallish, L., & Fletcher, K. (2002). The persistence of attention-deficit/hyperactivity disorder into young adulthood as a function of reporting source and definition of disorder. *Journal of Abnormal Psychology, 111*, 279–289.

Barkley, R. A., Fisher, M., Smallish, L., & Fletcher, K. (2003). Does the treatment of attention-deficit/hyperactivity disorder with stimulants contribute to drug use/abuse? A 13-year perspective study. *Pediatrics, 111*, 97–109.

Barkley, R. A., Grodzinsky, G. M., & DuPaul, G. J. (1992). Frontal lobe functions and attention deficit disorder with and without hyperactivity. A review and research report. *Journal of Abnormal Child Psychology, 20*, 163–188.

Barkley, R. A., Guevremont, D. C., Anastopolous, A. D., DuPaul, G. J., & Shelton, T. L. (1993). Driving related risks and outcomes of attention-deficit/hyperactivity disorder in adolescents and young adults: A 3–5 year follow-up survey. *Pediatrics, 92*, 212–218.

Barkley, R. A., Guevremont, D. C., Anastopolous, A. D., & Fletcher, K. E. (1992). A comparison of three family therapy programs for treating family conflicts in adolescents with attention-deficit hyperactivity disorder. *Journal of Consulting and Clinical Psychology, 60*, 450–462.

Barkley, R. A., McMurray, M. B., Edelbrock, C. S., & Robbins, K. (1990). The side effects of Ritalin in ADHD children: A systematic placebo-controlled evaluation of two doses. *Pediatrics, 86*, 184–192.

Barkley, R. A., & Murphy, K. R. (1998). *Attention-deficit/hyperactivity disorder: A clinical workbook* (2nd ed.). New York: Guilford Press.

Barkley, R. A., Murphy, K. R., DuPaul, G. I., & Bush, T. (2002). Driving in young adults with attention deficit hyperactivity disorder: Knowledge, performance, adverse outcomes, and the role of executive functioning. *Journal of the International Neuropsychological Society, 8*, 655–672.

Barkley, R. A., Shelton, T. L., Crosswait, C., Moorehouse, M., Fletcher, K., Barrett, S., et al. (2002). Preschool children with disruptive behavior: Three-year outcome as a function of adaptive disability. *Development and Psychopathology, 14*, 45–67.

Barr, C. L., Kroft, J., Feng, Y., Wigg, K., Roberts, W., Malone, M., et al. (2002). The norepinephrine transporter gene and attention deficit hyperactivity disorder. *American Journal of Medical Genetics, 114*, 255–259.

Bartell, S. S., & Solanto, M. V. (1995). Usefulness of the Rorschach inkblot test in the assessment of attention-deficit/hyperactivity disorder. *Perceptual and Motor Skills, 80*, 531–541.

Barthelemy, C., Bruneau, N., Cottet-Eymard, J. M., Domenech-Jouve, J., Garreau, B., Lelord, G., et al. (1988). Urinary free and conjugated catecholamines and metabolites in autistic children. *Journal of Autism and Developmental Disorders, 18*, 583–591.

Bauermeister, J. J., Barkley, R. A., Martinez, J. V., Cumba, E., Ramirez, R. R., Reina, G., et al. (2005). Time estimation and performance on reproduction tasks in subtypes of children with attention deficit hyperactivity disorder. *Journal of Clinical Child and Adolescent Psychology, 34*, 151–162.

Bauermeister, J. J., Matos, M., & Reina, G. (1999). Do the combined and inattentive types of ADHD have a similar impact on family life? *The ADHD Report, 7*, 6–8.

Baughman, F. A. (Producer). (2004). *ADHD-total 100% fraud* [Motion Picture]. (Available from Fred A. Baughman, Jr., 1303 Hidden Mountain Drive, El Cajon, CA 92019)

Baumgaertel, A., Wolraich, M. L., & Dietrich, M. (1995). Comparison of diagnostic criteria for attention deficit disorders in a German elementary school sample. *Journal of the American Academy of Child and Adolescent Psychiatry, 34,* 629–638.

Baving, L., Laucht, M., & Schmidt, M. H. (1999). Atypical frontal brain activation in ADHD: Preschool and elementary school boys and girls. *Journal of the American Academy of Child and Adolescent Psychiatry, 38,* 1363–1371.

Becker, K., Holtmann, M., Laucht, M., & Schmidt, M. H. (2004). Are regulatory problems in infancy precursors of later hyperkinetic symptoms? *Acta Paediatrica, 93,* 1463–1469.

Begun, R. W. (1995). *Social skills curriculum activities library.* Columbia, MO: Hawthorne.

Becker, K. B., & McCloskey, L. A. (2002). Attention and conduct problems in children exposed to family violence. *American Journal of Orthopsychiatry, 72,* 83–91.

Becker-Mattes, A., Mattes, J. A., Abikoff, H., & Brandt, L. (1985). State-dependent learning in hyperactive children receiving methylphenidate. *American Journal of Psychiatry, 142,* 455–459.

Beiser, M., Dion, R., & Gotowiec, A. (2000). The structure of attention-deficit and hyperactivity symptoms among Native and Non-Native elementary school children. *Journal of Abnormal Child Psychology, 28,* 425–437.

Bekle, B. (2004). Knowledge and attitudes about attention-deficit hyperactivity disorder (ADHD): A comparison between practicing teachers and undergraduate education students. *Journal of Attention Disorders, 7,* 151–161.

Belfiore, P. J., Grskovic, J. A., Murphy, A. M., & Zentall, S. S. (1996). The effects of antecedent color on reading for students with learning disabilities and co-occurring attention-deficit/hyperactivity disorder. *Journal of Learning Disabilities, 29,* 432–438.

Benjasuwantep, B., Ruangdaraganon, N., & Visudhipan, P. (2002). Prevalence and clinical characteristics of attention deficit hyperactivity disorder among primary school students in Bangkok. *Journal of the Medical Association of Thailand, 85*(Suppl. 4), S1232–S1240.

Berk, L. E., & Potts, M. K. (1991). Development and functional significance of private speech among attention-deficit hyperactivity disordered and normal boys. *Journal of Abnormal Child Psychology, 19,* 357–377.

Berkovitch, M., Pope, E., Phillips, J., et al. (1995). Pemoline-associated fulminant liver failure: Testing the evidence for causation. *Clinical Pharmacology and Therapeutics, 57,* 696–698.

Berman, T., Douglas, V. I., & Barr, R. G. (1999). Effects of methylphenidate on complex cognitive processing in attention-deficit hyperactivity disorder. *Journal of Abnormal Psychology, 108,* 90–105.

Berquin, P. C., Giedd, J. N., Jacobsen, L. K., Hamburger, S. D., Krain, A. L., Rapoport, J. L., et al. (1998). The cerebellum in attention-deficit/hyperactivity disorder: A morphometric study. *Neurology, 50,* 1087–1093.

Berry, C. A., Shaywitz, S. E., & Shaywitz, B. A. (1985). Girls with attention deficit disorder: A silent minority? A report on behavioral and cognitive characteristics. *Pediatrics, 76,* 801–809.

Bhatara, V., Feil, M., Hoagwood, K., Vitiello, B., & Zima, B. (2004). National trends in concomitant psychotropic medication with stimulants in pediatric visits: Practice versus knowledge. *Journal of Attention Disorders, 7,* 217–226.

Bhatara, V. S., Kumer, M., McMillin, M. J., & Bandettini, F. (1994). Screening for thyroid disease in ADHD. *The ADHD Report, 2,* 7–9.

Bhatia, M. S., Nigam, V. R., Bohra, N., & Malik, S. C. (1991). Attention deficit disorder with hyperactivity among pediatric outpatients. *Journal of Child Psychology and Psychiatry, 32,* 297–306.

Bhutta, A. T., Cleves, M. A., Casey, P. H., Cradock, M. M., & Anand, K. J. (2002). Cognitive and behavioral outcomes of school-aged children who were born preterm: A meta-analysis. *Journal of the American Medical Association, 288,* 728–737.

Bickett, L., & Milich, R. (1990). First impressions formed of boys with learning disabilities and attention deficit disorder. *Journal of Learning Disabilities, 23,* 253–259.

Biederman, J. (2004). Impact of comorbidity in adults with attention-deficit/hyperactivity disorder. *Journal of Clinical Psychiatry, 65*(Suppl. 3), 3–7.

Biederman, J. (2005). Attention-deficit/hyperactivity disorder: A selective overview. *Biological Psychiatry, 57,* 1215–1220.

Biederman, J., & Faraone, S. V. (2002). Current concepts on the neurobiology of attention-deficit/hyperactivity disorder. *Journal of Attention Disorders, 6*(Suppl. 1), S7–S16.

Biederman, J., & Faraone, S. V. (2004). The Massachusetts General Hospital studies of gender influences on attention-deficit/hyperactivity disorder in youth and relatives. *Psychiatric Clinics of North America, 27,* 225–232.

Biederman, J., Faraone, S. V., & Chen, W. J. (1993). Social adjustment inventory for children and adolescents: Concurrent validity in ADHD children. *Journal of the American Academy of Child and Adolescent Psychiatry, 32,* 1059–1064.

Biederman, J., Faraone, S. V., Mick, E., Spencer, T., Wilens, T., Kiely, K., et al. (1995). High risk for attention-deficit/hyperactivity disorder among children of parents with childhood onset of the disorder: A pilot study. *American Journal of Psychiatry, 152,* 431–435.

Biederman, J., Faraone, S. V., Mick, E., Williamson, S., Wilens, T. E., Spencer, T. J., et al. (1999). Clinical correlates of ADHD in females: Findings from a large group of girls ascertained from pediatric and psychiatric referral sources. *Journal of the American Academy of Child and Adolescent Psychiatry, 38,* 966–975.

Biederman, J., Faraone, S., Milberger, S., Curtis, S., Chen, L., Marrs, A., et al. (1996). Predictors of persistence and remission of ADHD into adolescence: Results from a four-year prospective follow-up study. *Journal of the American Academy of Child and Adolescent Psychiatry, 35,* 343–351.

Biederman, J., Faraone, S. V., Milberger, M. S., & Doyle, A. (1993). Diagnoses of attention deficit/hyperactivity disorder from parent reports predict diagnoses based on teacher reports. *Journal of the American Academy of Child and Adolescent Psychiatry, 32,* 315–317.

Biederman, J., Faraone, S. V., Milberger, S., Guite, J., Mick, E., Chen, L., et al. (1996). A prospective 4-year follow-up study of attention-deficit/hyperactivity and related disorders. *Archives of General Psychiatry, 53,* 437–446.

Biederman, J., Faraone, S. V., Monuteaux, M. C., Bober, M., & Cadogen, E. (2004). Gender effects on attention-deficit/hyperactivity disorder in adults, revisited. *Biological Psychiatry, 55,* 692–700.

Biederman, J., Faraone, S. V., Spencer, T., & Wilens, T. (1993). Patterns of psychiatric comorbidity, cognition, and psychological functioning in adults with attention deficit hyperactivity disorder. *American Journal of Psychiatry, 150,* 1792–1798.

Biederman, J., Faraone, S. V., Wozniak, J., Mick, E., Kwon, A., Cayton, G. A., et al. (2005). Clinical correlates of bipolar disorder in a large, referred sample of children and adolescents. *Journal of Psychiatric Research, 39,* 611–622.

Biederman, J., Heiligenstein, J. H., Faries, D. E., Galil, N., Dittmann, R., Emslie, G. J., et al. (2002). Efficacy of atomoxetine versus placebo in school-age girls with attention-deficit/hyperactivity disorder. *Pediatrics, 110,* e75.

Biederman, J., Kwon, A., Aleardi, M., Chouinard, V. A., Marino, T., Cole, H., et al. (2005). Absence of gender effects on attention deficit hyperactivity disorder: Findings in nonreferred subjects. *American Journal of Psychiatry, 162,* 1083–1089.

Biederman, J., Mick, E., & Faraone, S. V. (2000). Age-dependent decline of symptoms of attention deficit hyperactivity disorder: Impact of remission definition and symptom type. *American Journal of Psychiatry, 157,* 816–818.

Biederman, J., Mick, E., Faraone, S. V., Braaten, E., Doyle, A., Spencer, T., et al. (2002). Influence of gender on attention deficit hyperactivity disorder in children referred to a psychiatric clinic. *American Journal of Psychiatry, 159,* 36–42.

Biederman, J., Monuteaux, M. C., Kendrick, E., Klein, K. L., & Faraone, S. V. (2005). The CBCL as a screen for psychiatric comorbidity in paediatric patients with ADHD. *Archives of Disease in Childhood, 90,* 1010–1015.

Biederman, J., & Spencer, T. (2002). Methylphenidate in treatment of adults with attention-deficit/hyperactivity disorder. *Journal of Attention Disorders, 6*(Suppl. 1), S101–107.

Biederman, J., Wilens, T., Mick, E., Spencer, T., & Faraone, S. V. (1999). Pharmacotherapy of attention-deficit/hyperactivity disorder reduces risk for substance use disorder. *Pediatrics, 104,* e20.

Bjornstad, G., & Montgomery, P. (2005). Family therapy for attention-deficit disorder or attention-deficit/hyperactivity disorder in children and adolescents. *Cochrane Database of Systematic Reviews, 18,* CD005042.

Blachman, D. R., & Hinshaw, S. P. (2002). Patterns of friendship among girls with and without attention-deficit/hyperactivity disorder. *Journal of Abnormal Child Psychology, 30,* 625–640.

Block, M. A. (1996). *No more Ritalin: Treating ADHD without drugs.* New York: Kensington.

Block, M. A. (2001). *No more ADHD: 10 steps to help improve your child's attention and behavior without drugs.* Hurst, TX: Block Books.

Bobb, A. J., Castellanos, F. X., Addington, A. M., & Rapoport, J. L. (2005). Molecular genetic studies of ADHD: 1991 to 2004. *American Journal of Medical Genetics Part B-Neuropsychiatric Genetics, 132,* 109–125.

Bonafina, M. A., Newcorn, J. H., McKay, K. E., Koda, V. H., & Halperin, J. M. (2000). ADHD and reading disabilities: A cluster analytic approach for distinguishing subgroups. *Journal of Learning Disabilities, 33,* 297–307.

Boonstra, A. M., Kooij, J. J., Oosterlaan, J., Sergeant, J. A., & Buitelaar, J. K. (2005). Does methylphenidate improve inhibition and other cognitive abilities in adults with childhood-onset ADHD? *Journal of Clinical and Experimental Neuropsychology, 27,* 278–298.

Borger, N., & van der Meer, J. (2000). Motor control and state regulation in children with ADHD: A cardiac response study. *Biological Psychology, 51,* 247–267.

Borger, N., van der Meer, J., Ronner, A., Alberts, E., Geuze, R., & Bogte, H. (1999). Heart rate variability and sustained attention in ADHD children. *Journal of Abnormal Child Psychology, 27*(1), 25–33.

Boris, M., & Mandel, F. S. (1994). Foods and additives are common causes of the attention deficit hyperactive disorder in children. *Annals of Allergy, 72,* 462–468.

Boucugnani, L. L., & Jones, R. W. (1989). Behaviors analogous to frontal lobe dysfunction in children with attention-deficit/hyperactivity disorder. *Archives of Clinical Neuropsychology, 4,* 161–173.

Boyajian, A. E., DuPaul, G. J., Handler, M. W., Eckert, T. L., & McGoey, K. E. (2001). The use of classroom-based brief functional analyses with preschoolers at-risk for attention deficit hyperactivity disorder. *School Psychology Review, 30,* 278–293.

Breggin, P. R. (1998a). *Talking back to Ritalin.* New York: Common Courage Press.

Breggin, P. R. (1998b, November). [Letter to the editor]. *APA Monitor.*

Breggin, P. R. (2001). MTA study has flaws. *Archives of General Psychology, 58,* 1184.

Breslau, N., Brown, G. G., DelDotto, J. E., Kumary, S., Exhuthachan, S., Andreski, P., et al. (1996). Psychiatric sequelae of low birth weight at six years of age. *Journal of Abnormal Child Psychology, 24,* 385–400.

Broderick, P., & Benjamin, A. B. (2004). Caffeine and psychiatric symptoms: A review. *Journal of the Oklahoma State Medical Association, 97,* 538–542.

Brook, U., Watemberg, N., & Geva, D. (2000). Attitude and knowledge of attention deficit hyperactivity disorder and learning disability among high school teachers. *Patient Education and Counseling, 40,* 247–252.

Brooks, U., & Boaz, M. (2005a). Attention deficit and hyperactivity disorder (ADHD) and learning disabilities (LD): Adolescent perspective. *Patient Education and Counseling, 58,* 187–191.

Brooks, U., & Boaz, M. (2005b). Attention deficit and hyperactivity disorder/learning disabilities (ADHD/LD): Parental characterization and perception. *Patient Education and Counseling, 57,* 96–100.

Broussard, C. D., & Northup, J. (1995). An approach to functional analysis and assessment in regular classrooms. *School Psychology Quarterly, 10,* 151–164.

Broussard, C. D., & Northup, J. (1997). The use of functional analysis to develop peer interventions for disruptive classroom behavior. *School Psychology Quarterly, 12,* 65–76.

Brown, R. T., Amler, R. W., Freeman, W. S., Perrin, J. M., Stein, M. T., Clements, S. D., et al. (1962). Minimal brain dysfunction in the school-age child. *Archives of General Psychiatry, 6,* 197.

Brown, R. T., Amler, R. W., Freeman, W. S., Perrin, J. M., Stein, M. T., Feldman, H. M., et al. (2005). Treatment of attention-deficit/hyperactivity disorder: Overview of the evidence. *Pediatrics, 115,* e749–757.

Brown, T. E. (1996). *Brown attention deficit disorder scales manual.* San Antonio, TX: Psychological Corporation.

Brown, T. E. (1999). Does ADHD diagnosis require impulsivity-hyperactivity? A response to Gordon and Barkley. *The ADHD Report, 7,* 1–7.

Brownell, M. D., & Yogendran, M. S. (2001). Attention-deficit hyperactivity disorder in Manitoba children: Medical diagnosis and psychostimulant treatment rates. *Canadian Journal of Psychiatry, 46,* 264–272.

Brue, A. W., & Oakland, T. D. (2002). Alternative treatments for attention-deficit/hyperactivity disorder: Does evidence support their use? *Alternative Therapies in Health and Medicine, 8,* 68–70, 72–74.

Buchsbaum, M. S., Haier, R., Sostek, A. J., Weingartner, H., Zahn, T. P., Siever, L. J., et al. (1985). Attention dysfunction and psychopathology in college men. *Archives of General Psychiatry, 42,* 354–360.

Bussing, R., & Gary, F. A. (2001). Practice guidelines and parental ADHD treatment evaluations: Friends or foes? *Harvard Review of Psychiatry, 9,* 223–233.

Bussing, R., Gary, F. A., Mills, T. L., & Garvan, C. W. (2003). Parental explanatory models of ADHD: Gender and cultural variations. *Social Psychiatry and Psychiatric Epidemiology, 38,* 563–575.

Bussing, R., Zima, B. T., Gary, F. A., & Garvan, C. W. (2002). Use of complementary and alternative medicine for symptoms of attention-deficit hyperactivity disorder. *Psychiatric Services, 53,* 1096–1102.

Bussing, R., Zima, B. T., Mason, D., Hou, W., Garvan, C. W., & Forness, S. (2005). Use and persistence of pharmacotherapy for elementary school students with attention-deficit/hyperactivity disorder. *Journal of Child and Adolescent Psychopharmacology, 15,* 78–87.

Butte, N. F., Treuth, M. S., Voigt, R. G., Llorente, A. M., & Heird, W. C. (1999). Stimulant medications decrease energy expenditure and physical activity in children with attention-deficit/hyperactivity disorder. *Journal of Pediatrics, 135,* 203–207.

Byrne, J. M., Bawden, H. N., Beattie, T. L., & DeWolfe, N. A. (2000). Preschoolers classified as having attention-deficit hyperactivity disorder (ADHD): DSM-IV symptom endorsement pattern. *Journal of Child Neurology, 15,* 533–538.

Byrne, J. M., Bawden, H. N., Beattie, T. L., & DeWolfe, N. A. (2003). Risk for injury in preschoolers: Relationship to attention deficit hyperactivity disorder. *Child Neuropsychology, 9,* 142–151.

Campbell, S. B. (1990). *Behavior problems in preschoolers: Clinical and developmental issues.* New York: Guilford Press.

Campbell, S. B., & Ewing, L. J. (1990). Follow-up of hard-to-manage preschoolers: Adjustment at age nine years and predictors of continuing symptoms. *Journal of Child Psychology and Psychiatry, 31,* 891–910.

Cantwell, D. P., & Baker, L. (1987). Differential diagnosis of hyperactivity. Response to commentary. *Journal of Developmental Behavioral Pediatrics, 8,* 159–165, 169–170.

Cantwell, D. P., & Baker, L. (1991). Association between attention-deficit/hyperactivity disorder and learning disorders. *Journal of Learning Disabilities, 24,* 88–95.

Cantwell, D. P., Lewinsohn, P. M., Rhode, P., & Seeley, J. (1997). Correspondence between adolescent report and parent report of psychiatric diagnostic data. *Journal of the American Academy of Child and Adolescent Psychiatry, 36,* 610–619.

Carlson, C. L., & Mann, M. (2002). Sluggish cognitive tempo predicts a different pattern of impairment in the attention deficit hyperactivity disorder, predominately inattentive type. *Journal of Clinical Child and Adolescent Psychology, 31,* 123–129.

Carlson, C. L., & Tamm, L. (2000). Responsiveness of children with attention deficit-hyperactivity disorder to reward and response cost: Differential impact on performance and motivation. *Journal of Consulting and Clinical Psychology, 68,* 73–83.

Carlson, C. L., Tamm, L., & Gaub, M. (1997). Gender differences in children with ADHD, ODD, and co-occurring ADHD/ODD identified in a school population. *Journal of the American Academy of Child and Adolescent Psychiatry, 36,* 1706–1714.

Carlson, N. (1998). *Physiology of behavior* (6th ed.). Needham Heights, MA: Allyn & Bacon.

Carroll, K. M., & Rounsaville, B. J. (1993). History and significance of childhood attention deficit disorder in treatment-seeking cocaine abusers. *Comprehensive Psychiatry, 34,* 75–82.

Carter, C. M., Urbanowicz, M., Hemsely, R., Mantilla, L., Strobel, S., Graham, P. J., et al. (1993). Effects of a few food diet in attention deficit disorder. *Archives of Disease in Childhood, 69,* 564–568.

Castellanos, F. X. (1999). The psychobiology of attention-deficit/hyperactivity disorder. In H. C. Quay & A. E. Hogan (Eds.), *Handbook of disruptive behavior disorders* (pp. 179–198). New York: Kluwer Academic/Plenum.

Castellanos, F. X., Giedd, J. N., Berquin, P. C., Walter, J. M., Sharp, W., Tran, T., et al. (2001). Quantitative brain magnetic resonance imaging in girls with attention-deficit/hyperactivity disorder. *Archives of General Psychiatry, 58,* 289–295.

Castellanos, F. X., Giedd, J. N., Eckburg, P., Marsh, W. L., Vaituzis, C., Kaysen, D., et al. (1994). Quantitative morphology of the caudate nucleus in attention-deficit/hyperactivity disorder. *American Journal of Psychiatry, 151,* 1791–1796.

Castellanos, F. X., Lee, P. P., Sharp, W., Jeffries, N. O., Greenstein, D. K., Clasen, L. S., et al. (2002). Developmental trajectories of brain volume abnormalities in children and adolescents with attention-deficit/hyperactivity disorder. *Journal of the American Medical Association, 288,* 1740–1748.

Castellanos, F. X., Sharp, W. S., Gottesman, R. F., Greenstein, D. K., Giedd, J. N., & Rapoport, J. L. (2003). Anatomic brain abnormalities in monozygotic twins discordant for attention deficit hyperactivity disorder. *American Journal of Psychiatry, 160,* 1693–1696.

Castellanos, F. X., Sonuga-Barke, E. J., Milham, M. P., & Tannock, R. (in press). Characterizing cognition in ADHD: Beyond executive dysfunction. *Trends in Cognitive Sciences.*

Centers for Disease Control and Prevention. (2005). Prevalence of diagnosis and medication treatment for attention-deficit/hyperactivity disorder—United States, 2003. *Morbidity and Mortality Weekly Report, 54,* 842–847.

Chabot, R. A., & Serfontein, G. (1996). Quantitative electroencephalographic profiles of children with attention deficit disorder. *Biological Psychiatry, 40,* 951–963.

CH.A.D.D. (Children and Adults with Attention Deficit Disorders). (1992). Testimony to the senate and U.S. house of representatives subcommittee on appropriations. *CH.A.D.D., 6,* 24.

Chae, P. K. (1999). Correlation study between WISC-III scores and TOVA performance. *Psychology in the Schools, 36,* 179–185.

Chan, E., Hopkins, M. R., Perrin, J. M., Herrerias, C., & Homer, C. J. (2005). Diagnostic practices for attention deficit hyperactivity disorder: A national survey of primary care physicians. *Ambulatory Pediatrics, 5,* 201–208.

Chan, E., Rappaport, L. A., & Kemper, K. J. (2003). Complementary and alternative therapies in childhood attention and hyperactivity problems. *Journal of Developmental and Behavioral Pediatrics, 24,* 4–8.

Chang, C. C., Tsou, K. S., Shen, W. W., Wong, C. C., & Chao, C. C. (2004). A social skills training program for preschool children with attention-deficit/hyperactivity disorder. *Chang Gung Medical Journal, 27,* 918–923.

Chen, W. J., Faraone, S. V., Biederman, J., & Tsuang, M. T. (1994). Diagnostic accuracy of the Child Behavior Checklist scales for attention-deficit hyperactivity disorder: A receiver-operating characteristic analysis. *Journal of Consulting and Clinical Psychology, 62,* 1017–1025.

Chilcoat, H. D., & Breslau, N. (1999). Pathways from ADHD to early drug use. *Journal of the American Academy of Child and Adolescent Psychiatry, 38,* 1347–1362.

Chronis, A. M., Lahey, B. B., Pelham, W. E., Jr., Kipp, H. L., Baumann, B. L., & Lee, S. S. (2003). Psychopathology and substance abuse in parents of young children with attention-deficit/hyperactivity disorder. *Journal of the American Academy of Child and Adolescent Psychiatry, 42,* 1424–1432.

Clark, A., Barry, R., McCarthy, R., & Selikowitz, M. (2001). Excess beta activity in children with attention-deficit/hyperactivity disorder: An atypical electrophysiological group. *Psychiatry Research, 103,* 205–218.

Clay, R. A. (1998). New laws aid children with disabilities. *APA Monitor, 29*(1), 18.

Clements, S. D., & Peters, J. E. (1962). Minimal brain dysfunctions in the school-age child. Diagnosis and treatment. *Archives of General Psychiatry, 6,* 185–197.

Coger, R. W., Moe, K. L., & Serafetinides, E. A. (1996). Attention deficit disorder in adults and nicotine dependence: Psychobiological factors in resistance to recovery? *Journal of Psychoactive Drugs, 28,* 229–240.

Cohen, H. C., & Bailer, B. (1999). Lazy, crazy, or stupid? *Fire Chief, 8,* 74–76.

Cohen, M., Becker, M. G., & Campbell, R. (1990). Relationships among four methods of assessment of children with attention-deficit/hyperactivity disorder. *Journal of School Psychology, 28,* 189–202.

Collett, B. R., Ohan, J. L., & Myers, K. M. (2003). Ten-year review of rating scales: Scales assessing attention-deficit/hyperactivity disorder. *Journal of the American Academy of Child and Adolescent Psychiatry, 42,* 1015–1037.

Collings, R. D. (2003). Differences between ADHD inattentive and combined types on the CPT. *Journal of Psychopathology and Behavioral Assessment, 25,* 177–189.

Conners, C. K. (1980). *Food additives and hyperactive children.* New York: Plenum.

Conners, C. K. (1997). *Conners' rating scales—revised (CRS–R).* North Tonawanda, NY: Multi-Health Systems.

Conners, C. K. (1999a). *Conners' adult ADHD rating scales (CAARS).* North Tonawanda, NY: Multi-Health Systems.

Conners, C. K. (1999b). *Conners' continuous performance test*. North Tonawanda, NY: Multi-Health Systems.

Conners, C. K. (2004). *Conners' continuous performance test II (CPT-II)*. North Tonawanda, NY: Multi-Health Systems.

Conners, C. K., & Wells, K. (1997). *Conners-Wells adolescent self-report scale*. Tonawanda, NY: Multi-Health Systems.

Connor, D. F. (2002). Preschool attention deficit hyperactivity disorder: A review of prevalence, diagnosis, neurobiology, and stimulant treatment. *Developmental and Behavioral Pediatrics, 23*, S1–S9.

Connor, D. F., Edwards, G., Fletcher, K. E., Baird, J., Barkley, R. A., & Steingard, R. J. (2003). Correlates of comorbid psychopathology in children with ADHD. *Journal of the American Academy of Child and Adolescent Psychiatry, 42*, 193–200.

Connor, D. F., Fletcher, K., & Swanson, J. (1999). A meta-analysis of clonidine for symptoms of attention-deficit/hyperactivity disorder. *Journal of the American Academy of Child and Adolescent Psychiatry, 38*, 1551–1559.

Corkum, P., Moldofsky, H., Hogg-Johnson, S., Humphries, T., & Tannock, R. (1999). Sleep problems in children with attention-deficit/hyperactivity disorder: Impact of subtype, comorbidity, and stimulant medication. *Journal of the American Academy of Child and Adolescent Psychiatry, 38*, 1285–1293.

Corkum, P. V., & Siegel, L. S. (1993). Is the continuous performance task a valuable research tool for use with children with attention-deficit/hyperactivity disorder? *Journal of Child Psychology and Psychiatry, 34*, 1217–1239.

Costantino, G., Colon-Malgady, G., Malgady, R. G., & Perez, A. (1991). Assessment of attention deficit disorder using a thematic apperception technique. *Journal of Personality Assessment, 57*, 87–95.

Costello, E. J., Edelbrock, C. S., & Costello, A. J. (1985). Validity for the NIMH diagnostic interview schedule for children: A comparison between psychiatric and pediatric referral. *Journal of Abnormal Child Psychology, 13*, 579–595.

Coull, J. T., Middleton, H. C., Robbins, T. S., & Sahakian, B. J. (1995). Contrasting effects of clonidine and diazepam on tests of working memory and planning. *Psychopharmacology, 122*, 311–321.

Couzin, J. (2004). Pediatric study of ADHD drug draws high-level public-review. *Science, 305*, 1088–1089.

Crabtree, V. M., Ivanenko, A., & Gozal, D. (2003). Clinical and parental assessment of sleep in children with attention-deficit/hyperactivity disorder referred to a pediatric sleep medicine center. *Clinical Pediatrics, 42*, 807–813.

Culbert, T. P., Kajander, R. L., & Reaney, J. B. (1996). Biofeedback with children and adolescents: Clinical observations and patient perspectives. *Developmental and Behavioral Pediatrics, 17*, 342–350.

Cunningham, C. E. (1998). A large-group, community-based family systems approach to parent training. In R. A. Barkley (Ed.), *Attention-deficit/hyperactivity disorder: A handbook for diagnosis and treatment* (2nd ed., pp. 491–509). New York: Guilford Press.

Cunningham, C. E., & Boyle, M. H. (2002). Preschoolers at risk for attention-deficit hyperactivity disorder and oppositional defiant disorder: Family, parenting, and behavioral correlates. *Journal of Abnormal Psychology, 30*, 555–569.

Davila, R., Williams, M., & MacDonald, J. (1991). *Clarification of policy to address the needs of children with attention deficit disorders within general and/or special education*. Washington, DC: U.S. Department of Education.

Dane, A. V., Schachar, R. J., & Tannock, R. (2000). Does actigraphy differentiate ADHD subtypes in a clinical setting? *Journal of the American Academy of Child and Adolescent Psychiatry, 39*, 752–760.

Daviss, W. B., Bentivoglio, P., Racusin, R., Brown, K. M., Bostic, J. Q., & Wiley, L. (2001). Bupropion sustained release in adolescents with comorbid attention-deficit/hyperactivity disorder and depression. *Journal of the American Academy of Child and Adolescent Psychiatry, 40,* 307–314.

Demaray, M. K., Elting, J. E., & Schaefer, K. (2003). Assessment of attention-deficit/hyperactivity disorder (ADHD): A comparative evaluation of five, commonly used, published rating scales. *Psychology in the Schools, 40,* 341–360.

Demaray, M. K., Schaefer, K., & Delong, L. K. (2003). Attention-deficit/hyperactivity disorder (ADHD): A national survey of training and current assessment practices in the schools. *Psychology in the Schools, 40,* 583–597.

Dick, D. M., Viken, R. J., Kaprio, J., Pulkkinen, L., & Rose, R. J. (2005). Understanding the covariation among childhood externalizing symptoms: Genetic and environmental influences on conduct disorder, attention deficit hyperactivity disorder, and oppositional defiant disorder symptoms. *Journal of Abnormal Child Psychology, 33,* 219–229.

Dosreis, S., Zito, J. M., Safer, D. J., Soeken, K. L., Mitchell, J. W., Jr., & Ellwood, L. C. (2003). Parental perceptions and satisfaction with stimulant medication for attention-deficit hyperactivity disorder. *Journal of Developmental and Behavioral Pediatrics, 24,* 155–162.

Doyle, A. E., Biederman, J., Seidman, L. J., Reske-Nielsen, J. J., & Faraone, S. V. (2005). Neuropsychological functioning in relatives of girls with and without ADHD. *Psychological Medicine, 35,* 1121–1132.

Doyle, A. E., Faraone, S. V., & Seidman, L. J. (2005). Are endophenotypes based on measures of executive functions useful for molecular genetic studies of ADHD? *Journal of Child Psychology & Psychiatry, 46,* 778–803.

Doyle, A. E., Willcutt, E. G., Seidman, L. J., Biederman, J., Chouinard, V. A., Silva, J., et al. (2005). Attention-deficit/hyperactivity disorder endophenotypes. *Biological Psychiatry, 57,* 1324–1335.

Dowdy, C. A., Patton, J. R., Smith, T., & Polloway, E. A. (1998). *Attention-deficit/hyperactivity disorder in the classroom: A practical guide for teachers.* Austin, TX: PRO-ED.

Drechsler, R., Brandeis, D., Foldenyi, M., Imhof, K., & Steinhausen, H. C. (2005). The course of neuropsychological functions in children with attention deficit hyperactivity disorder from late childhood to early adolescence. *Journal of Child Psychology and Psychiatry, 46,* 824–836.

Dubey, D. R., & O'Leary, S. G. (1975). Increasing reading comprehension of two hyperactive children: Preliminary investigation. *Perceptual and Motor Skills, 41,* 691–694.

Dunlap, G., dePerczel, M., Clarke, S., Wilson, D., Wright, S., White, R., et al. (1994). Choice making to promote adaptive behavior for students with emotional and behavioral challenges. *Journal of Applied Behavior Analysis, 27,* 505–518.

DuPaul, G. J. (1991). Parent and teacher rating of ADHD symptoms: Psychometric properties in a community-based sample. *Journal of Clinical Child Psychology, 20,* 245–253.

DuPaul, G. J., Anastopoulos, A. D., Kwasnik, D., Barkley, R. A., & McMurray, M. B. (1996). Methylphenidate effects on children with attention-deficit/hyperactivity disorder: Self report symptoms, side effects, and self-esteem. *Journal of Attention Disorders, 1,* 3–15.

DuPaul, G. J., Bankert, C. L., & Ervin, R. A. (1994). Classwide peer tutoring: A school-based academic intervention for ADHD. *The ADHD Report, 2,* 4–5.

DuPaul, G. J., & Barkley, R. A. (1990). Medication therapy. In R. A. Barkley, *Attention deficit/hyperactivity disorder: A handbook for diagnosis and treatment* (pp. 573–612). New York: Guilford Press.

DuPaul, G. J., & Barkley, R. A. (1993). Behavioral contribution to pharmacotherapy: The utility of behavioral methodology in medication treatment of children with attention deficit/hyperactivity disorder. *Behavior Therapy, 24,* 47–65.

DuPaul, G. J., Barkley, R. A., & Conner, D. F. (1998). Stimulants. In R. A. Barkley, *Attention deficit/hyperactivity disorder: A handbook for diagnosis and treatment* (2nd ed.). New York: Guilford Press.

DuPaul, G. J., & Eckert, T. L. (1998). Academic interventions for students with attention deficit/hyperactivity disorder: A review of the literature. *Reading and Writing Quarterly, 14,* 59–82.

DuPaul, G. J., & Ervin, R. A. (1996). Functional assessment of behaviors related to attention deficit/hyperactivity disorder: Linking assessment to intervention design. *Behavior Therapy, 27,* 601–622.

DuPaul, G. J., Ervin, R. A., Hook, C. L., & McGoey, K. E. (1998). Peer tutoring for children with attention deficit hyperactivity disorder: Effects on classroom behavior and academic performance. *Journal of Applied Behavior Analysis, 31,* 579–592.

DuPaul, G. J., & Henningson, P. N. (1993). Peer tutoring effects of the classroom performance of children with attention deficit/hyperactivity disorder. *School Psychology Review, 22,* 134–143.

DuPaul, G. J., McGoey, K. E., Eckert, T. L., & Van Brackle, J. (2001). Preschool children with attention-deficit/hyperactivity disorder: Impairments in behavioral, social, and school functioning. *The Journal of the American Academy of Child and Adolescent Psychiatry, 40,* 508–515.

DuPaul, G. J., Power, T. J., Anastopoulos, A. D., & Reid, R. (1998). *ADHD rating scale-IV: Checklists, norms, and clinical interpretation.* New York: Guilford Press.

DuPaul, G. J., Rapport, M. D., & Perriello, L. M. (1991). Teacher ratings of academic skills: The development of the academic performance rating scale. *School Psychology Review, 20,* 284–300.

DuPaul, G. J., Schaughency, E., Weyandt, L., & Ota, K. (1998, November). *Attention deficit/hyperactivity disorder symptoms among U.S. college students.* Paper presented at the 32nd annual convention of the Association for the Advancement of Behavior Therapy, Washington, DC.

DuPaul, G. J., Schaughency, E. A., Weyandt, L. L., Tripp, G., Kiesner, J., Ota, K., et al. (2001). Self-report of ADHD symptoms in university students: Cross-gender and cross-national prevalence. *Journal of Learning Disabilities, 34,* 370–379.

DuPaul, G. J., & Stoner, G. (1994). *ADHD in the schools: Assessment and intervention strategies.* New York: Guilford Press.

DuPaul, G. J., & Stoner, G. (2003). *ADHD in the schools: Assessment and intervention strategies* (2nd ed.). New York: Guilford Press.

DuPaul, G. J., Stoner, G., Tilly, W. D., & Putnam, D. (1991). Interventions for attention problems. In G. Stoner, M. R. Shinn, & H. M. Walker (Eds.), *Interventions for achievement and behavior problems.* Silver Spring, MD: National Association of School Psychologists.

DuPaul, G. J., & Weyandt, L. L. (in press-a). School-based interventions for children and adolescents with attention-deficit/hyperactivity disorder: Enhancing academic and behavioral outcomes. *Education and Treatment of Children.*

DuPaul, G. J., & Weyandt, L. L. (in press-b). School-based intervention for children with attention-deficit/hyperactivity disorder: Effects on academic, social, and behavioural functioning. *International Journal of Disability, Development and Education.*

Durston, S., Tottenham, N. T., Thomas, K. M., Davidson, M. C., Eigsti, I. M., Yang, Y., et al. (2003). Differential patterns of striatal activation in young children with and without ADHD. *Biological Psychiatry, 53,* 871–878.

Dykman, K. D., & Dykman, R. A. (1998). Effect of nutritional supplements on attention deficit/hyperactivity disorder. *Integrative Physiological and Behavioral Science, 33,* 49–60.

Dykman, K. D., & McKinley, R. (1997). Effect of glyconutritionals on the severity of ADHD. *Proceedings of the Fisher Institute for Medical Research, 1,* 24–25.

Dykman, R. A. (2005). Historical aspects of attention deficit hyperactivity disorder. In D. Gozal & D. L. Molfese (Eds.), *Attention deficit hyperactivity disorder: From genes to parents* (pp. 1–40). Totowa, NJ: Humana Press.

Efron, D., Jarman, F., & Barker, M. (1997). Methylphenidate versus dexamphetamine in children with attention deficit hyperactivity disorder: A double-blind, crossover trial. *Pediatrics, 100,* E6.

Egger, J., Carter, C. M., Graham, P. J., Gumley, D., & Soothill, J. F. (1985). Controlled trial of oligoantigenic treatment in the hyperkinetic syndrome. *Lancet, 1,* 540–545.

Einfeld, S., Hall, W., & Levy, F. (1991). Hyperactivity and fragile X syndrome. *Journal of Abnormal Child Psychology, 19,* 253–263.

El-Zein, R. A., Abdel-Rahman, S. Z., Hay, M. J., Lopez, M. S., Bondy, M. L., Morris, D. L., et al. (2005). Cytogentic effects in children treated with methylphenidate. *Cancer Letters, 230,* 284–291.

Emslie, G. J., Walkup, J. T., Pliszka, S. R., & Ernst, M. (1999). Nontricyclic antidepressants: Current trends in children and adolescents. *Journal of the American Academy of Child and Adolescent Psychiatry, 38,* 517–528.

Epstein, J. N., Erkanli, A., Conners, C. K., Klaric, J., Costello, J. E., & Angold, A. (2003). Relations between Continuous Performance Test performance measures and ADHD behaviors. *Journal of Abnormal Child Psychology, 31,* 543–554.

Erhardt, D., & Hinshaw, S. P. (1994). Initial sociometric impressions of attention-deficit hyperactivity disorder and comparison boys: Predictions from social behaviors and from nonbehavioral variables. *Journal of Consulting and Clinical Psychology, 62,* 833–842.

Ervin, R. A., DuPaul, G. J., Kern, L., & Friman, P. C. (1998). Classroom-based functional and adjunctive assessments: Proactive approaches to intervention selection for adolescents with attention deficit hyperactivity disorder. *Journal of Applied Behavior Analysis, 31,* 65–78.

Escobar, R., Soutullo, C. A., Hervas, A., Gastaminza, X., Polavieja, P., & Gilaberte, I. (2005). Worse quality of life for children with newly diagnosed attention-deficit/hyperactivity disorder, compared with asthmatic and healthy children. *Pediatrics, 116,* e364–369.

Evans, S. W., Pelham., W., & Grudber, M. V. (1995). The efficacy of note taking to improve behavior and comprehension of adolescents with attention-deficit/hyperactivity disorder. *Exceptionality, 5,* 1–17.

Evans, S. W., Pelham, W. E., Smith, B. H., Bukstein, O., Gnagy, E. M., Greiner, A. R., et al. (2001). Dose-response effects of methylphenidate on ecologically valid measures of academic performance and classroom behavior in adolescents with ADHD. *Experimental and Clinical Psychopharmacology, 9,* 163–175.

Eyestone, L. L., & Howell, R. J. (1994). An epidemiological study of attention deficit/hyperactivity disorders and major depression in a male prison population. *Bulletin of the American Academy of Psychiatry and Law, 22,* 181–193.

Faraone, S. V., & Biederman, J. (2002). Efficacy of Adderall® for attention-deficit/hyperactivity disorder: A meta-analysis. *Journal of Attention Disorders, 6,* 69–75.

Faraone, S. V., Biederman, J., Lehman, B., Keenan, K., Norman, D., & Seidman, L. J. (1993). Evidence for the independent familial transmission of attention-deficit/hyperactivity disorder and learning disabilities: Results from a family genetic study. *American Journal of Psychiatry, 150,* 891–895.

Faraone, S. V., Biederman, J., Lehman, B. K., Spencer, T., Norman, D., Seidman, L. J., et al. (1993). Intellectual performance and school failure in children with attention-deficit/hyperactivity disorder and their siblings. *Journal of Abnormal Psychology, 102,* 616–623.

Faraone, S. V., Biederman, J., Mennin, D., Wozniak, J., & Spencer, T. (1997). Attention deficit/hyperactivity disorder with bipolar disorder. A familial subtype? *Journal of the American Academy of Child and Adolescent Psychiatry, 36,* 1378–1387.

Faraone, S. V., Biederman, J., & Milberger, S. (1995). How reliable are maternal reports of their children's psychopathology? One-year recall of psychiatric diagnoses of

ADHD children. *Journal of the American Academy of Child and Adolescent Psychiatry, 34*, 1001–1008.

Faraone, S. V., Biederman, J., & Monuteaux, M. C. (2002). Further evidence for the diagnostic continuity between child and adolescent ADHD. *Journal of Attention Disorders, 6*, 5–13.

Faraone, S. V., Perlis, R. H., Doyle, A. E., Smoller, J. W., Goralnick, J. J., Holmgren, M. A., et al. (2005). Molecular genetics of attention-deficit/hyperactivity disorder. *Biological Psychiatry, 57*, 1313–1323.

Fehlings, D. L., Roberts, W., Humphries, T., & Dawe, G. (1990). An evaluation of the effectiveness of cognitive behavioral therapy to improve home behavior in boys with ADHD. *Journal of Developmental and Behavioral Pediatrics, 11*, 216.

Feingold, B. (1975). *Why your child is hyperactive*. New York: Random House.

Field, T. M., Quintino, O., Hernandez-Reif, M., & Koslovsky, G. (1998). Adolescents with attention-deficit/hyperactivity disorder benefit from massage therapy. *Adolescence, 33*, 103–108.

Filipek, P. A. (1999). Neuroimaging in the developmental disorders: The state of the science. *Journal of Child Psychology and Psychiatry, 40*, 113–128.

Fiore, T. A., & Becker, E. A. (1993). Classroom interventions for children with ADD. *NASP Communique, 22*, insert.

Findling, R. L., Short, E. J., & Manos, M. J. (2001). Developmental aspects of psychostimulant treatment in children and adolescents with attention-deficit/hyperactivity disorder. *Journal of the American Academy of Child and Adolescent Psychiatry, 40*, 1441–1447.

Firestone, P., Davey, J., Goodman, J. T., & Peters, S. (1978). The effects of caffeine and methylphenidate on hyperactive children. *Journal of the American Academy of Child and Adolescent Psychiatry, 17*, 445–456.

Firestone, P., Lewy, F., & Douglas, V. I. (1976). Hyperactivity and physical anomalies. *Canadian Psychiatric Association Journal, 21*, 23–26.

Fischer, M., Barkley, R. A., Fletcher, K. E., & Smallish, L. (1993). The adolescent outcome of hyperactive children: Predictors of psychiatric academic, social, and emotional adjustment. *American Academy of Child and Adolescent Psychiatry, 32*, 324–332.

Fischer, M., Barkley, R. A., Smallish, L., & Fletcher, K. (2005). Executive functioning in hyperactive children as young adults: Attention, inhibition, response perseveration, and the impact of comorbidity. *Developmental Neuropsychology, 27*, 107–133.

Flood, W. A., Wilder, D. A., Flood, A. L., & Masuda, A. (2002). Peer-mediated reinforcement plus prompting as treatment for off-task behavior in children with attention deficit hyperactivity disorder. *Journal of Applied Behavior Analysis, 35*, 199–204.

Fogelman, Y., Vinker, S., Guy, N., & Kahan, E. (2003). Prevalence of and change in the prescription of methylphenidate in Israel over a 2-year period. *CNS Drugs, 17*, 915–919.

Foy, J. M., & Earls, M. F. (2005). A process for developing community consensus regarding the diagnosis and management of attention-deficit/hyperactivity disorder. *Pediatrics, 115*, e97–104.

Frame, K. (2004). The STARS program: Social empowerment training for preadolescents with attention deficit hyperactivity disorder (ADHD). *Journal of School Nursing, 20*, 257–261.

Frankel, F., Myatt, R., Cantwell, D. P., & Feinberg, D. T. (1997). Parent-assisted transfer of children's social skills training: Effects on children with and without attention deficit/hyperactivity disorder. *Journal of the American Academy of Child and Adolescent Psychiatry, 36*, 1056–1064.

Fraser, K. M. (2002). Too young for attention deficit disorder? Views from preschool. *Journal of Developmental and Behavioral Pediatrics, 23*, S46–S50.

Frauenglass, S., & Routh, D. K. (1999). Assessment of disruptive behavior disorders: Dimensional and categorical approaches. In H. Quay & A. E. Hogan (Eds.), *Handbook of disruptive behavior disorders* (pp. 49–71). New York: Kluwer Academic/Plenum.

Frederick, B. P., & Olmi, D. J. (1994). Children with attention-deficit/hyperactivity disorder: A review of the literature on social skill deficits. *Psychology in the Schools, 31,* 288–296.

Frei, H., Everts, R., von Ammon, K., Kaufmann, F., Walther, D., Hsu-Schmitz, S. F., et al. (2005). Homeopathic treatment of children with attention deficit hyperactivity disorder: A randomised, double blind, placebo controlled crossover trial. *European Journal of Pediatrics, 164,* 758–767.

Frick, P., Lahey, B. B., Christ, M. A., Loeber, R., & Green, S. (1991). History of childhood behavior problems in biological relatives of boys with attention-deficit/hyperactivity disorder and conduct disorder. *Journal of Clinical Child Psychology, 20,* 445–451.

Fuchs, L. S., & Fuchs, D. (1987). The relation between methods of graphing student performance data and achievement: A meta-analysis. *Journal of Special Education Technology, 8,* 5–13.

Funk, J. B., Chessare, J. B., Weaver, M. T., & Exley, A. R. (1993). Attention-deficit/ hyperactivity disorder, creativity, and the effects of methylphenidate. *Pediatrics, 91,* 816–819.

Gadow, K. D., Nolan, E. E., Litcher, L., Carlson, G. A., Panina, N., Golovakha, E., et al. (2000). Comparison of attention-deficit/hyperactivity disorder symptom subtypes in Ukrainian schoolchildren. *Journal of the American Academy of Child and Adolescent Psychiatry, 39,* 1520–1527.

Gadow, K. D., Sprafkin, J., & Nolan, E. E. (2001). DSM-IV symptoms in community and clinic preschool children. *Journal of the American Academy of Child and Adolescent Psychiatry, 40,* 1383–1392.

Garfinkel, B. D., Webster, C. D., & Sloman, L. (1981). Responses to methylphenidate and varied does of caffeine in children with attention deficit disorder. *Canadian Journal of Psychiatry, 26,* 395–401.

Gaub, M., & Carlson, C. L. (1997). Gender differences in ADHD: A meta-analysis and critical review. *Journal of the American Academy of Child and Adolescent Psychiatry, 36,* 1036–1045.

Gaultney, J. F., Terrell, D. F., & Gingras, J. L. (2005). Parent-reported periodic limb movement, sleep disordered breathing, bedtime resistance behaviors, and ADHD. *Behavioral Sleep Medicine, 3,* 32–43.

Gayan, J., Willcutt, E. G., Fisher, S. E., Francks, C., Cardon, L. R., Olson, R. K., et al. (2005). Bivariate linkage scan for reading disability and attention-deficit/hyperactivity disorder localizes pleiotropic loci. *Journal of Child Psychology and Psychiatry, 46,* 1045–1056.

Geller, B., Reising, D., Leonard, H., Riddle, M. A., & Walsh, T. B. (1999). Critical review of tricyclic antidepressant use in children and adolescents. *Journal of the American Academy of Child and Adolescent Psychiatry, 38,* 513–516.

Geller, D. A., Biederman, J., Faraone, S. V., Spencer, T., Doyle, R., Mullin, B., et al. (2004). Re-examining comorbidity of obsessive-compulsive and attention-deficit hyperactivity disorder using an empirically derived taxonomy. *European Child and Adolescent Psychiatry, 13,* 83–91.

Geller, D. A., Coffrey, B., Faraone, S., Hagermoser, L., Zaman, N. K., Farrell, C. L., et al. (2003). Does comorbid attention-deficit/hyperactivity disorder impact the clinical expression of pediatric obsessive-compulsive disorder? *CNS Spectrums, 8,* 259–264.

George, R. A., & Mortimer, D. B. (1998). Identification and medical treatment of ADHD in the juvenile justice setting. *The ADHD Report, 6,* 1–9.

Gershon, J. (2002). A meta-analytic review of gender differences in ADHD. *Journal of Attention Disorders, 5,* 143–154.

Gibbs, D. P., & Cooper, E. B. (1989). Prevalence of communication disorders in students with learning disabilities. *Journal of Learning Disabilities, 22*, 60–63.

Giedd, J. N., Castellanos, F. X., Casey, B. J., Kozuch, P., King, A. C., Hamburger, S. D., et al. (1994). Quantitative morphology of the corpus callosum in attention deficit/hyperactivity disorder. *American Journal of Psychiatry, 151*, 655–669.

Gillberg, C., Melander, H., von Knorring, A., Janols, L., Thernlund, G., et al. (1997). Long-term stimulant treatment of children with attention-deficit/hyperactivity disorder symptoms. *Archives of General Psychiatry, 54*, 857–864.

Gjone, H., Stevenson, J., & Sundet, J. M. (1996). Genetic influence on parent-reported attention-related problems in a Norwegian general population twin sample. *Journal of the American Academy of Child and Adolescent Psychiatry, 35*, 588–598.

Glass, C. S., & Wegar, K. (2000). Teacher perceptions of the incidence and management of attention deficit hyperactivity disorder. *Education, 121*, 412–420.

Gol, D., & Jarus, T. (2005). Effect of a social skills training group on everyday activities of children with attention-deficit-hyperactivity disorder. *Developmental Medicine and Child Neurology, 47*, 539–545.

Goldman, L. S., Genel, M., Bezman, R. J., & Slanetz, P. J. (1998). Diagnosis and treatment of attention-deficit/hyperactivity disorder in children and adolescents. *Journal of the American Medical Association, 279*, 1100–1107.

Goldman, J. A., Lerman, R. H., Contois, J. H., & Udall, J. N. (1986). Behavioral effects of sucrose on preschool children. *Journal of Abnormal Child Psychology, 14*, 565–577.

Goldstein, S. (1988). *Social skills assessment questionnaire.* Salt Lake City, UT: Neurology, Learning, and Behavior Center.

Goldstein, S., & Goldstein, M. (1998). *Managing attention-deficit/hyperactivity disorder in children: A guide for practitioners.* New York: Wiley.

Goldstein, S., & Teeter-Ellison, A. T. (2002). *Clinician's guide to adult ADHD: Assessment and intervention.* Boston: Academic Press.

Goodman, R., & Stevenson, J. (1989). A twin study of hyperactivity: II. The aetiological role of genes, family relationships, and perinatal adversity. *Journal of Child Psychology and Psychiatry, 30*, 691–709.

Gordon, M. (1988). *The Gordon diagnostic system.* Dewitt, NY: Gordon Systems.

Gordon, M., Antshel, K., Faraone, S., Barkley, R., Lewandowski, L., Hudziak, M. D., et al. (2005). Symptoms versus impairment: The case for respecting DSV-IV's Criterion D. *The ADHD Report, 13*, 1–9.

Gordon, M., & Barkley, R. A. (1999). Is all inattention ADD/ADHD? *The ADHD Report, 7*, 1–8.

Gordon, M., Barkley, R. A., & Murphy, K. R. (1997). ADHD on trial. *The ADHD Report, 5*, 1–4.

Gordon, S. M., Tulak, F., & Troncale, J. (2004). Prevalence and characteristics of adolescents patients with co-occurring ADHD and substance dependence. *Journal of Addictive Diseases, 23*, 31–40.

Graetz, B. W., Sawyer, M. G., & Baghurst, P. (2005). Gender differences among children with DSM-IV ADHD in Australia. *Journal of the American Academy of Child and Adolescent Psychiatry, 44*, 159–168.

Graetz, B. W., Sawyer, M. G., Hazell, P. L., Arney, F., & Baghurst, P. (2001). Validity of DSM-IV ADHD subtypes in a nationally representative sample of Australian children and adolescents. *Journal of the American Academy of Child and Adolescent Psychiatry, 40*, 1410–1417.

Greenberg, L. M. (1990). *Test of variables of attention (TOVA).* Los Alamitos, CA: Universal Attention Disorders.

Greenhill, L. (2001). Clinical effects of stimulant mediation in ADHD. In M. Solanto, A. Arnsten, & F. Castellano (Eds.), *Stimulant drugs and ADHD* (pp. 31–71). New York: Oxford University Press, Inc.

Greenhill, L. L., Halperin, J. M., & Abikoff, H. (1999). Stimulant medications. *Journal of the American Academy of Child and Adolescent Psychiatry, 38,* 503–512.

Greenhill, L. L., & Osman, B. B. (1999). *Ritalin: Theory and practice* (2nd ed.). New York: Mary Liebert, Inc.

Guevara, J. P., Mandell, D. S., Rostain, A. L., Zhao, H., & Hadley, T. R. (2003). National estimates of health services expenditures for children with behavioral disorders: An analysis of the medical expenditure panel survey. *Pediatrics, 112,* e440.

Guevremont, D. C. (1990). Social skills and peer relationship training. In R. A. Barkley (Ed.), *Attention-deficit/hyperactivity disorder: A handbook for diagnosis and treatment* (pp. 540–572). New York: Guilford Press.

Gureasko-Moore, D. P., DuPaul, G. J., & Power, T. J. (2005). Stimulant treatment for attention-deficit/hyperactivity disorder: Medication monitoring practices of school psychologists. *School Psychology Review, 34,* 232–245.

Habel, L. A., Schaefer, C. A., Levine, P., Bhat, A. K., & Elliott, G. (2005). Treatment with stimulants among youths in a large California health plan. *Journal of Child and Adolescent Psychopharmacology, 15,* 62–67.

Hall, J., Marshall, R., Vaughn, M., Hynd, G. W., & Riccio, C. (1997). Intervention strategies for preschool children with ADHD. In W. N. Bender (Ed.), *Understanding ADHD: A practical guide for teachers and parents.* Upper Saddle River, NJ: Prentice-Hall.

Hall, K. M., Irwin, M. M., Bowman, K. A., Frankenberger, W., & Jewett, D. C. (2005). Illicit use of prescribed stimulant medication among college students. *Journal of American College Health, 53,* 167–174.

Halperin, J. M., Gittelman, R., Katz, S., & Struve, F. A. (1986). Relationship between stimulant effect, electroencephalogram, and clinical neurological findings in hyperactive children. *Journal of the American Academy of Child Psychiatry, 25,* 820–825.

Halperin, J., Newcorn, J. H., Kopstein, I., McKay, K. E., Schwartz, S. T., Siever, L. J., et al. (1997). Serotonin, aggression, and parental psychopathology in children with attention-deficit/hyperactivity disorder. *Journal of the American Academy of Child and Adolescent Psychiatry, 36,* 1391–1398.

Hamlett, K. W., Pellegrini, D. S., & Conners, C. K. (1987). An investigation of executive processes in the problem solving of attention-deficit-disorder-hyperactive children. *Journal of Pediatric Psychology, 12,* 227–240.

Handen, B. L., Feldman, H. M., Lurier, A., & Huzar-Murray, P. J. (1999). Efficacy of methylphenidate among preschool children with developmental disabilities and ADHD. *Journal of the American Academy of Child and Adolescent Psychiatry, 38,* 805–812.

Hanna, G. L., Ornitz, E. M., & Hariharan, M. (1996). Urinary catecholamine excretion and behavioral differences in ADHD and normal boys. *Journal of Child and Adolescent Psychopharmacology, 6,* 63–73.

Harding, K. L., Judah, R. D., & Gant, C. (2003). Outcome-based comparison of Ritalin versus food-supplement treated children with AD/HD. *Alternative Medicine Review, 8,* 319–330.

Harrison, C., & Sofronoff, K. (2002). ADHD and parental psychological distress: Role of demographics, child behavioral characteristics, and parental cognitions. *Journal of the American Academy of Child and Adolescent Psychiatry, 41,* 703–711.

Hart, E. L., Lahey, B. B., Loeber, R., Applegate, B., & Frick, P. J. (1995). Developmental changes in attention-deficit/hyperactivity disorder in boys: A four-year longitudinal study. *Journal of Abnormal Child Psychology, 23,* 729–749.

Hartmann, T. (1993). *Attention deficit disorder: A different perception.* Novato, CA: Underwood Miller.

Hartsough, C. S., & Lambert, N. M. (1985). Medical factors in hyperactive and normal children: Prenatal, developmental, and health history findings. *American Journal of Orthopsychiatry, 55,* 190–210.

Hartung, C. M., Willcutt, E. G., Lahey, B. B., Pelham, W. E., Loney, J., Stein, M. A., et al. (2002). Sex differences in young children who meet criteria for attention deficit hyperactivity disorder. *Journal of Clinical Child and Adolescent Psychology, 31,* 453–464.

Hauser, P., Zametkin, A. J., Martinez, P., Vitiello, B., Matochik, J., Mixson, J. A., et al. (1993). Attention-deficit/hyperactivity disorder in people with generalized resistance to thyroid hormone. *New England Journal of Medicine, 328,* 997–1001.

Hauser, P., Zametkin, A. J., Martinez, P., Vitiello, B., Matochik, J. A., Mixson, J. A., et al. (1994). ADHD and the thyroid controversy. *Journal of the American Academy of Child and Adolescent Psychiatry, 33,* 756–757.

Havey, J. M., Olson, J. M., McCormick, C., & Cates, G. L. (2005). Teachers' perceptions of the incidence and management of attention-deficit hyperactivity disorder. *Applied Neuropsychology, 12,* 120–127.

Hazell, P. L., & Stuart, J. E. (2003). A randomized controlled trail of clonidine added to psychostimulant medication for hyperactive and aggressive children. *Journal of the American Academy of Child and Adolescent Psychiatry, 42,* 886–894.

Healey, D., & Rucklidge, J. J. (2005). An exploration into the creative abilities of children with ADHD. *Journal of Attention Disorders, 8,* 88–95.

Healy, M. T. (2000, March). *The presenting profile of college students diagnosed with attention-deficit/hyperactivity disorder.* Unpublished master's thesis, Central Washington University.

Hechtman, L. (1996). Families of children with attention-deficit/hyperactivity disorder: A review. *Canadian Journal of Psychiatry, 41,* 350–360.

Hechtman, L., Abikoff, H., Klein, R. G., Greenfield, B., Etcovitch, J., Cousins, L., et al. (2004). Children with ADHD treated with long-term methylphenidate and multimodal psychosocial treatment: Impact on parental practices. *Journal of the American Academy of Child and Adolescent Psychiatry, 43,* 830–838.

Hechtman, L., Abikoff, H., Klein, R. G., Weiss, G., Respitz, C., Kouri, J., et al. (2004). Academic achievement and emotional status of children with ADHD treated with long-term methylphenidate and multimodal psychosocial treatment. *Journal of the American Academy of Child and Adolescent Psychiatry, 43,* 812–819.

Hechtman, L., Weiss, G., Perlman, T., & Amsel, R. (1984). Hyperactives as young adults: Initial predictors of outcome. *Journal of the American Academy of Child Psychiatry, 23,* 250–260.

Heffron, W. A., Martin, C. A., Welsh, R. J., & Perry, P. (1987). Hyperactivity and child abuse. *Canadian Journal of Psychiatry, 32,* 384–386.

Heiligenstein, E., Conyers, L. M., Berns, A. R., & Smith, M. A. (1998). Preliminary normative data on *DSM-IV* attention-deficit/hyperactivity disorder in college students. *Journal of College Health, 46,* 185–188.

Heiligenstein, E., & Keeling, R. P. (1995). Presentation of unrecognized attention deficit hyperactivity disorder in college students. *Journal of the American College Health Association, 43,* 226–228.

Hermens, D. F., Cooper, N. J., Kohn, M., Clarke, S., & Gordon, E. (2005). Predicting stimulant medication response in ADHD: Evidence from an integrated profile of neuropsychological, psychophysiological and clinical factors. *Journal of Integral Neuroscience, 4,* 107–121.

Hermens, D. F., Kohn, M. R., Clarke, S. D., Gordon, E., & Williams, L. M. (2005). Sex differences in adolescent ADHD: Findings from concurrent EEG and EDA. *Clinical Neurophysiologist, 116,* 1455–1463.

Hesslinger, B., Tebartz van Elst, L., Nyberg, E., Dykierek, P., Richter, H., Berner, M., et al. (2002). Psychotherapy of attention deficit hyperactivity disorder in adults—a pilot study using a structured skills training program. *European Archives of Psychiatry and Clinical Neuroscience, 252,* 177–184.

Hines, A. M., & Shaw, G. A. (1993). Intrusive thoughts, sensation seeking, and drug use in college students. *Bulletin of the Psychonomic Society, 31*, 541–544.

Hinshaw, S. P. (2002). Preadolescent girls with attention-deficit/hyperactivity disorder: I. Background characteristics, comorbidity, cognitive and social functioning, and parenting practices. *Journal of Consulting and Clinical Psychology, 70*, 1086–1098.

Hinshaw, S. P., Henker, B., & Whalen, C. K. (1984). Cognitive-behavioral and pharmacologic interventions for hyperactive boys: Comparative and combined effects. *Journal of Consulting and Clinical Psychology, 52*, 739–749.

Hinshaw, S. P., Owens, E. B., Wells, K. C., Kraemer, H. C., Abikoff, H. B., Arnold, L. E., et al. (2000). Family processes and treatment outcome in the MTA: Negative/ineffective parenting practices in relation to multimodal treatment. *Journal of Abnormal Child Psychology, 28*, 555–568.

Hoagwood, K., Jensen, P. S., Feil, M., Vitiello, B., & Bhatara, V. S. (2000). Medication management of stimulants in pediatric practice settings: A national perspective. *Journal of Developmental and Behavioral Pediatrics, 21*, 322–331.

Hoagwood, K., Kelleher, K. J., Feil, M., & Comer, D. M. (2000). Treatment services for children with ADHD: A national perspective. *Journal of the American Academy of Child and Adolescent Psychiatry, 39*, 198–206.

Hodgens, J. B., Cole, J., & Boldizar, J. (2000). Peer-based differences among boys with ADHD. *Journal of Clinical and Child Psychology, 29*, 443–452.

Hoff, K. E., Ervin, R. A., & Friman, P. C. (2005). Refining functional behavioral assessment: Analyzing the separate and combined effects of hypothesized controlling variables during ongoing classroom routines. *School Psychology Review, 34*, 45–57.

Hoover, J. J., & Patton, J. R. (1995). *Teaching students with learning problems to use study skills: A teacher's guide.* Austin, TX: PRO-ED.

Horner, R. H. (1994). Functional assessment: Contributions and future directions. *Journal of Applied Behavior Analysis, 27*, 401–404.

Houck, G. M., King, M. C., Tomlinson, B., Vrabel, A., & Wecks, K. (2002). Small group intervention for children with attention disorders. *Journal of School Nursing, 18*, 196–200.

Howell, D. C., Huessy, H. R., & Hassuk, B. (1985). Fifteen-year follow-up of a behavioral history of attention deficit disorder. *Pediatrics, 76*, 185–191.

Hoza, B., Mrug, S., Gerdes, A. C., Hinshaw, S. P., Bukowski, W. M., Gold, J. A., et al. (2005). What aspects of peer relationships are impaired in children with attention-deficit/hyperactivity disorder? *Journal of Consulting and Clinical Psychology, 73*, 411–423.

Hoza, B., Pelham, W., Dobbs, J., Owens, J., & Pillow, D. (2002). Do boys with attention-deficit/hyperactivity disorder have positive illusory self-concepts? *Journal of Abnormal Psychology, 111*, 268–278.

Hoza, B., Pelham, W., Milich, R., Pillow, D., & McBride, K. (1993). The self-perceptions and attributions of ADHD and nonreferred boys. *Journal of Abnormal Child Psychology, 21*, 271–286.

Hudziak, J. J., Wadsworth, M. E., Heath, A. C., & Achenbach, T. (1999). Latent class analysis of child behavior checklist attention problems. *Journal of the American Academy of Child and Adolescent Psychiatry, 38*, 985–991.

Hyman, I. A., Wojtowicz, A., Lee, K. D., Haffner, M. E., Fiorello, C. A., Storlazzi, J. J., et al. (1998). School-based methylphenidate placebo protocols: Methodological and practical issues. *Journal of Learning Disabilities, 31*, 581–594, 614.

Hynd, G. W., Hern, K. L., Novey, E. S., Eliopulos, D., Marshall, R., Gonzalez, J. J., et al. (1993). Attention-deficit/hyperactivity disorder and asymmetry of the caudate nucleus. *Journal of Child Neurology, 8*, 339–347.

Hynd, G. W., Semrud-Clikeman, M., Lorys, A. R., Novey, E. S., Eliopulos, D., & Lyytinen, H. (1991). Corpus callosum morphology in attention-deficit/hyperactivity disorder: Morphometric analysis of MRI. *Journal of Learning Disabilities, 24,* 141–146.

Hynd, G. W., & Willis, W. G. (1988). *Pediatric neuropsychology.* Boston: Allyn & Bacon.

Individuals with Disabilities Education Act of 1990, 20 U.S.C. § 1400–1485.

Individuals with Disabilities Education Act of 1997, 20 U.S.C. § 1400–1485.

Individuals with Disabilities Education Act of 2004, 20 U.S.C. § 1400–1485.

Ingersoll, B., & Goldstein, S. (1993). *Attention deficit disorder and learning disabilities: Realities, myths, and controversial treatment.* New York: Wiley.

International consensus statement on ADHD. (2002). *Clinical Child and Family Psychology Review, 5,* 89–90.

Iovino, I., Fletcher, J. M., Breitmeyer, B. G., & Foorman, B. R. (1998). Colored overlays for visual perceptual deficits in children with reading disability and attention deficit/hyperactivity disorder: Are they differentially effective? *Journal of Clinical and Experimental Neuropsychology, 20,* 791–806.

Iwaszuk, W., Weyandt, L. L., Schepman, S., Fouts, H., Graff, Y., Hays, B., et al. (1997, March). *Development of the internal restlessness scale.* Poster session presented at the annual meeting of the Western Psychological Association, Seattle, WA.

Jackson, N. A. (2003). A survey of music therapy methods and their role in the treatment of early elementary school children with ADHD. *Journal of Music Therapy, 40,* 302–323.

Jarratt, K. P., Riccio, C. A., & Siekierski, B. M. (2005). Assessment of attention deficit hyperactivity disorder (ADHD) using the BASC and BRIEF. *Applied Neuropsychology, 12,* 83–93.

Javorsky, J., & Gussin, B. (1994). College students with attention-deficit/hyperactivity disorder: An overview and description of services. *Journal of College Student Development, 35,* 170–177.

Jensen, P. (2002). Longer term effects of stimulant treatments for attention-deficit/hyperactivity disorder. *Journal of Attention Disorders, 6*(Suppl. 1), S45–56.

Jensen, P. S. (2000). Commentary: The NIH ADHD consensus statement: Win, lose, or draw? *Journal of the American Academy of Child and Adolescent Psychiatry, 39,* 194–197.

Jensen, P. S., Garcia, J. A., Glied, S., Crowe, M., Foster, M., Schlander, M., et al. (2005). Cost-effectiveness of ADHD treatments: Findings from the multimodal treatments study of children with ADHD. *American Journal of Psychiatry, 162,* 1628–1636.

Jensen, P. S., Hinshaw, S. P., Kraemer, H. C., Lenora, N., Newcorn, J. H., Abikoff, H. B., et al. (2001). ADHD comorbidity findings from the MTA study: Comparing comorbid subgroups. *Journal of the American Academy of Child and Adolescent Psychiatry, 40,* 147–158.

Jensen, P. S., Hinshaw, S. P., Swanson, J. M., Greenhill, L. L., Conners, C. K., Arnold, L. E., et al. (2001). Findings from the NIMH multimodal treatment study of ADHD (MTA): Implications and applications for primary care providers. *Journal of Behavior Pediatrics, 22,* 60–73.

Jensen, P. S., & Kenny, D. T. (2004). The effects of yoga on the attention and behavior of boys with attention-deficit/hyperactivity disorder (ADHD). *Journal of Attention Disorders, 7,* 205–216.

Jensen, P. S., Kettler, L., Roper, M., Sloan, M. T., Dulcan, M. K., Hoven, C., et al. (1999). Are stimulants overprescribed? Treatment of ADHD in four U.S. communities. *Journal of the American Academy of Child and Adolescent Psychiatry, 38,* 797–804.

Jensen, P. S., Shevette, R. E., Xenakis, S. N., & Richters, J. (1993). Anxiety and depressive disorders in attention-deficit/hyperactivity disorder: New findings. *American Journal of Psychiatry, 150,* 1203–1209.

Jerome, L., Gordon, M., & Hustler, P. (1994). A comparison of American and Canadian teachers' knowledge and attitudes towards attention deficit hyperactivity disorder (ADHD). *Canadian Journal of Psychiatry, 39,* 563–567.

Jitendra, A. K., Edwards, L. L., Starosta, K., Sacks, G., Jacobson, L. A., & Choutka, C. M. (2004). Early reading instruction for children with reading difficulties: Meeting the needs of diverse learners. *Journal of Learning Disabilities, 37,* 421–439.

Jonsdottir, S., Bouma, A., Sergeant, J. A., & Scherder, E. J. (2005). The impact of specific language impairment on working memory in children with ADHD combined subtype. *The Archives of Clinical Neuropsychology, 20,* 443–456.

Kadesjö, C., Kadesjö, B., Hägglöf, B., & Gillberg, C. (2001). ADHD in Swedish 3- to 7-year-old children. *Journal of the American Academy of Child and Adolescent Psychiatry, 40,* 1021–1028.

Kadesjö, C., Hägglöf, B., Kadesjö, B., & Gillberg, C. (2003). Attention-deficit-hyperactivity disorder with and without oppositional defiant disorder in 3- to 7-year-old children. *Developmental Medicine and Child Neurology, 45,* 693–699.

Kadison, R. (2005). Getting an edge—Use of stimulants and antidepressants in college. *New England Journal of Medicine, 353,* 1089–1091.

Kaidar, I., Wiener, J., & Tannock, R. (2003). The attributions of children with attention-deficit/hyperactivity disorder for their problem behaviors. *Journal of Attention Disorders, 6,* 99–109.

Kanarek, R. B. (1994). Does sucrose or aspartame cause hyperactivity in children? *Nutrition Reviews, 52,* 173–175.

Kanbayashi, Y., Nakata, Y., Fujii, K., Kita, M., & Wada, K. (1994). ADHD-related behavior among nonreferred children: Parents' ratings of *DSM-III-R* symptoms. *Child Psychiatry and Human Development, 25,* 13–29.

Kaneko, M., Hoshino, Y., Hashimoto, S., Okano, T., & Kumashiro, H. (1993). Hypothalamicpituitary-adrenal axis function in children with attention-deficit/hyperactivity disorder. *Journal of Autism and Developmental Disorders, 23,* 59–65.

Kaplan, S., Heiligenstein, J., West, S., Busner, J., Harder, D., Dittman, R., et al. (2004). Efficacy and safety of atomoxetine in childhood attention-deficit/hyperactivity disorder with comorbid oppositional defiant disorder. *Journal of Attention Disorders, 8,* 45–52.

Kato, P. M., Nichols, M. L., Kerivan, A. S., & Huffman, L. C. (2001). Identifying characteristics of older and younger females with attention-deficit hyperactivity disorder. *Journal of Developmental and Behavioral Pediatrics, 22,* 306–315.

Katusic, S. K., Barbaresi, W. J., Colligan, R. C., Weaver, A. L., Leibson, C. L., & Jacobsen, S. L. (2005). Case definition in epidemiological studies of AD/HD. *Annals of Epidemiology, 15,* 430–437.

Kavale, K. A., & Forness, S. R. (1983). Hyperactivity and diet treatment: A meta–analysis of the Feingold hypothesis. *Journal of Learning Disabilities, 16,* 324–330.

Kelley, M. L., & McCain, A. P. (1995). Promoting academic performance in inattentive children. The relative efficacy of school-home notes with and without response cost. *Behavior Modification, 19,* 357–375.

Kelly, P. C., Cohen, M. L., Walker, W. O., Caskey, O. L., & Atkinson, A. W. (1989). Self-esteem in children medically managed for attention deficit disorder. *Pediatrics, 83,* 211–217.

Kelsey, D. K., Sumner, C. R., Casat, C. D., Coury, D. L., Quintana, H., Saylor, K. E., et al. (2004). Once-daily atomoxetine treatment for children with attention-deficit/hyperactivity disorder, including an assessment of evening and morning behavior: A double-blind, placebo-controlled trial. *Pediatrics, 114,* e1–8.

Kendall, J., Hatton, D., Beckett, A., & Leo, M. (2003). Children's accounts of attention-deficit/hyperactivity disorder. *Advances in Nursing Science, 26,* 114–130.

Kendall, P. C. (1992). *Cognitive-behavioral therapy for impulsive children: The manual.* (Available from P. C. Kendall, 238 Meeting House Lane, Merion Station, PA, 19066)

Kendall, P. C., & Braswell, L. (1982). Cognitive-behavior self-control therapy for children: A components analysis. *Journal of Consulting and Clinical Psychology, 50,* 672–689.

Kennemer, K., & Goldstein, S. (2005). Incidence of ADHD in adults with severe mental health problems. *Applied Neuropsychology, 12,* 77–82.

Kent, L. (2004). Recent advances in the genetics of attention deficit hyperactivity disorder. *Current Psychiatry Report, 6,* 143–148.

Kessler, R. C., Adler, L. A., Barkley, R., Biederman, J., Conners, C. K., Faraone, S. V., et al. (2005). Patterns and predictors of attention-deficit/hyperactivity disorder persistence into adulthood: Results from the national comorbidity survey replication. *Biological Psychiatry, 57,* 1442–1451.

Khilnani, S., Field, T., Hernandez-Reif, M., & Schanberg, S. (2003). Massage therapy improves mood and behavior of students with attention-deficit/hyperactivity disorder. *Adolescence, 38,* 624–638.

Kirley, A., Hawi, Z., Daly, G., McCarron, M., Mullins, C., Millar, N., et al. (2002). Dopaminergic system genes in ADHD: Toward a biological hypothesis. *Neuropsychopharmacology, 27,* 607–619.

Kitchens, S. A., Rosen, L. A., & Braaten, E. B. (1999). Differences in anger, aggression, depression, and anxiety between ADHD and non-ADHD children. *Journal of Attention Disorders, 3,* 77–83.

Klassen, A. F., Miller, A., & Fine, S. (2004). Health-related quality of life in children and adolescents who have a diagnosis of attention-deficit/hyperactivity disorder. *Pediatrics, 114,* e541–e547.

Kleiman, G., Humphrey, M., & Lindsay, P. H. (1981). Microcomputers and hyperactive children. *Creative Computing, 7,* 93–94.

Klorman, R., Hazel-Fernandez, G. A., Shaywitz, S. E., Fletcher, J. M., Marchione, K. E., Holahan, J. M., et al. (1999). Executive functioning deficits in Attention Deficit Hyperactivity Disorder are independent of oppositional defiant or reading disorder. *Journal of the American Academy of Child and Adolescent Psychiatry, 38,* 1148–1155.

Kløve, H. (1989). The hypoarousal hypothesis: What is the evidence? In T. Sagvolden & T. Archer (Eds.), *Attention Deficit Disorder: Clinical and basic research.* Hillsdale, NJ: Lawrence Erlbaum Associates.

Kolko, D. J., Bukstein, O. G., & Barron, J. (1999). Methylphenidate and behavior modification in children with ADHD and comorbid ODD or CD: Main and incremental effects across settings. *Journal of the American Academy of Child and Adolescent Psychiatry, 38,* 578–586.

Kollins, S. H. (2003). Comparing the abuse potential of methylphenidate versus other stimulants: A review of available evidence and relevance to the ADHD patient. *Journal of Clinical Psychiatry, 64*(Suppl. 11), 14–18.

Kooij, J. J., Buitelaar, J. K., van den Oord, E. J., Furer, J. W., Rijnders, C. A., & Hodiamont, P. P. (2005). Internal and external validity of attention-deficit hyperactivity disorder in a population-based sample of adults. *Psychological Medicine, 35,* 817–827.

Kooij, J. J., Burger, H., Boonstra, A. M., Van der Linden, L., & Buitelaar, J. K. (2004). Efficacy and safety of methylphenidate in 45 adults with attention-deficit/hyperactivity disorder. A randomized placebo-controlled double-blind cross-over trial. *Psychological Medicine, 34,* 973–982.

Kos, J. M., Richdale, A. L., & Jackson, M. S. (2004). Knowledge about attention deficit/hyperactivity disorder: A comparison of in-service and pre-service teachers. *Psychology in the Schools, 41,* 517–526.

Kotkin, R. (1998). The Irvine Paraprofessional Program: Promising practice for serving students with ADHD. *Journal of Learning Disabilities, 31,* 556–564.

Kratochvil, C. J., Heiligenstein, J. H., Dittmann, R., Spencer, T. J., Biederman, J., Wernicke, J., et al. (2002). Atomoxetine and methylphenidate treatment in children with ADHD: A prospective, randomized, open-label trial. *Journal of the American Academy of Child and Adolescent Psychiatry, 41,* 776–784.

Krummel, D. A., Seligson, F. H., & Guthrie, H. A. (1996). Hyperactivity: Is candy causal? *Critical Reviews in Food Science and Nutrition, 36,* 31–47.

Kuntsi, J., Rijsdijk, F., Ronald, A., Asherson, P., & Plomin, R. (2005). Genetic influences on the stability of attention-deficit/hyperactivity disorder symptoms from early to middle childhood. *Biological Psychiatry, 57,* 647–654.

Kuo, F. E., & Taylor, A. F. (2004). A potential natural treatment for attention-deficit/hyperactivity disorder: Evidence from a national study. *American Journal of Public Health, 94,* 1580–1586.

Lahey, B. B., Pelham, W. E., Loney, J., Lee, S. S., & Willcutt, E. (2005). Instability of the DSM-IV subtypes of ADHD from preschool through elementary school. *Archives of General Psychiatry, 62,* 896–902.

Lahoste, G. J., Swanson, J. M., Wigal, S. B., Glabe, C., Wigal, T., et al. (1996). Dopamine D4 receptor gene polymorphism is associated with attention deficit/hyperactivity disorder. *Molecular Psychiatry, 1,* 121–124.

Landau, S., & Moore, L. A. (1991). Social skill deficits in children with attention deficit/hyperactivity disorder. *School Psychology Review, 20,* 235–251.

Larsson, J. O., Larsson, H., & Lichtenstein, P. (2004). Genetic and environmental contributions to stability and change of ADHD symptoms between 8 and 13 years of age: A longitudinal twin study. *Journal of the American Academy of Child and Adolescent Psychiatry, 43,* 1267–1275.

Latham, P., & Latham, P. (1992). *ADD and the law.* Washington, DC: JKL Communications.

Latham, P. S., & Latham, P. H. (1999). ADHD views from the courthouse. *The ADHD Report, 7,* 9–11, 14.

Latham, P. S., & Latham, P. H. (2002). What clinician's need to know about legal issues relative to ADHD. In S. Goldstein, & A. T. Ellison (Eds.), *Clinician's Guide to Adult ADHD: Assessment and Intervention* (pp. 205–219). Boston: Academic Press.

Lavigne, J. V., Gibbons, R. D., Christoffel, K. K., Arend, R., Rosenbaum, D., Binns, H., et al. (1996). Prevalence rates and correlates of psychiatric disorders among preschool children. *Journal of the American Academy of Child and Adolescent Psychiatry, 35,* 204–214.

Law, S. F., & Schachar, R. J. (1999). Do typical clinical doses of methylphenidate cause tics in children treated for attention-deficit/hyperactivity disorder? *Journal of the American Academy of Child and Adolescent Psychiatry, 38,* 944–951.

Lawrence, V., Houghton, S., Tannock, R., Douglas, G., Durkin, K., & Whiting, K. (2002). ADHD outside the laboratory: Boys' executive function performance on tasks in videogame play and on a visit to the zoo. *Journal of Abnormal Child Psychology, 30,* 447–462.

LeFever, G. B., Butterfoss, F. D., & Vislocky, N. F. (1999). High prevalence of attention deficit disorder: Catalyst for development of a school health coalition. *Community Health, 22,* 38–49.

Leon, R. M. (2000). Effects of caffeine on cognitive, psychomotor, and affective performance of children with attention-deficit/hyperactivity disorder. *Journal of Attention Disorders, 4,* 27–47.

Levin, H. S., & Hanten, G. (2005). Executive functions after traumatic brain injury in children. *Pediatric Neurology, 33,* 79–93.

Levy, F., Hay, D. A., Bennett, K. S., & McStephen, M. (2005). Gender differences in ADHD subtype comorbidity. *Journal of the American Academy of Child and Adolescent Psychiatry, 44,* 368–376.

Levy, F., Hay, D., McStephen, M., Wood, C., & Waldman, I. (1997). Attention-deficit hyperactivity disorder: A category or a continuum? Genetic analysis of a large-scale twin study. *Journal of the American Academy of Child and Adolescent Psychiatry, 36,* 737–744.

Lezak, M. D. (1995). *Neuropsychological assessment* (3rd ed.). New York: Oxford University Press.

Lijffijt, M., Kenemans, J. L., Wal, A. T., Quik, E. H., Kemner, C., Westenberg, H., et al. (in press). Dose-related effect of methylphenidate on stopping and changing in children with attention-deficit/hyperactivity disorder. *European Psychiatry.*

Lin, C. H., Hsiao, C. K., & Chen, W. J. (1999). Development of sustained attention assessed using the continuous performance test among children 6 to 15 years of age. *Journal of Abnormal Child Psychology, 27,* 403–412.

Linterman, I., & Weyandt, L. (2001). Divided attention skills in college students with ADHD: Is it advantageous to have ADHD? *The ADHD Report, 9,* 1–6.

Liu, Y., & Reichelt, K. L. (2001). A serotonin uptake-stimulating tetra-peptide found in urines from ADHD children. *World Journal of Biological Psychiatry, 2,* 144–148.

Lloyd, J. W., Landrum, T., & Hallahan, D. P. (1991). Self-monitoring applications for classroom intervention. In G. Stoner, M. R. Shinn, & H. M. Walker (Eds.), *Interventions for achievement and behavior problems* (pp. 201–213). Washington, DC: National Association of School Psychologists.

Lomas, B., & Gartside, P. S. (1997). Attention-deficit/hyperactivity disorder among homeless veterans. *Psychiatric Services, 48,* 1331–1333.

Loney, J., Kramer, J., & Milich, R. (1981). The hyperkinetic child grows up: Predictors for symptoms, delinquency, and achievement at follow-up. In K. Gadow & J. Loney (Eds.), *Psychosocial aspects of drug treatment for hyperactivity* (pp.). Boulder, CO: Westview Press.

Loo, S. K., & Barkley, R. A. (2005). Clinical utility of EEG in attention deficit hyperactivity disorder. *Applied Neuropsychology, 12,* 64–76.

Lorch, E. P., Milich, R., Sanchez, R. P., van den Broek, P., Baer, S., Hooks, K., et al. (2000). Comprehension of televised stories in boys with attention deficit/hyperactivity disorder and nonreferred boys. *Journal of Abnormal Psychology, 109,* 321–330.

Lou, H. C., Henriksen, L., & Bruhn, P. (1984). Focal cerebral hypoperfusion in children with dysphasia and/or attention deficit disorder. *Archives of Neurology, 41,* 825–829.

Lou, H. C., Henriksen, L., Bruhn, P., Borner, H., & Nielsen, J. B. (1989). Striatal dysfunction in attention deficit and hyperkinetic disorder. *Archives of Neurology, 46,* 48–52.

Low, K. G., & Gendaszek, A. E. (2002). Illicit use of psychostimulants among college students: A preliminary study. *Psychology, Health, & Medicine, 7,* 283–287.

Lubar, J. F. (1991). Discourse on the development of EEG diagnostics and biofeedback for attention-deficit/hyperactivity disorders. *Biofeedback and Self-Regulation, 16,* 201–225.

Lucker, J. R., Geffner, D., & Koch, W. (1996). Perception of loudness in children with ADD and without ADD. *Child Psychiatry and Human Development, 26,* 181–190.

Luk, S. L., Leung, P. W. L., & Lee, P. L. M. (1988). Conners' Teaching Rating Scale in Chinese children in Hong Kong. *Journal of Child Psychology and Psychiatry, 29,* 165–174.

Luman, M., Oosterlaan, J., & Sergeant, J. A. (2005). The impact of reinforcement contingencies on AD/HD: A review and theoretical approach. *Clinical Psychology Review, 25,* 183–213.

Magnusson, P., Smari, J. Gretarsdottir, H., & Prandardottir, H. (1999). Attention-deficit/hyperactivity symptoms in Icelandic schoolchildren: Assessment with the Attention-Deficit/Hyperactivity Rating Scale-IV. *Scandinavian Journal of Psychology, 40,* 301–306.

Mahone, E. M., Pillion, J. P., Hoffman, J., Hiemenz, J. R., & Denckla, M. B. (2005). Construct validity of the auditory continuous performance test for preschoolers. *Developmental Neuropsychology, 27,* 11–33.

Mann, C. A., Lubar, J. F., Zimmerman, B., Miller, K., & Muenchen, A. (1990). Quantitative analysis of EEG in boys with attention-deficit/hyperactivity disorder: Controlled with clinical implications. *Pediatric Neurology, 8,* 30–36.

Mannuzza, S., Gittelman-Klein, R., Bessler, A., Malloy, P., & LaPadula, M. (1993). Adult outcome of hyperactive boys: Educational achievement, occupational rank, and psychiatric status. *Archives of General Psychiatry, 50,* 565–576.

Mannuzza, S., Klein, R. G., Abikoff, H., & Moulton, J. L. (2004). Significance of childhood conduct problems to later development of conduct disorder among children with ADHD: A prospective follow-up study. *Journal of Abnormal Child Psychology, 32,* 565–573.

Mannuzza, S., Klein, R. G., Bessler, A., & Malloy, P. (1993). Adult outcome of hyperactive boys: Educational achievement, occupational rank, and psychiatric status. *Archives of General Psychiatry, 50,* 565–576.

Mannuzza, S., Klein, R. G., Bessler, A., Malloy, P., & Hynes, M. E. (1997). Educational and occupational outcome of hyperactive boys grown up. *Journal of the American Academy of Child and Adolescent Psychiatry, 36,* 1222–1227.

Manos, M. J., Short, E. J., & Findling, R. L. (1999). Differential effectiveness of methylphenidate and Adderall in school-age youths with attention-deficit/hyperactivity disorder. *Journal of the American Academy of Child and Adolescent Psychiatry, 38,* 813–819.

Mariani, M., & Barkley, R. A. (1997). Neuropsychological functioning in preschool children with attention-deficit/hyperactivity disorder. *Developmental Neuropsychology, 13,* 111–129.

Marks, D. J., Himelstein, J., Newcorn, J. H., & Halperin, J. M. (1999). Identification of AD/HD subtypes using laboratory-based measures: A cluster analysis. *Journal of Abnormal Child Psychology, 27,* 167–175.

Marotta, P. J., & Roberts, E. A. (1998). Pemoline hepatotoxity in children. *Journal of Pediatrics, 132,* 894–897.

Marshall, R. M., Hynd, G. W., Handwerk, M. J., & Hall, J. (1997). Academic underachievement in ADHD subtypes. *Journal of Learning Disabilities, 30,* 635–642.

Martin, A. J., Linfoot, K., & Stephenson, J. (1999). How teachers respond to concerns about misbehavior in their classroom. *Psychology in the Schools, 36,* 347–358.

Martinussen, R., Hayden, J., Hogg-Johnson, S., & Tannock, R. (2005). A meta-analysis of working memory impairments in children with attention-deficit/hyperactivity disorder. *Journal of the American Academy of Child and Adolescent Psychiatry, 44,* 377–384.

Mash, E. J., & Johnston, C. (1983). Parental perceptions of child behavior problems, parenting self-esteem, and mothers reported stress in younger and older hyperactive and normal children. *Journal of Consulting and Clinical Psychology, 51,* 68–99.

Masi, G., Millepiedi, S., Mucci, M., Poli, P., Bertini, N., & Milantoni, L. (2004). Generalized anxiety disorder in referred children and adolescents. *Journal of the American Academy of Child and Adolescent Psychiatry, 43,* 752–760.

Massello, W., 3rd, & Carpenter, D. A. (1999). A fatality due to the intranasal abuse of methylphenidate (Ritalin). *Journal of Forensic Science, 44,* 220–221.

McBurnett, K., Pfiffner, L. J., Willcutt, E., Tamm, L., Lerner, M., Ottolini, Y. L., et al. (1999). Experimental cross-validation of *DSM-IV* subtypes of attention deficit/hyperactivity disorder. *Journal of the American Academy of Child and Adolescent Psychiatry, 38,* 17–24.

McCabe, S. E., Knight, J. R., Teter, C. J., & Wechsler, H. (2005). Non-medical use of prescription stimulants among US college students: Prevalence and correlates from a national survey. *Addiction, 99,* 96–106.

McCabe, S. E., Teter, C. J., & Boyd, C. J. (2004). The use, misuse and diversion of prescription stimulants among middle and high school students. *Substance Use and Misuse, 39,* 1095–1116.

McCarney, S. B. (1995). *The attention deficit disorders evaluation scales (ADDES).* Columbia, MO: Hawthorne.

McGee, R. A., Clark, S. E., & Symons, D. K. (2000). Does the Conners' Continuous Performance Test aid in ADHD diagnosis? *Journal of Abnormal Child Psychology, 28,* 415–424.

McGough, J. J., Pataki, C. S., & Suddath, R. (2005). Dexmethylphenidate extended-release capsules for attention deficit hyperactivity disorder. *Expert Review of Neurotherapeutics, 5,* 437–441.

McGough, J. J., Smalley, S. L., McCracken, J. T., Yang, M., Del'Homme, M., Lynn, D. E., et al. (2005). Psychiatric comorbidity in adult attention deficit hyperactivity disorder: Findings from multiplex families. *American Journal of Psychiatry, 162,* 1621–1627.

McGrath, M. M., Sullivan, M., Devin, J., Fontes-Murphy, M., Barcelos, S., DePalma, J. L., et al. (2005). Early precursors of low attention and hyperactivity in a preterm sample at age four. *Issues of Comprehensive Pediatric Nursing, 28,* 1–15.

McLaughlin-Crabtree, V., Ivaneko, A., O'Brien, L. M., & Gonzal, D. (2003). Periodic limb movement disorder of sleep in children. *Journal of Sleep Research, 12,* 73–81.

McNeil, C. B. (1995). *The ADHD classroom kit: An inclusive approach to behavior management* (pp. 800, 962–1141). King of Prussia, PA: Center for Applied Psychology.

Merrell, K. W. (1999). *Behavioral, social, and emotional assessment of children and adolescents.* Mahwah, NJ: Lawrence Erlbaum Associates.

Mick, E., Faraone, S. V., & Biederman, J. (2004). Age-dependent expression of attention-deficit/hyperactivity disorder symptoms. *Psychiatric Clinics of North America, 27,* 215–224.

Mikkelsen, E., Lake, R. C., Brown, G. L., Ziegler, M. G., & Ebert, M. H. (1981). The hyperactive child syndrome: Peripheral sympathetic nervous system function and the effect of d-amphetamine. *Psychiatry Research, 4,* 157–169.

Milberger, S., Biederman, J., Faraone, S. V., Chen, L., & Jones, J. (1996). Is maternal smoking during pregnancy a risk factor for attention-deficit/hyperactivity disorder in children? *American Journal of Psychiatry, 153,* 1138–1142.

Milich, R., Balentine, A. C., & Lynam, D. R. (2002). ADHD combined type and ADHD predominantly inattentive type are distinct and unrelated disorders. *Clinical Psychology Science Practice, 8,* 463–488.

Mill, J., Xu, X., Ronald, A., Curran, S., Price, T., Knight, J., et al. (2005). Quantitative trait locus analysis of candidate gene alleles associated with attention deficit hyperactivity disorder (ADHD) in five genes: DRD4, DAT1, DRD5, SNAP-25, and 5HT1B. *American Journal of Medical Genetics Part B-Neuropsychiatric Genetics, 133,* 68–73.

Miranda, A., Presentacion, M. J., & Soriano, M. (2002). Effectiveness of a school-based multicomponent program for the treatment of children with ADHD. *Journal of Learning Disabilities, 35,* 546–562.

Mithaug, D. K., & Mithaug, D. E. (2003). Effects of teacher-directed versus student-directed instruction on self-management of young children with disabilities. *Journal of Applied Behavior Analysis, 36,* 133–136.

Mitsis, E. M., McKay, K. E., Schulz, K. P., Newcorn, J. H., & Halperin, J. M. (2000). Parent-teacher concordance for *DSM-IV* attention-deficit/hyperactivity disorder in a clinic-referred sample. *Journal of the American Academy of Child and Adolescent Psychiatry, 39,* 308–313.

Molina, B., & Pelham, W. E. (2003). Childhood predictors of adolescent substance use in a longitudinal study of children with ADHD. *Journal of Abnormal Psychology, 112,* 497–507.

Monastra, V. J., Linden, M., Phillips, A., Lubar, J. F., VanDeusen, P., Wing, W., et al. (1999). Assessing attention-deficit/hyperactivity disorder via quantitative electroencephalography: An initial validation study. *Neuropsychology, 13,* 424–433.

Morgan, A. E., Hynd, G. W., Riccio, C. A., & Hall, J. (1996). Validity of *DSM-IV* ADHD predominately inattentive and combined types: Relationship to previous *DSM* diagnoses/subtype differences. *Journal of the American Academy of Child and Adolescent Psychiatry, 35*, 325–333.

Mousain-Bosc, M., Roche, M., Rapin, J., & Bali, J. P. (2004). Magnesium VitB6 intake reduces central nervous system hyperexcitability in children. *Journal of the American College of Nutrition, 23*, 545S–548S.

MTA Cooperative Group. (2004). National Institute of Mental Health multimodal treatment study of ADHD follow-up: 24-month outcomes of treatment strategies for attention-deficit/hyperactivity disorder. *Pediatrics, 113*, 754–761.

Mugnaini, D., Masi, G., Brovedani, P., Chelazzi, C., Matas, M., Romagnoli, C., et al. (2005). Teacher reports of ADHD symptoms in Italian children at the end of first grade. *European Psychiatry*.

Mulligan, S. (2001). Classroom strategies used by teachers of students with attention deficit hyperactivity disorder. *Physical & Occupational Therapy in Pediatrics, 20*, 25–44.

Murphy, B., & Johnson, G. (1988). *Managing ADD in the classroom*. DePaul Northshore Hospital, Covington, LA.

Murphy, K., & Barkley, R. A. (1996). Attention-deficit/hyperactivity disorder in adults. *Comprehensive Psychiatry, 37*, 393–401.

Murphy, K., & Gordon, M. (2006). Assessment of adults with ADHD. In R. Barkley (Ed.), *ADHD: A handbook for diagnosis and treatment* (3rd ed., pp. 425–450).

Murphy, K. R., Barkley, R. A., & Bush, T. (2002). Young adults with attention deficit hyperactivity disorder: Subtype differences in comorbidity, educational, and clinical history. *The Journal of Nervous and Mental Disease, 190*, 147–157.

Murphy, P., & Schachar, R. (2000). Use of self-ratings in the assessment of symptoms of attention deficit hyperactivity disorder in adults. *American Journal of Psychiatry, 157*, 1156–1159.

Musser, C. J., Ahmann, P. A., Theye, F. W., Mundt, P., Broste, S. K., & Mueller-Rizner, N. (1998). Stimulant use and the potential for abuse in Wisconsin as reported by school administrators and longitudinally followed children. *Journal of Developmental and Behavioral Pediatrics, 19*, 187–192.

Nadeau, K. (1995). *A comprehensive guide to adults with attention deficit disorder*. New York: Brunner/Mazel.

Naglieri, J. A., & Das, J. P. (1997). *Das-Naglieri cognitive assessment system (CAS)*. Itasca, IL: Riverside.

Naglieri, J. A., Goldstein, S., Delauder, B. Y., & Schwebach, A. (2005). Relationship between the WISC-III and the Cognitive Assessment System with Conners' Rating Scales and Continuous Performance Tests. *Archives of Clinical Neuropsychology, 20*, 385–401.

Najt, P., Glahn, D., Bearden, C. E., Hatch, J. P., Monkul, E. S., Kaur, S., et al. (2005). Attention deficits in bipolar disorder: A comparison based on the Continuous Performance Test. *Neuroscience Letters, 379*, 122–126.

National Institutes of Health (NIH). (2000). Consensus and development conference statement: Diagnosis and treatment of attention-deficit/hyperactivity disorder. *Journal of the American Academy of Child and Adolescent Psychiatry, 39*, 182–193.

Neef, N. A., Marckel, J., Ferreri, S., Jung, S., Nist, L., & Armstrong, N. (2004). Effects of modeling versus instructions on sensitivity to reinforcement schedules. *Journal of Applied Behavior Analysis, 37*, 267–281.

Nelson, R., Roberts, M., & Smith, D. (1998). *Conducting functional behavioral assessments: A practical guide*. Longmont, CO: Sopris West.

Newby, R. S., Fischer, M., & Roman, M. A. (1991). Parent training for families of children with ADHD. *School Psychology Review, 20*, 252–265.

Newcorn, J. H., Halperin, J. M., Jensen, P. S., Abikoff, H. B., Arnold, L. E., Cantwell, D. P., et al. (2001). Symptom profiles in children with ADHD: Effects of comorbidity and gender. *Journal of the American Academy of Child and Adolescent Psychiatry, 40,* 137–146.

Nierenberg, A. A., Miyahara, S., Spencer, T., Wisniewski, S. R., Otto, M. W., Simon, N., et al. (2005). Clinical and diagnostic implications of lifetime attention-deficit/hyperactivity disorder comorbidity in adults with bipolar disorder: Data from the first 1000 STEP-BD participants. *Biological Psychiatry, 57,* 1467–1473.

Nietfeld, J. L., & Hunt, A. A. (2005). Elementary and pre-service teachers' strategies for working with students with hyperactivity. *Current Issues in Education, 8,* 1–14.

Nigg, J. T., & Hinshaw, S. P. (1998). Parent personality traits and psychopathology associated with antisocial behaviors in childhood attention-deficit/hyperactivity disorder. *Journal of Child Psychology and Psychiatry, 39,* 145–159.

Nigg, J. T., Willcutt, E. G., Doyle, A. E., & Sonuga-Barke, E. J. (2005). Causal heterogeneity in attention-deficit/hyperactivity disorder: Do we need neuropsychologically impaired subtypes? *Biological Psychiatry, 57,* 1224–1230.

Noell, G. H., Witt, J. C., Gilbertson, D. N., Ranier, D. D., & Freeland, J. T. (1997). Increasing teacher intervention implementation in general education settings through consultation and performance feedback. *School Psychology Quarterly, 12,* 77–88.

Noell, G. W., Witt, J. C., LaFleur, L. H., Mortenson, B. P., Ranier, D. D., & LeVelle, J. (2000). Increasing intervention implementation in general education following consultation: A comparison of two follow-up strategies. *Journal of Applied Behavior Analysis, 33,* 271–284.

Nolan, E. D., Gadow, K. D., & Sprafkin, J. (2001). Teacher reports of DSM-IV ADHD, ODD, and CD symptoms in schoolchildren. *Journal of Child and Adolescent Psychiatry, 40,* 241–249.

North, J., Broussard, C., Jones, K., George, T., Vollmer, T. R., & Herring, M. (1995). The differential effects of teacher and peer attention on the disruptive classroom behavior of three children with a diagnosis of attention deficit hyperactivity disorder. *Journal of Applied Behavior Analysis, 28,* 277–229.

Northrup, J., Broussard, C., Jones, K., & George, T. (1995). A preliminary comparison of reinforces assessment methods for children with ADHD. *Journal of Applied Behavior Analysis, 28,* 99–100.

Northrup, J., Jones, K., Broussard, D., DiGiovanni, G., Herring, M., Fusilier, I., et al. (1997). A preliminary analysis of interactive effects between common classroom contingencies and methylphenidate. *Journal of Applied Behavior Analysis, 30,* 121–125.

Nussbaum, N. L., Grant, M. L., Roman, M. J., Poole, J. H., & Bigler, E. D. (1990). Attention deficit disorder and the mediating effect of age on academic and behavioral variables. *Developmental and Behavioral Pediatrics, 11,* 22–26.

Oades, R. D. (2000). Differential measures of 'sustained attention' in children with attention-deficit/hyperactivity or tic disorders: Relations to monoamine metabolism. *Psychiatry Research, 93,* 165–178.

Oades, R. D. (2002). Dopamine may be 'hyper' with respect to noradrenaline metabolism, but 'hypo' with respect to serotonin metabolism in children with attention-deficit hyperactivity disorder. *Behavioural Brain Research, 130,* 97–102.

Oades, R. D., Sadile, A. G., Sagvolden, T., Viggiano, D., Zuddas, A., Devoto, P., et al. (2005). The control of responsiveness in ADHD by catecholamines: Evidence for dopaminergic, noradrenergic and interactive roles. *Developmental Science, 8,* 122–131.

Ohan, J. L., & Johnston, C. (2002). Are the performance overestimates given by boys with ADHD self-protection? *Journal of Clinical Child Psychology, 31,* 230–241.

Oosterlaan, J., & Sergeant, J. A. (1998). Effects of reward and response cost on response inhibition in AD/HD, disruptive, anxious, and normal children. *Journal of Abnormal Child Psychology, 26,* 161–174.

Ornoy, A., Uriel, L., & Tennenbaum, A. (1993). Inattention, hyperactivity, and speech delay at two–four years of age as a predictor for ADD–ADHD syndrome. *Israel Journal of Psychiatry and Related Sciences, 30*, 155–163.

Orvaschel, H. (1985). Psychiatric interviews suitable for use in research with children and adolescents. *Psychological Bulletin, 21*, 737–745.

Orvaschel, H., & Walsh, G. (1984). *The assessment of adaptive functioning in children: A review of existing measures suitable for epidemiological and clinical services research.* Washington, DC: US Department of Health and Human Services, NIMH, Division of Biometry and Epidemiology.

Owens, J., & Hoza, B. (2003). Diagnostic utility of DSM-IV-TR symptoms in the prediction of DSM-IV-TR ADHD subtypes and ODD. *Journal of Attention Disorders, 7*, 11–27.

Palacios, E. D., & Semrud-Clikeman, M. (2005). Delinquency, hyperactivity, and phonological awareness: A comparison of adolescents with ODD and ADHD. *Applied Neuropsychology, 12*, 94–105.

Palumbo, D., Spencer, T., Lynch, J., Co-Chien, H., & Faraone, S. V. (2004). Emergence of tics in children with ADHD: Impact of once-daily OROS methylphenidate therapy. *Journal of Child and Adolescent Psychopharmacology, 14*, 185–194.

Paolitto, A. W. (1999). Clinical validation of the cognitive assessment system with children with ADHD. *The ADHD Report, 7*, 1–5.

Parker, J. G., & Asher, S. R. (1987). Peer relations and later personal adjustment. Are low accepted children at risk? *Psychological Bulletin, 102*, 357–389.

Pastor, P. N., & Reuben, C. A. (2002). Attention deficit disorder and learning disability: United States, 1997–98. *Vital and Health Statistics, 10*, 1–12.

Pelham, W. E., Jr., Fabiano, G. A., & Massetti, G. M. (2005). Evidence-based assessment of attention deficit hyperactivity disorder in children and adolescents. *Journal of Clinical Child and Adolescent Psychology, 34*, 449–476.

Pelham, W. E., Jr., Gnagy, E. M., Greiner, A. R., Hoza, B., Hinshaw, S. P., Swanson, J. M., et al. (2000). Behavioral versus behavioral and pharmacological treatment in ADHD children attending a summer treatment program. *Journal of Abnormal Child Psychology, 28*, 507–525.

Pelham, W. E., Jr., McBurnett, K., Murphy, D. A., Clinton, J., & Thiele, C. (1990). Methylphenidate and baseball playing in ADHD children: Who's on first? *Journal of Consulting and Clinical Psychology, 146*, 130–133.

Pelham, W. E., Jr., Wheeler, T., & Chronis, A. (1998). Empirically supported psychosocial treatments for attention-deficit/hyperactivity disorder. *Journal of Clinical Child Psychology, 27*, 190–205.

Pennington, B. F., Groisser, D., & Welsh, M. C. (1993). Contrasting cognitive deficits in attention-deficit/hyperactivity disorder versus reading disability. *Developmental Neuropsychology, 29*, 512–523.

Perla, M. (1996, November). Using Kendall's *Stop and Think* program with ADHD students. *National Association of School Psychologists' Communique*, 16–17.

Perugini, E. M., Harvey, E. A., Lovejoy, D. W., Sandstrom, K., & Webb, A. H. (2000). The predictive power of combined neuropsychological measures for attention-deficit/hyperactivity disorder in children. *Child Neuropsychology, 6*, 101–114.

Perwien, A. R., Faries, D. E., Kratochvil, C. J., Sumner, C. R., Kelsey, D. K., & Allen, A. J. (2004). Improvement in health-related quality of life in children with ADHD: An analysis of placebo controlled studies of atomoxetine. *Journal of Developmental and Behavioral Pediatrics, 25*, 264–271.

Pfiffner, L. J., & Barkley, R. A. (1990). Educational placement and management. In R. A. Barkley (Ed.), *Attention-deficit/hyperactivity disorder: A handbook for diagnosis and treatment* (pp. 498–539). New York: Guilford Press.

Pfiffner, L. J., & O'Leary, S. G. (1987). The efficacy of all-positive management as a function of the prior use of negative consequences. *Journal of Applied Behavior Analysis, 20*, 265–271.

Physician's Desk Reference. (2006). Montvale, NJ: Medical Economics Data.

Pineda, D., Ardila, A., Rosselli, M., Arias, B. E., Henao, G. C., Gomez, L. F., et al. (1999). Prevalence of attention-deficit/hyperactivity disorder symptoms in 4- to 17-year-old children in the general population. *Journal of Abnormal Child Psychology, 27*, 455–462.

Pisecco, S., Huzinec, C., & Curtis, D. (2001). The effect of child characteristics on teachers' acceptability of classroom-based behavioral strategies and psychostimulant medication for the treatment of ADHD. *Journal of Clinical Child Psychology, 30*, 413–421.

Pisecco, S., Wristers, K., Swank, P., Silva, P. A., & Barker, D. B. (2001). The effect of academic self-concept on ADHD and antisocial behaviors in early adolescence. *Journal of Learning Disabilities, 34*, 450–461.

Pisterman, S., McGrath, P., Firestone, P., Goodman, J. T., Webster, I., Mallory, R., & et al. (1992). The role of parent training in treatment of preschoolers with ADHD. *American Journal of Orthopsychiatry, 62*, 397–408.

Pitcher, T. M., Piek, J. P., & Hay, D. A. (2003). Fine and gross motor ability in males with ADHD. *Developmental Medicine and Child Neurology, 45*, 525–535.

Platzman, K. A., Stay, M. R., Brown, R. T., Coles, C. D., Smith, I. E., & Falek, A. (1992). Review of observational methods in attention deficit hyperactive Disorder (ADHD): Implications of a Diagnosis. *School Psychology Quarterly, 7*, 155–177.

Pliszka, S. R. (2003). *Neuroscience for the Mental Health Clinician*. New York: Guilford Press.

Pliszka, S. R. (2005). The neuropsychopharmacology of attention-deficit/hyperactivity disorder. *Biological Psychiatry, 57*, 1385–1390.

Pliszka, S. R., Browne, R. G., Olvera, R. L., & Wynne, S. K. (2000). A double-blind, placebo-controlled study of adderall and methylphenidate in the treatment of attention-deficit/hyperactivity disorder. *Journal of the American Academy of Child and Adolescent Psychiatry, 39*, 619–626.

Pliszka, S. R., McCracken, J. T., & Mass, J. W. (1996). Catecholamines in attention deficit/hyperactivity disorder: Current perspectives. *Journal of the American Academy of Child and Adolescent Psychiatry, 35*, 264–272.

Pomerleau, C. S., Downey, K. K., Snedecor, S. M., Mehringer, A. M., Marks, J. L., & Pomerleau, O. F. (2003). Smoking patterns and abstinence effects in smokers with no ADHD, childhood ADHD, and adult ADHD symptomatology. *Addictive Behaviors, 28*, 1149–1157.

Popper, C. W. (2000). Pharmacologic alternatives to psychostimulants for the treatment of attention-deficit/hyperactivity disorder. *Child and Adolescent Psychiatric Clinics of North America, 9*, 605–646.

Porrino, L. J., Rapoport, J. L., Behar, D., Sceery, W., Ismond, D. R., & Bunney, W. E. (1983). A naturalistic assessment of the motor activity of hyperactive boys. I. Comparison with normal controls. *Archives of General Psychiatry, 40*, 681–687.

Potashkin, B. D., & Beckles, N. (1990). Relative efficacy of Ritalin and biofeedback treatments in the management of hyperactivity. *Biofeedback and Self-Regulation, 15*, 305–315.

Powell, S., & Nelson, B. (1997). Effects of choosing academic assignments on a student with attention deficit hyperactivity disorder. *Journal of Applied Behavior Analysis, 30*, 181–183.

Power, T. J., Hess, L. E., & Bennett, D. S. (1995). The acceptability of interventions for attention-deficit hyperactivity disorder among elementary and middle school teachers. *Journal of Developmental and Behavioral Pediatrics, 16*, 238–243.

Prifitera, A., & Dersh, J. (1993). Base rates of WISC-III diagnostic subtest patterns among normal, learning disabled, and ADHD samples. *Journal of Psychoeducational Assessment: WISC-III Monograph*, 43–55.

Purvis, K. L., & Tannock, R. (1997). Language abilities in children with attention deficit/hyperactivity disorder, reading disabilities, and normal controls. *Journal of Abnormal Child Psychology, 25*, 133–144.

Purvis, K. L., & Tannock, R. (2000). Phonological processing, not inhibitory control, differentiates ADHD and Reading Disability. *Journal of the American Academy of Child and Adolescent Psychiatry, 39*, 485–493.

Ramirez, C. A., Rosen, L. A., Deffenbacher, H., Hurst, H., Nicoletta, C., Rosencranz, T., et al. (1997). Anger and anger expression in adults with high ADHD symptoms. *Journal of Attention Disorders, 2*, 115–128.

Ranseen, J. D. (1998). Lawyers with ADHD: The special test accommodation controversy. *Professional Psychology: Research and Practice, 29*, 450–459.

Rappley, M. D., Mullan, P. B., Alvarez, F. J., et al. (1999). Diagnosis of attention deficit/hyperactivity disorder and use of psychotropic medication in very young children. *Archives of Pediatric and Adolescent Medicine, 153*, 1039–1045.

Rapport, M. D., Chung, K., Shore, G., & Isaacs, P. (2001). A conceptual model of child psychopathology: Implications for understanding attention deficit hyperactivity disorder and treatment efficacy. *Journal of Clinical Child Psychology, 30*, 48–58.

Rapport, M. D., & Denney, C. B. (1999). Attention-deficit/hyperactivity disorder and methylphenidate: Assessment and prediction of clinical response. In L. Greenhill & B. Osman (Eds.), *Ritalin: Theory and practice* (pp. 45–70). New York: Mary Ann Liebert, Inc.

Rapport, M. D., DuPaul, G. J., & Kelly, K. L. (1989). Attention-deficit/hyperactivity disorder and methylphenidate: The relationship between gross body weight and drug response in children. *Psychopharmacology Bulletin, 25*, 285–290.

Rapport, M. D., DuPaul, G. J., Stoner, G., & Jones, J. T. (1986). Comparing classroom and clinic measures of attention deficit disorder: Differential, idiosyncratic, and dose-response effects of methylphenidate. *Journal of Consulting and Clinical Psychology, 54*, 334–341.

Rapport, M. D., & Gordon, M. (1987). *The attention training system (ATS): User's manual*. DeWitt, NY: Gordon Systems.

Rapport, M. D., & Moffitt, C. (2002). Attention deficit/hyperactivity disorder and methylphenidate: A review of height/weight, cardiovascular, and somatic complaint side effects. *Clinical Psychology Review, 22*, 1107–1131.

Rapport, M. D., Murphy, H. A., & Bailey, J. S. (1982). Ritalin vs. response cost in the control of hyperactive children: A within-subject comparison. *Journal of Applied Behavior Analysis, 15*, 205–216.

Rapport, M. D., Quinn, S. O., DuPaul, G. J., Quinn, E. P., & Kelly, K. L. (1989). Attention deficit disorder with hyperactivity and methylphenidate: The effects of dose and mastery level on children's learning performance. *Journal of Abnormal Child Psychology, 17*, 669–689.

Rapport, M. D., Randall, R., & Moffitt, C. (2002). Attention-deficit/hyperactivity disorder and methylphenidate: A dose-response analysis and parent-child comparison of somatic complaints. *Journal of Attention Disorders, 6*, 15–24.

Rapport, M. D., Tucker, S. B., DuPaul, G. J., Merlo, M., & Stoner, G. (1986). Hyperactivity and frustration: The influence of size and control over rewards in delaying gratification. *Journal of Abnormal Child Psychology, 14*, 192–204.

Rasmussen, K., Almvik, R., & Levander, S. (2001). Attention deficit hyperactivity disorder, reading disability, and personality disorders in a prison population. *Journal of the American Academy of Psychiatry and the Law, 29*, 186–193.

Reader, M. J., Harris, E. L., Schuerholz, L. J., & Denkla, M. B. (1994). Attention deficit/hyperactivity disorder and executive dysfunction. *Developmental Neuropsychology, 10,* 493–512.

Reid, R., Casat, C. D., Norton, H. J., Anastopoulos, A. D., & Temple, E. P. (2001). Using behavior rating scales for ADHD across ethnic groups: The IOWA Conners. *Journal of Emotional and Behavioral Disorders, 9,* 210–218.

Reid, R., Hakendorf, P., & Prosser, B. (2002). Use of psychostimulant medication for ADHD in South Australia. *Journal of the American Academy of Child and Adolescent Psychiatry, 41,* 906–913.

Reid, R., Maag, J. W., Vasa, F. S., & Wright, G. (1994). Who are the children with attention deficit/hyperactivity disorder? A school-based survey. *The Journal of Special Education, 2,* 117–137.

Reid, R., Vasa, F. S., Maag, J. W., & Wright, G. (1994). An analysis of teachers' perceptions of attention-deficit/hyperactivity disorder. *The Journal of Research and Development in Education, 27,* 195–202.

Retz, W., Retz-Junginger, P., Hengesch, G., Schneider, M., Thome, J., Pajonk, F. G., et al. (2004). Psychometric and psychopathological characterization of young male prison inmates with and without attention deficit/hyperactivity disorder. *European Archives of Psychiatry and Clinical Neuroscience, 254,* 201–208.

Reynolds, C. R., & Kamphaus, R. W. (1992). *Behavior assessment system for children.* Circle Pines, MN: American Guidance Service.

Reynolds, C. R., & Kamphaus, R. W. (2004). *Behavior assessment system for children, second edition.* Circle Pines, MN: American Guidance Service.

Riccio, C. A., Hynd, G. W., Cohen, M. J., Hall, J., & Molt, L. (1994). Comorbidity of central auditory processing disorder and attention-deficit/hyperactivity disorder. *Journal of the American Academy of Child Psychiatry, 33,* 849–857.

Rice, J. A., & Weyandt, L. (2000). Performance on measures of executive function in adults with Tourette's syndrome. *The ADHD Report, 8,* 1–7.

Richards, T., Deffenbacher, J., & Rosen, L. (2002). Driving anger and other driving-related behaviors in high and low ADHD symptom college students. *Journal of Attention Disorders, 6,* 25–38.

Rief, S. (1993). *How to reach and teach ADD/ADHD children.* San Francisco, CA: Jossey-Bass.

Roberts, M., & DuPaul, G. (2005). Evaluating medication effects for students with attention deficit hyperactivity disorder. www.nasponline.org/publications, 28(6).

Robin, A. L. (1998). *ADHD in adolescents: Diagnosis and treatment.* New York: Guilford Press.

Robin, A. L., Koepke, T., & Moye, A. (1990). Multidimensional assessment of parent-adolescent relations. *Psychological Assessment: A Journal of Consulting and Clinical Psychology, 2,* 451–459.

Robinson, L. M., Sclar, D. A., Skaer, T. L., & Galin, R. S. (1999). National trends in the prevalence of attention-deficit/hyperactivity disorder and the prescribing of methylphenidate among school-age children: 1990–1995. *Clinical Pediatrics (Philadelphia), 38,* 209–17.

Robinson, L. M., Sclar, D. A., Skaer, T. L., & Galin, R. S. (2004). Treatment modalities among US children diagnosed with attention-deficit hyperactivity disorder: 1995–99. *International Clinical Psychopharmacology, 19,* 17–22.

Robinson, L. M., Skaer, T. L., Sclar, D. A., & Galin, R. S. (2002). Is attention deficit hyperactivity disorder increasing among girls in the US? Trends in diagnosis and the prescribing of stimulants. *CNS Drugs, 16,* 129–137.

Robinson, P. W., Newby, T. J., & Gazell, S. L. (1981). A token system for a class of underachieving hyperactive children. *Journal of Applied Behavior Analysis, 14,* 307–315.

Rohde, L. A., Barbosa, G., Polanczyk, G., Eizirik, M., Rasmussen, E. R., Neuman, R. J., et al. (2001). Factor and latent class analysis of DSM-IV ADHD symptoms in a school sample of Brazilian adolescents. *Journal of the American Academy of Child and Adolescent Psychiatry, 40,* 711–718.

Rohde, L. A., Biederman, J., Busnello, E., Zimmerman, H., Schmitz, M., Martins, S., et al. (1999). ADHD in a sample of Brazilian adolescents: A study of prevalence, comorbid conditions, and impairments. *Journal of the American Academy of Child and Adolescent Psychiatry, 38,* 716–722.

Rojas, N. L., & Chan, E. (2005). Old and new controversies in the alternative treatment of attention-deficit hyperactivity disorder. *Mental Retardation and Developmental Disabilities Research Reviews, 11,* 116–130.

Rosa-Neto, P., Lou, H. C., Cumming, P., Pryds, O., Karrebaek, H., Lunding, J., et al. (2005). Methylphenidate-evoked changes in striatal dopamine correlate with inattention and impulsivity in adolescents with attention deficit hyperactivity disorder. *Neuroimage, 25,* 868–876.

Rosenbaum, A. K., O'Leary, D., & Jacob, R. G. (1975). Behavioral intervention with hyperactive children: Group consequences as a supplement to individual contingencies. *Behavior Therapy, 6,* 315–323.

Rosenfeld, P., Lambert, N. M., & Black, A. (1985). Desk arrangement effects on pupil classroom behavior. *Journal of Educational Psychology, 77,* 101–108.

Rosler, M., Retz, W., Retz-Junginger, P., Hengesch, G., Schneider, M., Supprian, T., et al. (2004). Prevalence of attention deficit-/hyperactivity disorder (ADHD) and comorbid disorders in young male prison inmates. *European Archives of Psychiatry and Clinical Neuroscience, 254,* 365–371.

Rovet, J. F., & Hepworth, S. L. (2001). Dissociating attention deficits in children with ADHD and congenital hypothyroidism using multiple CPTs. *Journal of Child Psychology and Psychiatry, 42,* 1049–1056.

Rowland, A. S., Lesesne, C. A., & Abramowitz, A. J. (2002). The epidemiology of attention-deficit/hyperactivity disorder (ADHD): A public health view. *Mental Retardation and Developmental Disabilities, 8,* 162–170.

Rubia, K., Overmeyer, S., Taylor, E., Brammer, M., Williams, S. C., Simmons, A., & Bullmore, E. T. (1999). Hypofrontality in attention deficit hyperactivity disorder during higher-order motor control: A study with functional MRI. *American Journal of Psychiatry, 156,* 891–896.

Rucklidge, J. J., & Kaplan, B. J. (1997). Psychological functioning of women identified in adulthood with attention-deficit/hyperactivity disorder. *Journal of Attention Disorders, 2,* 167–176.

Rucklidge, J. J., & Tannock, R. (2001). Psychiatric, psychosocial, and cognitive functioning of female adolescents with ADHD. *Journal of the American Academy of Child and Adolescent Psychiatry, 40,* 530–540.

Safer, D. J. (1973). A familial factor in minimal brain dysfunction. *Behavior Genetics, 3,* 175–186.

Safer, D. J., & Allen, R. (1976). *Hyperactive children.* Baltimore: University Park Press.

Safer, D. J., & Krager, J. M. (1994). The increased rate of stimulant treatment for hyperactive/inattentive students in secondary schools. *Pediatrics, 94,* 462–464.

Safer, D. J., & Zito, J. M. (1996, October). *Increased methylphenidate usage for attention deficit disorder in the 1990s.* Paper presented at the 43rd annual meeting of the American Academy of Child and Adolescent Psychiatry, Philadelphia.

Safer, D. J., Zito, J. M., & Fine, E. M. (1996). Increased methylphenidate usage for attention deficit disorder in the 1990s. *Pediatric, 98,* 1084–1088.

Samuel, V. J., George, P., Thornell, A., Curtis, S., Taylor, A., Brome, D., et al. (1999). A pilot controlled family study of DSM-III-R and DSM-IV ADHD in African-American children. *Journal of the American Academy of Child and Adolescent Psychiatry, 38,* 34–39.

Sangal, R. B., & Sangal, J. M. (2004). Attention-deficit/hyperactivity disorder: Cognitive evoked potential (P300) topography predicts treatment response to methylphenidate. *Clinical Neurophysiology, 115,* 188–193.

Satterfield, J. H., & Dawson, W. E. (1971). Electrodermal correlates of hyperactivity in children. *Psychophysiology, 8,* 191–198.

Satterfield, J. H., Satterfield, B. T., & Cantwell, D. P. (1980). Multimodality treatment: A two year evaluation of 61 hyperactive boys. *Archives of Psychiatry, 37,* 915–919.

Satterfield, J. H., Satterfield, B. T., & Cantwell, D. P. (1981). Three-year multimodality treatment study of 100 hyperactive boys. *Journal of Pediatrics, 98,* 650–655.

Sattler, J. M. (1992). *Assessment of children—Updated and revised* (3rd ed.). San Diego, CA: Author.

Sattler, J. M. (1998). *Clinical and forensic interviewing of children and their families.* San Diego, CA: Author.

Sattler, J. M. (2002). *Assessment of children* (4th ed.). San Diego, CA: Author.

Sattler, J. M. (2006). *Assessment of children* (5th ed.). San Diego, CA: Author.

Sattler, J. M., Weyandt, L., & Willis, J. O. (2006). Attention-deficit/hyperactivity disorder. In J. M. Sattler (Ed.), *Assessment of children* (6th ed., pp. XX). San Diego, CA: Author.

Sayal, K., Taylor, E., & Beecham, J. (2003). Parental perception of problems and mental health service use for hyperactivity. *Journal of the American Academy of Child and Adolescent Psychiatry, 42,* 1410–1414.

Schachar, R., & Ickowicz, A. (1999). Pharmacological treatment of attention-deficit/hyperactivity disorder. In H. C. Quay & A. E. Hogan, *Handbook of disruptive behavior disorders* (pp. 221–254). New York: Kluwer Academic/Plenum.

Schaughency, E., McGee, R., Raja, S. N., Feehan, M., & Silva, P. (1994). Self-reported inattention, impulsivity, and hyperactivity in ages 15 and 18 years in the general population. *Journal of the American Academy of Child and Adolescent Psychiatry, 33,* 173–183.

Schaughency, E. A., & Rothlind, J. (1991). Assessment and classification of attention deficit/hyperactivity disorders. *School Psychology Review, 20,* 197–202.

Schertz, M., Adesman, A. R., Alfieri, N. E., & Bienkowski, R. S. (1996). Predictors of weight loss in children with attention deficit hyperactivity disorder treated with stimulant medication. *Pediatrics, 98,* 763–769.

Schilling, D. L., Washington, K., Billingsley, F. F., & Deitz, J. (2003). Classroom seating for children with attention deficit hyperactivity disorder: Therapy balls versus chairs. *American Journal of Occupational Therapy, 57,* 534–541.

Schmidt, M. H., Mocks, P., Lay, B., Eisert, H. G., Fojkar, R., Fritz-Sigmund, D., et al. (1997). Does oligoantigenic diet influence hyperactive/ conduct disordered children?—A controlled trial. *European Child and Adolescent Psychiatry, 6,* 88–95.

Schmitz, M., Cadore, L., Paczko, M., Kipper, L., Chaves, M., Rohde, L., et al. (2002). Neuropsychological performance in DSM-IV ADHD subtypes: An exploratory study with untreated adolescents. *Canadian Journal of Psychiatry, 47,* 863–869.

Schnoll, R., Burshteyn, D., & Cea-Aravena, J. (2003). Nutrition in the treatment of attention-deficit hyperactivity disorder: A neglected but important aspect. *Applied Psychophysiology and Biofeedback, 28,* 63–75.

Schrimsher, G. W., Billingsley, R. L., Jackson, E. F., & Moore, B. D., III. (2002). Caudate nucleus volume asymmetry predicts attention-deficit hyperactivity disorder (ADHD) symptomatology in children. *Journal of Child Neurology, 17,* 877–884.

Schubiner, H. (1998). Medical interventions. In A. Robin (Ed.), *ADHD in adolescents: Diagnosis and treatment* (pp. 224–253). New York: Guilford Press.

Schubiner, H. (2005). Substance abuse in patients with attention-deficit hyperactivity disorder: Therapeutic implications. *CNS Drugs, 19,* 643–655.

Schweitzer, J. B., Lee, D. O., Hanford, R. B., Tagamets, M. A., Hoffman, J. M., Grafton, S. T., et al. (2003). A positron emission tomography study of methylphenidate in adults with ADHD: Alterations in resting blood flow and predicting treatment response. *Neuropsychopharmacology, 28,* 967–973.

Sciutto, M. J., Terjesen, M. D., & Bender-Frank, A. S. (2000). Teachers' knowledge and misperceptions of attention-deficit/hyperactivity disorder. *Psychology in the Schools, 37*, 115–122.

Section 504 of the Rehabilitation Act of 1973, 29 U.S.C. § 794.

Seidman, L. J., Biederman, J., Monuteaux, M. C., Doyle, A. E., & Faraone, S. V. (2001). Learning disabilities and executive dysfunction in boys with attention-deficit/hyperactivity disorder. *Neuropsychology, 15*, 544–556.

Seidman, L. J., Biederman, J., Monuteaux, M. C., Valera, E., Doyle, A. E., & Faraone, S. V. (2005). Impact of gender and age on executive functioning: Do girls and boys with and without attention deficit hyperactivity disorder differ neuropsychologically in preteen and teenage years? *Developmental Neuropsychology, 27*, 79–105.

Seidman, L. J., Valera, E. M., & Makris, N. (2005). Structural brain imaging of attention-deficit/hyperactivity disorder. *Biological Psychiatry, 57*, 1263–1272.

Semrud-Clikeman, M., Nielsen, K. H., Clinton, A., Sylvester, L., Parle, N., & Connor, R. T. (1999). An intervention approach for children with teacher- and parent-identified attentional difficulties. *Journal of Learning Disabilities, 32*, 581–590.

Semrud-Clikeman, M., Steingard, R. J., Filipek, P., Biederman, J., Bekken, K., & Renshaw, P. F. (2000). Using MRI to examine brain-behavior relationships in males with attention deficit hyperactivity disorder. *Journal of the American Academy of Child and Adolescent Psychiatry, 39*, 477–484.

Shapiro, E. S., DuPaul, G. J., & Bradley-Klug, K. L. (1998). Self-management as a strategy to improve the classroom behavior of adolescents with ADHD. *Journal of Learning Disabilities, 31*, 545–555.

Shaw, G. A., & Brown, G. (1990). Laterality and creativity concomitants of attention problems. *Developmental Neuropsychology, 6*, 39–57.

Shaw, G., & Giambra, L. (1993). Task-unrelated thoughts of college students diagnosed as hyperactive in childhood. *Developmental Neuropsychology, 9*, 17–30.

Shaw, K., Wagner, I., Eastwood, H., & Mitchell, G. (2003). A qualitative study of Australian GP's attitudes and practices in the diagnosis and management of attention-deficit/hyperactivity disorder (ADHD). *Family Practice, 20*, 129–134.

Shaw, R., Grayson, A., & Lewis, V. (2005). Inhibition, ADHD, and computer games: The inhibitory performance of children with ADHD on computerized tasks and games. *Journal of Attention Disorders, 8*, 160–168.

Shaywitz, B. A., Fletcher, J. M., & Shaywitz, S. E. (1995). Defining and classifying learning disabilities and ADHD. *Journal of Child Neurology, 10*, 50–57.

Shaywitz, B. A., Sullivan, C. M., Anderson, G. M., Gillespie, S. M., Sullivan, B., & Shaywitz, S. E. (1994). Aspartame, behavior, and cognitive function in children with attention deficit disorder. *Pediatrics, 93*, 70–75.

Shekim, W., Asarnow, R. F., Hess, E., Zaucha, K., & Wheeler, N. (1990). A clinical and demographic profile of a sample of adults with attention deficit disorder—residual type. *Comprehensive Psychiatry, 31*, 41–425.

Shekim, W. O., Dekirmenjian, H., Chapel, J. L., Javaed, S., & Dans, J. M. (1979). Norepinephrine metabolism and clinical response to dextro amphetamine in hyperactive boys. *Journal of Pediatrics, 95*, 389–394.

Sheridan, S. M., Dee, C. C., Morgan, J., McCormick, M., & Walker, D. (1996). A multimethod intervention for social skill deficits in children with ADHD and their parents. *School Psychology Review, 25*, 57–76.

Sherman, D. K., Iacono, W. G., & McGue, M. K. (1997). Attention-deficit/hyperactivity disorder dimensions: A twin study of inattention and impulsivity-hyperactivity. *Journal of the American Academy of Child and Adolescent Psychiatry, 36*, 745–753.

Short, E. J., Manos, M. J., Findlling, R. L., & Schubel, E. A. (2004). A prospective study of stimulant response in preschool children: Insights from ROC analyses. *Journal of the American Academy of Child and Adolescent Psychiatry, 43*, 251–259.

Shroyer, C., & Zentall, S. S. (1986). Effects of rate, nonrelevant information, and repetition on the listening comprehension of hyperactive children. *Journal of Special Education, 20,* 231–239.

Sieg, K. G., Gaffney, G. R., Preston, D. F., & Hellings, J. A. (1995). SPECT brain imaging abnormalities in attention-deficit/hyperactivity disorder. *Clinical Nuclear Medicine, 20,* 55–60.

Simpson, D., & Plosker, G. L. (2004). Atomoxetine: A review of its use in adults with attention deficit hyperactivity disorder. *Drugs, 64,* 205–222.

Sinha, D., & Efron, D. (2005). Complementary and alternative medicine use in children with attention deficit hyperactivity disorder. *Journal of Paediatrics and Child Health, 41,* 23–26.

Slaats-Willemse, D., de Sonneville, L., Swaab-Barneveld, H., & Buitelaar, J. (2005). Motor flexibility problems as a marker for genetic susceptibility to attention-deficit/hyperactivity disorder. *Biological Psychiatry, 58,* 233–238.

Slaats-Willemse, D., Swaab-Barneveld, H., De Sonneville, L., & Buitelaar, J. (2005). Familial clustering of executive functioning in affected sibling pair families with ADHD. *Journal of the American Academy of Child and Adolescent Psychiatry, 44,* 385–391.

Sleator, E. K., & Ullmann, R. K. (1981). Can the physician diagnose hyperactivity in the office? *Pediatrics, 67,* 13–17.

Sloan, M. T., Jensen, P. S., & Hoagwood, K. (1999). Assessing services for children with ADHD: Gaps and opportunities. *Journal of Attention Disorders, 3,* 19–29.

Slusarek, M., Velling, S., Bunk, D., & Eggers, C. (2001). Motivational effects on inhibitory control in children with ADHD. *Journal of the American Academy of Child and Adolescent Psychiatry, 40,* 355–363.

Smalley, S. (1997). Genetic influences in childhood-onset psychiatric disorders: Autism and attention-deficit/hyperactivity disorder. *American Journal of Human Genetics, 60,* 1276–1282.

Smith, B. H., Pelham, W. E., Jr., Gnagy, E., Molina, B., & Evans, S. (2000). The reliability, validity, and unique contributions of self-report by adolescents receiving treatment for attention-deficit/hyperactivity disorder. *Journal of Consulting and Clinical Psychology, 68,* 489–499.

Smith, T. E., Polloway, E. A., Patton, J. R., & Dowdy, C. A. (1995). *Teaching students with special needs in inclusive settings.* Boston: Allyn & Bacon.

Solanto, M. V., Arnsten, A., & Castellanos, F. X. (2001). *Stimulant drugs and ADHD: Basic and clinical neuroscience.* New York: Oxford University Press.

Sonuga-Barke, E., Daley, D., & Thompson, M. (2002). Does maternal ADHD reduce the effectiveness of parent training for preschool children's ADHD? *The Journal of the American Academy of Child and Adolescent Psychiatry, 41,* 696–702.

Sonuga-Barke, E., Daley, D., Thompson, M., Laver-Bradbury, C., & Weeks, A. (2001). Parent-based therapies for preschool attention-deficit/hyperactivity disorder: A randomized, controlled trial with a community sample. *Journal of the American Academy of Child and Adolescent Psychiatry, 40,* 402–408.

Sonuhara, G. A., Barr, C., Schachar, R. J., Tannock, R., Roberts, W., Malone, M. A., Jain, U. R., et al. (1997). *Association study of dopamine D4 receptor gene in children and adolescents with ADHD.* Paper presented at the annual meeting of the American Academy of Child and Adolescent Psychiatry, Toronto, Canada.

Sosne, J. (1988). *Classroom interventions with attention deficit disordered children.* (Available from Children's Program, P.C., 5331 S.W. Macadam Ave., Suite 210, Portland, OR, 97201).

Sowell, E. R., Thompson, P. M., Welcome, S. E., Henkenius, A. L., Toga, A. W., & Peterson, B. S. (2003). Cortical abnormalities in children and adolescents with attention-deficit hyperactivity disorder. *Lancet, 362,* 1699–1707.

Spencer, T. J. (2004). ADHD treatment across the life cycle. *Journal of Clinical Psychiatry, 65*(Suppl. 3), 22–26.

Spencer, T. J., Biederman, J., Wilens, T. E., & Faraone, S. V. (2002). Overview and neurobiology of attention-deficit/hyperactivity disorder. *Journal of Clinical Psychiatry, 63*, 3–9.

Spencer, T. J., Biederman, J., Wilens, T. E., Faraone, S. V., Prince, J., Gerard, K., et al. (2001). Efficacy of a mixed amphetamine salts compound in adults with attention-deficit/hyperactivity disorder. *Archives of General Psychiatry, 58*, 775–782.

Spencer, T., Biederman, J., Wilens, T., Harding, M., O'Donnel, B. A., & Griffin, S. (1996). Pharmacotherapy of attention-deficit/hyperactivity disorder across the life cycle. *Journal of the American Academy of Child and Adolescent Psychiatry, 35*, 409–432.

Spencer, T. J., Heiligenstein, J. H., Biederman, J., Faries, D. E., Kratochvil, C. J., Conners, C. K., et al. (2002). Results from 2 proof-of-concept, placebo-controlled studies of atomoxetine in children with attention-deficit/hyperactivity disorder. *Journal of Clinical Psychiatry, 63*, 1140–1147.

Spencer, T. J., Weber, W., Jetton, J., Kraus, I., Pert, J., & Zallen, B. (1999). Clinical correlates of ADHD in females: Findings from a large group of girls ascertained from pediatric and psychiatric referral sources. *Journal of the American Academy of Child and Adolescent Psychiatry, 38*, 966–975.

Sprich, S., Biederman, J., Crawford, M. H., Mundy, E., & Faraone, S. V. (2000). Adoptive and biological families of children and adolescents with ADHD. *Journal of the American Academy of Child and Adolescent Psychiatry, 39*, 1432–1437.

Starobrat-Hermelin, B., & Kozielec, T. (1997). The effects of magnesium physiological supplementation on the hyperactivity in children with attention deficit hyperactivity disorder (ADHD). Positive response to magnesium oral loading test. *Magnesium Research, 10*, 149–156.

Stephans, R. S., Pelham, W. E., & Skinner, R. (1984). State-dependent and main effects of methylphenidate and pemoline on paired-associate learning and spelling in hyperactive children. *Journal of Consulting and Clinical Psychology, 52*, 104–113.

Stevens, J., Harman, J. S., & Kelleher, K. J. (2004). Ethnic and regional differences in primary care visits for attention-deficit hyperactivity disorder. *Journal of Developmental and Behavioral Pediatrics, 25*, 318–325.

Stevens, J., Harman, J. S., & Kelleher, K. J. (2005). Race/ethnicity and insurance status as factors associated with ADHD treatment patterns. *Journal of Child and Adolescent Psychopharmacology, 15*, 88–96.

Stevens, J., Quittner, A. L., Zukerman, J. B., & Moore, S. (2002). Behavioral inhibition, self-regulation of motivation, and working memory in children with attention deficit hyperactivity disorder. *Developmental Neuropsychology, 21*, 117–139.

Stevenson, J., Asherson, P., Hay, D., Levy, F., Swanson, J., Thapar, A., et al. (2005). Characterizing the ADHD phenotype for genetic studies. *Developmental Science, 8*, 115–121.

Stevenson, J., Langley, K., Pay, H., Payton, A., Worthington, J., Ollier, W., et al. (2005). Attention deficit hyperactivity disorder with reading disabilities: Preliminary genetic findings on the involvement of the ADRA2A gene. *Journal of Child Psychology and Psychiatry, 46*, 1081–1088.

Stewart, M. A., Pitts, F. N., Craig, A. G., & Dieruf, W. (1966). The hyperactive child syndrome. *American Journal of Orthopsychiatry, 36*, 861–867.

Still, G. F. (1902). The Coulstonian lectures on some abnormal psychical conditions in children. *Lancet, 1*, 1008, 1077, 1082, 1163–1168.

Stockl, K. M., Hughes, T. E., Jarrar, M. A., Secnik, K., & Perwien, A. R. (2003). Physician perceptions of the use of medications for attention deficit hyperactivity disorder. *Journal of Managed Care and Pharmacy, 9*, 416–423.

Stoner, G., Carey, S. P., Ikeda, M. J., & Shinn, M. R. (1994). The utility of curriculum-based measurement for evaluating the effects of methylphenidate on academic performance. *Journal of Applied Behavior Analysis, 27,* 101–114.

Stormont-Spurgin, M. (1997). I lost my homework: Strategies for improving organization in students with ADHD. *Interventions in School and Clinic, 32,* 270–274.

Stormont-Spurgin, M., & Zentall, S. S. (1995). Contributing factors in the manifestation of aggression in preschoolers with hyperactivity. *Journal of Child Psychology and Psychiatry in Allied Disciplines, 36,* 491–509.

Strauss, A. A., & Lehtinen, L. E. (1947). *Psychopathology and education of the brain-injured child.* New York: Grune & Stratton.

Strayhorn, J. M., Jr., & Bickel, D. D. (2002). Reduction in children's symptoms of attention deficit hyperactivity disorder and oppositional defiant disorder during individual tutoring as compared with classroom instructions. *Psychology Report, 91,* 69–80.

Stroes, A., Alberts, E., & van der Meere, J. (2003). Boys with ADHD in social interaction with a nonfamiliar adult: An observational study. *Journal of the American Academy of Child and Adolescent Psychiatry, 42,* 295–302.

Suvarnakich, K., Rohitsuk, W., Patoommas, P., et al. (1999). Academic problems in primary schools in Bangkok. *Journal of the Psychiatric Association of Thailand, 44,* 55–63.

Sukhodolsky, D. G., do Rosario-Campos, M. C., Scahill, L., Katsovich, L., Pauls, D. L., Peterson, B. S., et al. (2005). Adaptive, emotional, and family functioning of children with obsessive-compulsive disorder and comorbid attention deficit hyperactivity disorder. *American Journal of Psychiatry, 162,* 1125–1132.

Sukhodolsky, D. G., Scahill, L., Zhang, H., Peterson, B. S., King, R. A., Lombroso, P. J., et al. (2003). Disruptive behavior in children with Tourette's Syndrome: Association with ADHD comorbidity, tic severity, and functional impairment. *Journal of the American Academy of Child and Adolescent Psychiatry, 42,* 98–105.

Swain, A. M., & Zentall, S. S. (1990). Behavioral comparisons of liked and disliked children in play contexts and the behavioral accommodations by their classmates. *Journal of Consulting and Clinical Psychology, 58,* 197–209.

Swanson, J. M., Flodman, P., Kennedy, J., Spence, M. A., Moyzis, R., Schuck, S., et al. (2000). Dopamine genes and ADHD. *Neuroscience and Biobehavioral Reviews, 24,* 21–25.

Swanson, J. M., Sunohara, G. A., Kennedy, J. L., Regino, R., Fineber, E., Wigal, T., et al. (1998). Association of the dopamine receptor D4 (DRD4) gene with a refined phenotype of attention-deficit/hyperactivity disorder (ADHD): A family-based approach. *Molecular Psychiatry, 3,* 38–41.

Szatmari, P. (1992). The epidemiology of attention-deficit/hyperactivity disorders. In G. Weiss (Ed.), *Child and adolescent psychiatry clinics of North America: Attention deficit disorder* (pp. 361–372). Philadelphia: Saunders.

Szatmari, P., Offord, D. R., & Boyle, M. H. (1989). Correlates, associated impairments, and patterns of service utilization of children with attention deficit disorders: Findings from the Ontario child health study. *Journal of Child Psychology and Psychiatry, 30,* 205–217.

Szatmari, P., Saigal, S., Rosenbaum, P., & Campbell, D. (1993). Psychopathology and adaptive functioning of extremely low birthweight children at eight years of age. *Developmental and Psychopathology, 5,* 345–357.

Tannock, R. (1998). Attention-deficit/hyperactivity disorder: Advances in cognitive, neurobiological, and genetic research. *Journal of Child Psychology and Psychiatry, 39,* 65–99.

Tantillo, M., Kesick, C. M., Hynd, G. W., & Dishman, R. K. (2001). The effects of exercise on children with attention-deficit hyperactivity disorder. *Medicine and Science in Sports and Exercise, 34,* 203–212.

Taylor, J. F. (1990). *Helping your hyperactive child.* Rocklin, CA: Prima Publishing and Communications.

Teicher, M. H., Ito, Y., Glod, C. A., & Barber, N. I. (1996). Objective measurement of hyperactivity and attention problems in ADHD. *Journal of the American Academy of Child and Adolescent Psychiatry, 35,* 334–342.

Tercyak, K. P., Lerman, C., & Audrain, J. (2002). Association of attention-deficit/hyperactivity disorder symptoms with levels of cigarette smoking in a community sample of adolescents. *Journal of the American Academy of Child and Adolescent Psychiatry, 41,* 799–805.

Teter, C. J., McCabe, S. E., Boyd, C. J., & Guthrie, S. K. (2003). Illicit methylphenidate use in an undergraduate student sample: Prevalence and risk factors. *Pharmacotherapy, 23,* 609–617.

Thomson, J. B., & Varley, C. K. (1998). Prediction of stimulant response in children with attention-deficit/hyperactivity disorder. *Journal of Child and Adolescent Psychopharmacology, 8,* 125–132.

Thunstrom, M. (2002). Severe sleep problems in infancy associated with subsequent development of attention-deficit/hyperactivity disorder at 5.5 years of age. *Acta Paediatrica, 91,* 584–592.

Tilson, P. W., & Bender, W. N. (1997). Teaching the secondary student with ADHD. In William N. Bender (Ed.), *Understanding ADHD: A practical guide for teachers and parents.* Upper Saddle River, NJ: Prentice-Hall.

Todd, R. D., Rasmussen, E. R., Neuman, R. J., Reich, W., Hudziak, J. J., Bucholz, K. K., et al. (2001). Familiality and heritability of subtypes of attention deficit hyperactivity disorder in a population sample of adolescent female twins. *American Journal of Psychiatry, 158,* 1891–1898.

Todd, R. D., Sitdhiraksa, N., Reich, W., Ji, T. H. C., Joyner, C. A., Heath, A. C., et al. (2002). Discrimination of DSM-IV and latent class attention-deficit/hyperactivity disorder subtypes by educational and cognitive performance in a population-based sample of child and adolescent twins. *Journal of the American Academy of Child and Adolescent Psychiatry, 41,* 820–827.

Tourette's Syndrome Study Group. (2002). Treatment of ADHD in children with tics: A randomized controlled trial. *Neurology, 26,* 527–536.

Trites, R. L., Tryphonas, H., & Ferguson, H. B. (1980). Diet treatment for hyperactive children with food allergies. In R. M. Knight & D. Bakker (Eds.), *Treatment of hyperactive and learning disordered children.* Baltimore: University Park Press.

Tutty, S., Gephart, H., & Wurzbacher, K. (2003). Enhancing behavioral and social skill functioning in children newly diagnosed with attention-deficit hyperactivity disorder in a pediatric setting. *Journal of Developmental and Behavioral Pediatrics, 24,* 51–57.

Umbreit, J. (1995). Functional assessment and intervention in a regular classroom setting for the disruptive behavior of a student with attention deficit hyperactivity disorder. *Behavioral Disorders, 20,* 267–278.

Urbain, E. S., & Kendall, P. C. (1980). Review of social-cognitive problem-solving interventions with children. *Psychological Bulletin, 88,* 109–143.

Vaidya, C. J., Austin, G., Kirkorian, G., Ridlehuber, H. W., Desmond, J. E., Glover, G. H., et al. (1998). Selective effects of methylphenidate in attention-deficit/hyperactivity disorder: A functional magnetic resonance study. *The National Academy of Sciences, 95,* 14494–14499.

Vaidya, C. J., Bunge, S. A., Dudukovic, N. M., Zalecki, C. A., Elliott, G. R., & Gabrieli, J. D. E. (2005). Altered neural substrates of cognitive control in childhood ADHD: Evidence from functional magnetic resonance imaging. *American Journal of Psychiatry, 162,* 1605–1613.

van der Meere, J. J., Vreeling, H. J., & Sergeant, J. A. (1992). A motor presetting study in hyperactives, learning disabled, and control children. *Journal of Child Psychology and Psychiatry, 34,* 1347–1354.

VandenBerg, N. L. (2001). The use of a weighted vest to increase on-task behavior in children with attention difficulties. *American Journal of Occupational Therapy, 55,* 621–628.

Vance, A., Maruff, P., & Barnett, R. (2003). Attention deficit hyperactivity disorder, combined type: Better executive function performance with longer-term psychostimulant medication. *Australian and New Zealand Journal of Psychiatry, 37,* 570–576.

Varley, C. K., Vincent, J., Varley, P., & Calderon, R. (2001). Emergence of tics in children with attention deficit hyperactivity disorder treated with stimulant medications. *Comprehensive Psychiatry, 42,* 228–233.

Voeller, K. S. (1991). Toward a neurobiologic nosology of attention-deficit/hyperactivity disorder. *Journal of Child Neurology, 6,* S2–S8.

Volkow, N. D., Fowler, J. S., Wang, G., Ding, Y., & Gatley, S. J. (2002). Mechanism of action of methylphenidate: Insights from PET imaging studies. *Journal of Attention Disorders, 6*(Suppl. 1), S31–43.

Volkow, N. D., Wang, G. J., Fowler, J. S., & Ding, Y. S. (2005). Imaging the effects of methylphenidate on brain dopamine: New model on its therapeutic actions for attention-deficit/hyperactivity disorder. *Biological Psychiatry, 57,* 1410–1415.

Volkow, N. D., Wang, G. J., Fowler, J. S., Logan, J., Gerasimov, M., Maynard, L., et al. (2001). Therapeutic doses of oral methylphenidate significantly increase extracellular dopamine in the human brain. *Journal of Neuroscience, 15,* RC121.

Volkow, N. D., Wang, G. J., Maynard, L., Fowler, J. S., Jayne, B., Telang, F., et al. (2002). Effects of alcohol detoxification on dopamine D2 receptors in alcoholics: A preliminary study. *Psychiatry Research, 116,* 163–172.

Waddell, D. (1991). Attention-deficit/hyperactivity disorder: A teacher handout (insert). *NASP Communique, 19.*

Walker, H., & McConnell, S. (1988). *Walker-McConnell scale of social competence.* Austin, TX: Pro-Ed.

Ward, M., Wender, P., & Reimher, F. (1993). The Wender Utah rating scale: An aid in retrospective diagnosis of children with ADHD. *American Journal of Psychiatry, 160,* 245–256.

Waschbusch, D. A., Pelham, W. E., Jr., Jennings, J. R., Greiner, A. R., Tarter, R. E., & Moss, H. B. (2002). Reactive aggression in boys with disruptive behavior disorders: Behavior, physiology, and affect. *Journal of Abnormal Child Psychology, 30,* 641–656.

Waxmonsky, J. G. (2005). Nonstimulant therapies for attention-deficit hyperactivity disorder (ADHD) in children and adults. *Essent Psychopharmacology, 6,* 262–276.

Webb, J. T., & Latimer, D. (1993). ADHD and children who are gifted. *Exceptional Children,* 183–184.

Wechsler, D. (1989). *Weschler intelligence scale for children–third edition.* San Antonio, TX: Psychological Corporation.

Webster-Stratton, C., Reid, J., & Hammond, M. (2001). Social skills and problem-solving training for children with early-onset conduct problems: Who benefits? *Journal of Child Psychology and Psychiatry, 42,* 943–952.

Weiler, M. D., Bellinger, D., Marmor, J., Rancier, S., & Waber, D. (1999). Mother and teacher reports of ADHD symptoms: *DSM-IV* questionnaire data. *Journal of the American Academy of Child and Adolescent Psychiatry, 38,* 1139–1147.

Weill, M. (1995, November). Helping children with attention problems: Strategies for parents (insert). *NASP Communique.*

Weinstein, R. S., Soule, C. R., Collins, F., Cone, J., Mehlhorn, M., & Simontacchi, K. (1991). Expectations and high school change: Teacher-researcher collaboration to prevent school failure. *American Journal of Community Psychology, 19,* 333–363.

Weiss, G., & Hechtman, L. (1993). *Hyperactive children grown up: ADHD in children, adolescents, and adults* (2nd ed., pp. XX). New York: Guilford Press.

Weiss, M., Tannock, R., Kratochvil, C., Dunn, D., Velez-Borras, J., Thomason, C., et al. (2005). A randomized, placebo-controlled study of once-daily atomoxetine in the school setting in children with ADHD. *Journal of the American Academy of Child and Adolescent Psychiatry, 44,* 647–655.

Werry, J. S., & Quay, H. C. (1971). The prevalence of behavior symptoms in younger elementary school children. *American Journal of Orthopsychiatry, 41,* 136–143.

Weyandt, L. L. (1995, November). ADHD in college students. *NASP Communique, 27–28.*

Weyandt, L. L. (2001). *An ADHD primer.* Boston: Allyn & Bacon.

Weyandt, L. L. (2004). The use of medication in the treatment of ADHD. *NASP Communique, 33,* 35–36.

Weyandt, L. L. (2005a). Executive function in children, adolescents, and adults with attention deficit hyperactivity disorder: Introduction to the special issue. *Developmental Neuropsychology, 27,* 1–10.

Weyandt, L. L. (2005b). Neuropsychological performance in adults with attention deficit hyperactivity disorder. In D. Gozal & D. L. Molfese (Eds.), *Hyperactivity disorder: From genes to patients* (pp. 457–486). Totowa, NJ: Humana Press.

Weyandt, L. L. (2006). *The physiological bases of cognitive and behavioral disorders.* Mahwah, NJ: Lawrence Erlbaum Associates.

Weyandt, L. (in press). [Letter to the editor]. *The ADHD Report.*

Weyandt, L. L., & DuPaul, J. G. (in press). ADHD in college students. *Journal of Attention Disorders.*

Weyandt, L. L., Iwaszuk, W., Fulton, K., Ollerton, M., Beatty, N., Fouts, H., et al. (2003). The Internal Restlessness Scale: Performance of college students with and without ADHD. *Journal of Learning Disabilities, 36,* 382–389.

Weyandt, L. L., Mitzlaff, L., & Thomas, L. (2002). The relationship between intelligence and performance on the Test of Variables of Attention (TOVA). *Journal of Learning Disabilities, 35,* 114–120.

Weyandt, L., Rice, J. A., & Linterman, I. (1995). Reported prevalence of attentional difficulties in a general sample of college students. *Journal of Psychopathology and Behavioral Assessment, 17,* 293–304.

Weyandt, L., Rice, J. A., Linterman, I., Mitzlaff, L., & Emert, E. (1998). Neuropsychological performance of a sample of adults with ADHD, developmental reading disorder, and controls. *Developmental Neuropsychology, 14,* 643–656.

Weyandt, L. L., & Willis, W. G. (1994). Executive functions in school-aged children: Potential efficacy of tasks in discriminating clinical groups. *Developmental Neuropsychology, 19,* 27–38.

Wheldall, K. (1991). Managing troublesome classroom behavior in regular schools: A positive teaching perspective. *International Journal of Disability, Development, and Education, 38,* 99–116.

White, M. A. (1975). Natural rates of teacher approval and disapproval in the classroom. *Journal of Applied Behavior Analysis, 8,* 367–372.

Wigal, T., Swanson, J. M., Douglas, V. I., Wigal, S. B., Wippler, C. M., & Cavoto, K. F. (1998). Effect of reinforcement on facial responsivity and persistence in children with attention-deficit hyperactivity disorder. *Behavior Modification, 22,* 143–166.

Wilens, T. E. (2004). Impact of ADHD and its treatment on substance abuse in adults. *Journal of Clinical Psychiatry, 65*(Suppl. 3), 38–45.

Wilens, T. E., Biederman, J., Brown, S., Monuteaux, M., Prince, J., & Spencer, T. J. (2002). Patterns of psychopathology and dysfunction in clinically referred preschoolers. *Journal of Developmental and Behavioral Pediatrics, 23,* S31–S36.

Wilens, T. E., Biederman, J., & Spencer, T. (1994). Clonidine for sleep disturbances associated with attention-deficit/hyperactivity disorder. *Journal of the American Academy of Child and Adolescent Psychiatry, 33,* 424–426.

Wilens, T. E., Biederman, J., & Spencer, T. J. (2002). Attention deficit/hyperactivity disorder across the lifespan. *Annual Review of Medicine, 53,* 113–31.

Wilens, T. E., Faraone, S. V., Biederman, J., & Gunawardene, S. (2003). Does stimulant therapy of attention-deficit/hyperactivity disorder beget later substance abuse? A meta-analytic review of the literature. *Pediatrics, 111,* 179–185.

Wilens, T. E., McBurnett, K., Stein, M., Lerner, M., Spencer, T., & Wolraich, M. (2005). ADHD treatment with once-daily OROS methylphenidate: Final results from a long-term open-label study. *Journal of the American Academy of Child and Adolescent Psychiatry, 44,* 1015–1023.

Wilens, T. E., Prince, J. B., Spencer, T., Van Pattern, S. L., Doyle, R., Girard, K., et al. (2003). An open trial of bupropion for the treatment of adults with attention-deficit/hyperactivity disorder and bipolar disorder. *Society of Biological Psychiatry, 54,* 9–16.

Willcutt, E. (in press). The etiology of ADHD: Behavioral and molecular genetic approaches. In D. Barch (Ed.), *Cognitive and affective neuroscience of psychopathology.* New York: Oxford University Press.

Willcutt, E. G., Brodsky, K., Chhabildas, N., Shanahan, M., Yerys, B., Scott, A., et al. (2005). The neuropsychology of attention deficit hyperactivity disorder: Validity of the executive function hypothesis. In D. Gozal & D. L. Molfese (Eds.), *Hyperactivity disorder: From genes to patients* (pp. 185–214). Totowa, NJ: Humana Press.

Willcutt, E. G., Pennington, B. F., & DeFries, J. C. (2000). Twin study of the etiology of comorbidity between reading disability and attention-deficit/hyperactivity disorder. *American Journal of Medical Genetics, 96,* 293–301.

Willcutt, E. G., Pennington, B. F., Olson, R. K., Chhabildas, N., & Hulslander, J. (2005). Neuropsychological analyses of comorbidity between reading disability and attention deficit hyperactivity disorder: In search of the common deficit. *Developmental Neuropsychology, 27,* 35–78.

Williams, R. J., Goodale, L. A., Shay-Fiddler, M. A., Gloster, S. P., & Chang, S. Y. (2004). Methylphenidate and dextroamphetamine abuse in substance-abusing adolescents. *American Journal of Addiction, 13,* 381–389.

Willis, W. G., & Weiler, M. D. (2005). Neural substrates of childhood attention deficit hyperactivity disorder: Electroencephalographic and magnetic resonance imaging evidence. *Developmental Neuropsychology, 27,* 135–182.

Wilson, J. J., & Levin, F. R. (2001). Attention deficit hyperactivity disorder (ADHD) and substance use disorders. *Current Psychiatric Reports, 3,* 497–506.

Wilson, J. M., & Marcotte, A. C. (1996). Psychosocial adjustment and educational outcome in adolescents with a childhood diagnosis of attention deficit disorder. *Journal of the American Academy of Child & Adolescent Psychiatry, 35,* 579–587.

Winsberg, B. G., & Comings, D. E. (1999). Association of dopamine transporter gene (DAT1) with poor methylphenidate response. *Journal of the American Academy of Child and Adolescent Psychiatry, 38,* 1474–1477.

Wirt, R. D., Lachar, D., Klinedinst, J. K., & Seat, P. S. (1990). *Personality Inventory for Children—1990 Edition.* Los Angeles: Western Psychological Services.

Wolf, L. (2001). College students with ADHD and other hidden disabilities. Outcomes and interventions. *Annals of the New York Academy of Sciences, 931,* 385–395.

Wolraich, M. L., Hannah, J. N., Baumgaertel, A., & Feurer, I. D. (1998). Examination of DSM-IV criteria for attention deficit/hyperactivity disorder in a country-wide sample. *Journal of Developmental and Behavioral Pediatrics, 19,* 162–168.

Wolraich, M. L., Hannah, J. N., Pinnock, T. Y., Baumgaertel, A., & Brown, J. (1996). Comparison of diagnostic criteria for attention-deficit/hyperactivity disorder in a country-wide sample. *Journal of the American Academy of Child and Adolescent Psychiatry, 35,* 319–324.

Wolraich, M. L., Lambert, E. W., Baumgaertel, A., Garcia-Tornel, S., Feurer, I. D., Bickman, L., et al. (2003). Teachers' screening for attention deficit/hyperactivity disorder: Comparing multinational samples on teacher ratings of ADHD. *Journal of Abnormal Child Psychology, 31,* 445–455.

Wolraich, M. L., Lambert, E. W., Bickman, L., Simmons, T., Doffing, M. A., & Worley, K. A. (2004). Assessing the impact of parent and teacher agreement on diagnosing attention-deficit hyperactivity disorder. *Developmental and Behavioral Pediatrics, 25,* 41–47.

Wolraich, M. L., Lambert, E. W., Doffing, M. A., Bickman, L., Simmons, T., & Worley, K. (2003). Psychometric properties of the Vanderbilt ADHD Diagnostic Parent Rating Scale in a referred population. *Journal of Pediatric Psychology, 28,* 559–568.

Wolraich, M. L., Lingren, S. D., Stumbo, P. J., Stegink, L. D., Appelbaum, M., & Kiristy, M. C. (1994). Effects of diets high in sucrose or aspartame on the behavior and cognitive performance of children. *The New England Journal of Medicine, 330,* 81–87.

Wolraich, M. L., Wibbelsman, C. J., Brown, T. E., Evans, S. W., Gotlieb, E. M., Knight, J. R., et al. (2005). Attention-deficit/hyperactivity disorder among adolescents: A review of the diagnosis, treatment, and clinical implications. *Pediatrics, 115,* 1734–1746.

Wolraich, M. L., Wilson, D. B., & White, J. W. (1995). The effect of sugar on behavior or cognition in children: A meta-analysis. *Journal of the American Medical Association, 274,* 1617–1621.

Woodcock, R. W., & Johnson, M. B. (1987). *Woodcock-Johnson psychoeducational battery–revised.* Allen, TX: Teaching Resources.

Woodcock, R., McGrew, K., & Mathes, N. (2001). *Woodcock-Johnson complete battery–third edition.* Hasca, IL: Riverside Publishing.

Woods, S. P., Lovejoy, D. W., Stutts, M. L., Ball, J. D., & Fals-Steward, W. (2002). Comparative efficiency of a discrepancy analysis for the classification of attention-deficit/hyperactivity disorder in adults. *Archives of Clinical Neuropsychology, 17,* 351–369.

Xu, X., Knight, J., Brookes, K., Mill, J., Sham, P., Craig, I., et al. (2005). DNA pooling analysis of 21 norepinephrine transporter gene SNPs with attention deficit hyperactivity disorder: No evidence for association. *American Journal of Medical Genetics Part B-Neuropsychiatry Genetics, 134,* 115–118.

Yang, P., Jong, Y. J., Chung, L. C., & Chen, C. S. (2004). Gender differences in a clinic-referred sample of Taiwanese attention-deficit/hyperactivity disorder children. *Psychiatry and Clinical Neurosciences, 58,* 619–623.

Yasutake, D., Lerner, J., & Ward, M. E. (1994). The need for teachers to receive training for working with students with attention deficit disorder. *B.C. Journal of Special Education, 18,* 81–84.

Zachor, D. A., Roberts, A. W., Bart Hodgens, J., Isaacs, J. S., & Merrick, J. (in press). Effects of long-term psychostimulant medication on growth of children with ADHD. *Research in Developmental Disabilities.*

Zametkin, A. J., Liebenauer, L. L., Fitzgerald, G. A., King, A. C., Minkunas, D. V., Herscovitch, P., et al. (1993). Brain metabolism in teenagers with attention-deficit/hyperactivity disorder. *Archives of General Psychiatry, 50,* 333–340.

Zentall, S. S. (1989). Attentional cuing in spelling tasks for hyperactive and comparison regular classroom children. *The Journal of Special Education, 23,* 83–93.

Zentall, S. S. (1993). Research on the educational implications of attention-deficit/hyperactivity disorder. *Exceptional Children, 60,* 143–153.

Zentall, S. S., & Meyer, M. J. (1987). Self-regulation of stimulation of ADD-H children between reading and vigilance task performance. *Journal of Abnormal Child Psychology, 15,* 519–536.

Zentall, S. S., & Shaw, J. H. (1980). Effects of classroom noise on performance of activity of second-grade hyperactive and control children. *Journal of Educational Psychology, 72,* 830–840.

Zentall, S. S., & Smith, Y. N. (1993). Mathematical performance and behavior of children with hyperactivity with and without coexisting aggression. *Behavior Research Therapy, 31,* 701–710.

Zhao, A. L., Su, L. Y., Zhang, Y. H., Tang, B. S., Luo, X. R., Huang, C. X., et al. (2005). Association analysis of serotonin transporter promoter gene polymorphism with ADHD and related symptomatology. *International Journal of Neuroscience, 115,* 1183–1191.

Zito, J. M., Safer, D. J., DosReis, S., Gardner, J. F., Boles, M., & Lynch, F. (2000). Trends in the prescribing of psychotropic medications to preschoolers. *Journal of the American Medical Association, 23,* 1025–1030.

Zito, J. M., Safer, D. J., DosReis, S., Magder, L. S., & Riddle, M. A. (1997). Methylphenidate patterns among Medicaid youths. *Psychopharmacology Bulletin, 30,* 143–147.

Zito, J. M., Safer, D. J., DosReis, S., Gardner, J. F., Magder, L., Soeken, K., et al. (2003). Psychotropic practice patterns for youth: A 10-year perspective. *Archives of Pediatric and Adolescent Medicine, 157,* 17–25.

INDEX

Page numbers of tables and figures are in italics

Inattention. *See* Attention problems
Increased incidence of ADHD, 10–11
Individual therapy, 97
Individualized education plan (IEP), 26
Individuals with Disabilities Education Act (IDEA), 25–26, *27*, 55
Individuals with Disabilities Education Act (IDEA)/Section 504 flow chart (Figure 1.1), *27*
Infancy and toddlerhood developmental stages, 11–13, *24*
Informed consent, 47
Ingersoll, Barbara, and Sam Goldstein, *Attention Deficit Disorder and Learning Disabilities: Realities, Myths, and Controversial Treatments*, 124
Insect repellents, 31
Instructional strategies, 75–83
Instructions, 77
Intangible rewards, 80
Intelligence, 15, 68
Internal restlessness, 17
Internal Restlessness Scale (Iwaszuk), 60
Internalized speech, 14, 40
Interpersonal relationships, 94, 96
Interpersonal skills, 95
Interventions. *See* Alternative treatments; Combined treatments; Counseling; Home-based interventions; Medication; School-based interventions
Interviews
  with the individual, 60–61
  with parents, 48–55
  with teachers, 55–57
Intrusive thoughts, 23
IQ tests, 15, 61

K

Key Questions for Assessing Comorbidity/ Differential Diagnosis (Robin), 142–148
Kiddie SADS-E (Orvaschel), 59

L

Laboratory measures in assessment of ADHD, 62–64
Language impairments, 67

"Lawyers with ADHD: The Special Test Accommodation Controversy" (Ranseen), 28
Lead poisoning, 50, 65
Learning disabilities, 6, 13, 26, 28, 44, 52, 64, 67–68
Legal issues in attention deficit/hyperactivity disorder (ADHD), 25–28
Lifelong condition, 1
Listening and reading comprehension, 78–79
Lithium, 119
Local organizations, 97

M

Magnetic resonance imaging (MRI), 36, 37, 65
Major depression, 69
  see also Depression
Marital problems, 101
Massage, 123–124
Matching Familiar Figures Test, 63
Maternal health, 50
Media attention, 11, 32, 105
Medical evaluation, 65
Medical history, 50
Medication, 20, 105–119
  alpha2 noradrenergic agonists, 119
  antidepressants, 117–119, *118*
  combined treatments, 119–120
  reactions to, 65
  research on, 71, 105, 107–108, 111, 113
  self-medication, 19
  side effects, 50, 112, 113–114
  stimulant, 35, 37, 63, 96
    benefits of, 108–109
    concerns about, 109–110
    controversy, 106
    long-term effects, 109, 116–117
    misconceptions, 114–116
    monitoring, 112–113, *113*
    pharmacology, 106–107
    rate of medication, 110–112
    school-based medication evaluation (Table 5.2), *113*
    side effects, 111, 113
    types of (Table 5.1), 107–108, *107*
    when to use, 110
  see also Ritalin
Megavitamin supplements, 31, 122